Java EE 7 Essentials

Arun Gupta

Beijing · Cambridge · Farnham · Köln · Sebastopol · Tokyo

Java EE 7 Essentials

by Arun Gupta

Copyright © 2013 Arun Gupta. All rights reserved.

Printed in the United States of America.

Published by O'Reilly Media, Inc., 1005 Gravenstein Highway North, Sebastopol, CA 95472.

O'Reilly books may be purchased for educational, business, or sales promotional use. Online editions are also available for most titles (*http://my.safaribooksonline.com*). For more information, contact our corporate/institutional sales department: 800-998-9938 or *corporate@oreilly.com*.

Editors: Mike Loukides and Meghan Blanchette	**Indexer:** Angela Howard
Production Editor: Kara Ebrahim	**Cover Designer:** Randy Comer
Copyeditor: Rachel Monaghan	**Interior Designer:** David Futato
Proofreader: Linley Dolby	**Illustrator:** Rebecca Demarest

August 2013:   First Edition

Revision History for the First Edition:

2013-08-08:   First release

See *http://oreilly.com/catalog/errata.csp?isbn=9781449370176* for release details.

Nutshell Handbook, the Nutshell Handbook logo, and the O'Reilly logo are registered trademarks of O'Reilly Media, Inc. *Java EE 7 Essentials*, the image of glassfish, and related trade dress are trademarks of O'Reilly Media, Inc.

Many of the designations used by manufacturers and sellers to distinguish their products are claimed as trademarks. Where those designations appear in this book, and O'Reilly Media, Inc., was aware of a trademark claim, the designations have been printed in caps or initial caps.

While every precaution has been taken in the preparation of this book, the publisher and author assume no responsibility for errors or omissions, or for damages resulting from the use of the information contained herein.

ISBN: 978-1-449-37017-6

[LSI]

To Menka, the eternal sunshine in my life. You make my days shine and life upbeat.

To Aditya and Mihir, your stories and games are invaluable to me.

Table of Contents

Foreword

As Java EE platform specification lead, I've been guiding the path of Java EE since its introduction in 1999. Arun has been a key member of the Java EE team from the beginning. The Java EE platform has evolved significantly over the last 13 years. The release of Java EE 5 in 2006 was just the beginning of a theme that continues today: making it easier to develop Java EE applications. Java EE 6 in 2009 contributed significantly to this theme with the inclusion of CDI. Java EE 7 is the latest release continuing this theme of focusing on developer productivity. Arun has been involved in several different areas of Java EE, but the common thread of his involvement has been understanding real developers and real applications. His background with Java EE, and his current role as technology evangelist for Java EE, make him uniquely qualified to introduce developers to the latest Java EE technology.

In this book, Arun surveys all the key technologies of the latest version of Java EE, giving developers a taste for these many new capabilities, and showing just how easy it is to write Java EE applications. Arun expands on his popular *Java EE 6 Pocket Guide* to cover more technologies in more depth. Particular attention is paid to technologies new to Java EE 7, and to new features of existing technologies. Developers with some Java EE experience, as well as developers new to Java EE, will find this a very helpful overview of Java EE 7.

Each chapter covers a Java EE technology in just enough depth to help you understand what the technology does, what it's best used for, and how to get started using it. While it's not a complete tutorial, an experienced developer will find that it provides just the right level of detail to understand the technology. The chapters are full of short code fragments that developers will appreciate.

After describing the key technologies of Java EE, in the last chapter of the book, Arun pulls it all together with a hands-on lab that walks you through the process of developing a real application that uses most of these technologies. This is where Arun's experience really shines. There's nothing like seeing the code for a running application to show you how these technologies actually work in practice.

Java EE is a rich platform that we've been developing over many years. It can be daunting to sort through all the old and new versions of technologies to find the best way to write Java EE applications. We've made it much easier to write Java EE applications in recent years, but sometimes that message doesn't come through when reading our many Java EE specifications. Arun's years of experience in working with application developers, teaching hands-on labs, and evangelizing Java EE put him in a unique position to provide all the key information at just the right depth. This book is a great way for developers to get an overview of the Java EE platform, and especially the new features in Java EE 7.

—Bill Shannon
Architect Java EE Platform Specification Lead, Oracle
June 2013

Preface

The Java EE 7 platform builds upon previous versions of the platform and focuses on higher productivity and embracing HTML5. This book is directed toward readers who want to get a quick overview of the platform and to keep coming back to review the basics.

This book provides an overview of the key specifications in the Java EE 7 platform (one specification per chapter). This book is by no means intended to be an exhaustive guide or tutorial that explains each and every concept of different specifications. However, the main concepts from the different specifications are explained using simple code samples. No prior knowledge of earlier versions of the platform is required, but you'll need some basic understanding of Java to understand the code.

A significant part of this book is derived from *Java EE 6 Pocket Guide* (O'Reilly). New chapters have been added to cover the new technologies in the platform. New sections have been added or existing sections updated to reflect the changes in the platform. If you have read the *Java EE 6 Pocket Guide*, then you can read this book at a much faster pace; otherwise, you can read this book from beginning to end. Alternatively, you can read specific chapters based upon your interest.

I also provide self-paced instructions on how to build an end-to-end application using most of the technologies described. This allows developers to understand the design patterns they can apply to build a real-life application using Java EE 7.

I hope you will enjoy the book!

Conventions Used in This Book

The following typographical conventions are used in this book:

Italic

Indicates new terms, URLs, email addresses, filenames, and file extensions.

Constant width

Used for program listings, as well as within paragraphs to refer to program elements such as variable or function names, databases, data types, environment variables, statements, and keywords.

Constant width italic

Shows text that should be replaced with user-supplied values or by values determined by context.

Using Code Examples

Supplemental material (code examples, exercises, etc.) is available for download at *http://oreil.ly/javaee7-files*.

This book is here to help you get your job done. In general, if this book includes code examples, you may use the code in your programs and documentation. You do not need to contact us for permission unless you're reproducing a significant portion of the code. For example, writing a program that uses several chunks of code from this book does not require permission. Selling or distributing a CD-ROM of examples from O'Reilly books does require permission. Answering a question by citing this book and quoting example code does not require permission. Incorporating a significant amount of example code from this book into your product's documentation does require permission.

We appreciate, but do not require, attribution. An attribution usually includes the title, author, publisher, and ISBN. For example: "*Java EE 7 Essentials* by Arun Gupta (O'Reilly). Copyright 2013 Arun Gupta, 978-1-449-37017-6."

If you feel your use of code examples falls outside fair use or the permission given above, feel free to contact us at *permissions@oreilly.com*.

Safari® Books Online

 Safari Books Online (*www.safaribooksonline.com*) is an ondemand digital library that delivers expert content in both book and video form from the world's leading authors in technology and business.

Technology professionals, software developers, web designers, and business and creative professionals use Safari Books Online as their primary resource for research, problem solving, learning, and certification training.

Safari Books Online offers a range of product mixes and pricing programs for organizations, government agencies, and individuals. Subscribers have access to thousands of books, training videos, and prepublication manuscripts in one fully searchable database from publishers like O'Reilly Media, Prentice Hall Professional, Addison-Wesley

Professional, Microsoft Press, Sams, Que, Peachpit Press, Focal Press, Cisco Press, John Wiley & Sons, Syngress, Morgan Kaufmann, IBM Redbooks, Packt, Adobe Press, FT Press, Apress, Manning, New Riders, McGraw-Hill, Jones & Bartlett, Course Technology, and dozens more. For more information about Safari Books Online, please visit us online.

How to Contact Us

Please address comments and questions concerning this book to the publisher:

O'Reilly Media, Inc.
1005 Gravenstein Highway North
Sebastopol, CA 95472
800-998-9938 (in the United States or Canada)
707-829-0515 (international or local)
707-829-0104 (fax)

We have a web page for this book, where we list errata, examples, and any additional information. You can access this page at *http://oreil.ly/javaee7*.

To comment or ask technical questions about this book, send email to *bookques tions@oreilly.com*.

For more information about our books, courses, conferences, and news, see our website at *http://www.oreilly.com*.

Find us on Facebook: *http://facebook.com/oreilly*

Follow us on Twitter: *http://twitter.com/oreillymedia*

Watch us on YouTube: *http://www.youtube.com/oreillymedia*

Acknowledgments

This book would not have been possible without support from a multitude of people.

First and foremost, many thanks to O'Reilly for trusting in me and providing an opportunity to write this book. Their team provided excellent support throughout the editing, reviewing, proofreading, and publishing process.

At O'Reilly, Meghan Blanchette provided excellent editorial help throughout all the stages, helping with interim reviews, providing feedback on styling, arranging technical reviews, and connecting me with the rest of the team when required.

Rachel Monaghan and Kara Ebrahim helped with copyediting and making sure to provide the finishing touches. And thanks to the rest of the O'Reilly team with whom I did not interact directly, but who were helping in many other ways.

The detailed proofreading and technical review by Markus Eisele (@myfear, *http://blog.eisele.net*), John Yeary (@jyeary, *http://javaevangelist.blogspot.com*), and Bert Ertman (@BertErtman, *http://bertertman.wordpress.com*) ensured that the relevant content was covered accurately. Their vast experience and knowledge showed in the depth of their comments.

I am grateful for the numerous discussions with developers around the world that helped me understand the technology better. Thanks to my colleagues at Oracle and the different JSR specification leads for explaining the intended use cases of different technologies. And thanks to everybody else in my life, who provided much-needed breaks from book writing.

CHAPTER 1

Java Platform, Enterprise Edition

Introduction

The Java Platform, Enterprise Edition (Java EE), provides a standards-based platform for developing web and enterprise applications. These applications are typically designed as multitier applications, with a frontend tier consisting of a web framework, a middle tier providing security and transactions, and a backend tier providing connectivity to a database or a legacy system. These applications should be responsive and capable of scaling to accommodate the growth in user demand.

The Java EE platform defines APIs for different components in each tier, and also provides some additional services such as naming, injection, and resource management that span across the platform. These components are deployed in containers that provide runtime support. Containers provide a federated view of the underlying Java EE APIs to the application components. Java EE application components never interact directly with other Java EE application components. They use the protocols and methods of the container for interacting with each other and with platform services. Interposing a container between the application components and the Java EE services allows the container to transparently inject the services required by the component, such as declarative transaction management, security checks, resource pooling, and state management. This container-based model and abstraction of resource access allows the platform to offload the developer from common infrastructure tasks.

Each component of the platform is defined in a separate specification that also describes the API, javadocs, and expected runtime behavior.

Java EE 7 was released in June 2013 and provides a simple, easy-to-use, and complete stack for building such web and enterprise applications. The previous versions of the platform, starting with Java EE 5 and continuing with Java EE 6, took the first steps in providing a simplified developer experience.

The Java EE 7 platform built upon the previous version with three main goals:

Embracing HTML5

> The WebSocket protocol, developed as part of the collection of technologies that make up HTML5, brings a new level of ease of development and network efficiency to modern, interactive web applications. It provides a two-way, full-duplex communication channel between a client and a server over a single TCP (transmission control protocol) channel. Java EE 7 defines a new standard API to develop and deploy WebSocket clients and endpoints.
>
> JSON is the lingua franca of the Web for lightweight data exchange. Until now, developers were required to bundle third-party libraries for JSON processing. Java EE 7 defines a new portable API to parse, generate, transform, and query JSON using a Streaming API or Object Model API.
>
> JavaServer Faces (JSF) introduces pass-through attributes and elements that allow near-total control over the user experience of each individual element in the view. This allows HTML5-friendly markup to be easily embedded in a page.

Higher productivity

> The JMS API has been greatly simplified. `JMSContext` provides the unified functionality of `Connection` and `Session` objects. In addition, several JMS interfaces implement `Autocloseable` and thus are automatically closed after use. Finally, correct error handling, runtime exceptions instead of checked exceptions, method chaining on `JMSProducer`, and simplified message sending are further examples of features that the JMS API has simplified.
>
> Without the Client API (introduced in JAX-RS 2), developers are required to use basic `HttpUrlConnection` APIs and write all the surrounding code.
>
> More defaults for the application's use—such as a preconfigured `DataSource` for accessing databases in operational environments, a preconfigured JMS `ConnectionFactory` for accessing a JMS provider, and a preconfigured `ManagedExecutorService`—provide a seamless out-of-the-box experience for new developers starting with the platform.
>
> The Contexts and Dependency Injection (CDI) specification is now a core component model, and is enabled by default. This makes the platform a lot more cohesive and integrated. CDI interceptors are now more widely applicable to beans. `@Transactional` annotation brings transactional semantics to POJOs (plain old Java objects), outside of an EJB (Enterprise JavaBean). Bean Validation allows automatic validation of method arguments and results using interceptors.
>
> Less boilerplate text, more defaults, and a cohesive integrated platform together boost developers' productivity when building applications using the latest version of the platform.

Enterprise demands

Batch Applications for the Java Platform is a new functionality in the platform and very important for enterprise customers. It allows developers to easily define non-interactive, bulk-oriented, long-running jobs in an item- or task-oriented way.

Concurrency Utilities for Java EE, another functionality new to the platform, is an extension of the Java SE Concurrency Utilities API, for use in the Java EE container-managed environment so that the proper container-managed runtime context can be made available for the execution of these tasks.

This functionality in the platform allows the developer to leverage the standard APIs and reduces the dependency on third-party frameworks.

Prior to Java EE 7, the Java EE 6 platform improved upon the developer productivity features and added a lot more functionality.

Deliverables

The Java EE 7 platform was developed as Java Specification Request (JSR) 342 (*http:// jcp.org/en/jsr/detail?id=342*) following JCP 2.9. The JCP process defines three key deliverables for any JSR:

Specification

A formal document that describes the proposed component and its features.

Reference Implementation (RI)

Binary implementation of the proposed specification. The RI helps to ensure that the proposed specifications can be implemented in a binary form and provides constant feedback to the specification process.

The RI of Java EE is built in the GlassFish community (*http://glassfish.org*).

Technology Compliance Kit (TCK)

A set of tests that verify that the RI is in compliance with the specification. This allows multiple vendors to provide compliant implementations.

Java EE 7 consists of the platform specification that defines requirements across the platform. It also consists of the following component specifications:

Web technologies

- JSR 45: Debugging Support for Other Languages 1.0
- JSR 52: Standard Tag Library for JavaServer Pages (JSTL) 1.2
- JSR 245: JavaServer Pages (JSP) 2.3
- JSR 340: Servlet 3.1
- JSR 341: Expression Language 3.0
- JSR 344: JavaServer Faces (JSF) 2.2

- JSR 353: Java API for JSON Processing (JSON-P) 1.0
- JSR 356: Java API for WebSocket 1.0

Enterprise technologies
- JSR 236: Concurrency Utilities for Java EE 1.0
- JSR 250: Common Annotations for the Java Platform 1.2
- JSR 316: Managed Beans 1.0
- JSR 318: Interceptors 1.2
- JSR 322: Java EE Connector Architecture (JCA) 1.7
- JSR 330: Dependency Injection for Java 1.0
- JSR 338: Java Persistence API (JPA) 2.1
- JSR 343: Java Message Service (JMS) 2.0
- JSR 345: Enterprise JavaBeans (EJB) 3.2
- JSR 346: Contexts and Dependency Injection (CDI) for the Java EE Platform 1.1
- JSR 349: Bean Validation 1.1
- JSR 352: Batch Applications for Java Platform 1.0
- JSR 907: Java Transaction API (JTA) 1.2
- JSR 919: JavaMail 1.5

Web service technologies
- JSR 93: Java API for XML Registries (JAXR) 1.0 (optional for Java EE 7)
- JSR 101: Java API for XML-based RPC (JAX-RPC) 1.1 (optional for Java EE 7)
- JSR 109: Implementing Enterprise Web Services 1.4
- JSR 181: Web Services Metadata for the Java Platform 2.1
- JSR 222: Java Architecture for XML Binding (JAXB) 2.2
- JSR 224: Java API for XML Web Services (JAX-WS) 2.2
- JSR 339: Java API for RESTful Web Services (JAX-RS) 2.0

Management and security technologies
- JSR 77: J2EE Management API 1.1
- JSR 88: Java Platform EE Application Deployment API 1.2 (optional for Java EE 7)
- JSR 115: Java Authorization Contract and Containers (JACC) 1.5

- JSR 196: Java Authentication Service Provider Inteface for Containers (JASPIC) 1.1

The different components work together to provide an integrated stack, as shown in Figure 1-1.

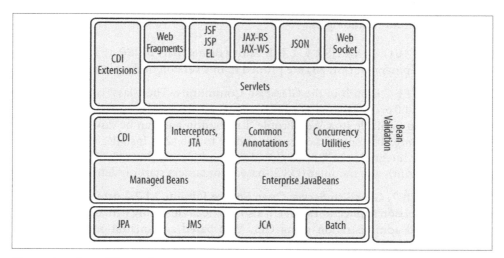

Figure 1-1. Java EE 7 architecture

In Figure 1-1:

- Different components can be logically divided into three tiers: backend tier, middle tier, and web tier. This is only a logical representation, and the components can be restricted to a different tier based upon the application's requirements.

- JPA and JMS provide the basic services such as database access and messaging. JCA allows connection to legacy systems. Batch is used for performing noninteractive, bulk-oriented tasks.

- Managed Beans and EJB provide a simplified programming model using POJOs to use the basic services.

- CDI, Interceptors, and Common Annotations provide concepts that are applicable to a wide variety of components, such as type-safe dependency injection, addressing cross-cutting concerns using interceptors, and a common set of annotations. Concurrency Utilities can be used to run tasks in a managed thread. JTA enables Transactional Interceptors that can be applied to any POJO.

- CDI Extensions allow you to extend the platform beyond its existing capabilities in a standard way.

- Web Services using JAX-RS and JAX-WS, JSF, JSP, and EL define the programming model for web applications. Web Fragments allow automatic registration of third-party web frameworks in a very natural way. JSON provides a way to parse and generate JSON structures in the web tier. WebSocket allows the setup of a bidirectional, full-duplex communication channel over a single TCP connection.

- Bean Validation provides a standard means to declare constraints and validate them across different technologies.

JAX-RPC (JSR 101), JAXR (JSR 93), EJB Entity Beans (part of JSR 153), and Java EE Application Deployment (JSR 88) are pruned in this version of the platform.

The RI of Java EE 7 is built in the GlassFish Community. The GlassFish Server Open Source Edition 4.0 provides a full Java EE 7–compliant, free, and open source application server. It is also available in a Web Profile distribution and can be downloaded from *http://glassfish.org*. The application server is easy to use (ZIP installer and NetBeans/Eclipse/IntelliJ integration), lightweight (downloads starting at 37 MB, small disk/memory footprint), and modular (OSGi-based, containers start on demand).

Prior to Java EE 7, GlassFish Server Open Source Edition 3.1.2.2 provides a Java EE 6–compliant version application server. It also provides clustering with high availability and centralized administration using CLI, Web-based administration console, and REST management/monitoring APIs. The Oracle GlassFish Server is Oracle's commercially supported GlassFish server distribution and can be downloaded from *http://oracle.com/goto/glassfish*. As of this writing, there are 18 Java EE 6–compliant application servers (*http://bit.ly/1bC2HA1*).

The TCK is available to all Java EE licensees for testing their respective implementations.

What's New in Java EE 7

Some new specifications have been added to improve the functionality and richness of the platform. Several existing component specifications were revised to make them simpler and easier to use.

The main features of the new specifications are described as follows:

Java API for WebSocket
- Enables a WebSocket client and server endpoint to be defined declaratively via annotations on a POJO, or programmatically via interface implementation.

- Provides server-specific configuration, such as mapping that identifies a WebSocket endpoint in the URI space of the container, subprotocols supported by the endpoint, and extensions required by the applications.

- Offers client-specific configurations such as providing custom configuration algorithms.

- Enables packaging and deployment on JDK or web containers.
- Allows for integration with existing Java EE technologies.

Java API for JSON Processing
- The streaming API provides a way to parse and generate JSON in a streaming fashion.
- The Object Model API creates a random-access, tree-like structure that represents the JSON data in memory.

Batch Applications for Java Platform
- Allows for description of a Batch Job using Job Specification Language defined by an XML schema. It defines a complete execution sequence of the jobs.
- Features the Batch Programming Model using interfaces, abstract classes, and field annotations.
- Offers the Chunked and Batchlet job-processing styles.

Concurrency Utilities for Java EE
- Provides concurrency capabilities to Java EE application components, without compromising container integrity.
- Defines managed objects: `ManagedExecutorService`, `ManagedScheduledExecutorService`, `ContextService`, and `ManagedThreadFactory`.

The main features of the updated specifications are described as follows:

Java API for RESTful Web Services
- Offers a new Client API that can be used to access web resources and provides integration with JAX-RS providers.
- Supports asynchronous processing in both the Client API and the Server API.
- Defines Message Filters and Entity Interceptors as extension points to customize the request/response processing on the client and server side.
- Supports new server-side content negotiation using qs factor.
- Enables declarative validation of fields, properties, and parameters injected using `@HeaderParam`, `@QueryParam`, etc. Resource classes may be annotated with constraint annotations.

Java Message Service
- Several changes have been made to make the API simpler and easier to use. For example, `Connection`, `Session`, and other objects with a `close` method now implement the `java.lang.Autocloseable` interface to allow them to be used in a Java SE 7 try-with-resources statement. New methods have been added to create a session without the need to supply redundant arguments. A new

method, `getBody`, has been added to allow an application to extract the body directly from a `Message` without the need to cast it first to an appropriate subtype.

- A message producer can now specify that a message must not be delivered until after a specified time interval.
- New send methods have been added to allow an application to send messages asynchronously.
- JMS providers must now set the `JMSXDeliveryCount` message property.

Expression Language
- Expression Language (EL) is a specification of its own. It can be configured and used outside of a Java EE container using `ELProcessor`.
- The lambda syntax is now included in EL. Using lambdas, a complete set of collection operations, such as map and filter is now supported.
- In addition to the usual arithmetic and comparison operators, new operators —such as an assignment operator and string concatenation operator—have been added to make EL more expressive.

Enterprise JavaBeans
- Support for EJB 2.1, EJB QL, and JAX-RPC-based Web Service endpoints and client view is now optional.
- Enhanced message-driven beans (MDBs) contract with a no-method message listener interface to expose all public methods as message listener methods. This will allow custom Resource Adapters for future MDBs.
- EJB API Groups have been defined with clear rules for an EJB Lite Container to support other API groups. This will help define how EJB features beyond EJB Lite can be officially added to a product that does not support full Java EE Profile.
- Asynchronous session bean invocations and nonpersistent EJB Timer Service are included in EJB Lite.
- An option has been added to disable passivation of stateful session beans.

Servlets
- Defines a standard mechanism to upgrade existing HTTP connection to a different protocol using `HttpUpgradeHandler`.
- Offers nonblocking request and response processing for async servlets.
- Defines rules for which HTTP methods are covered by `<security-constraint>`.

JavaServer Faces

- Faces Flow provides an encapsulation of related views/pages with application-defined entry and exit points.

- Resource Library Contracts enable developers to apply facelet templates to an entire application in a reusable and interchangeable manner.

- HTML5-friendly markup allows near-total control over the user experience of each individual element in the view.

- Stateless Views mean developers no longer have to save the `UIComponent` state. This allows applications with JavaScript components to manage the state instead of JSF doing it for them.

Java Persistence

- Database schema and tables may be generated by using `javax.persistence.schema-generation.*` properties.

- Unsynchronized Persistence Contexts mean a persistence context does not have to be enlisted in a transaction. Such persistence contexts can explicitly join a transaction.

- Bulk update/delete is supported via `Criteria` API.

- Predefined and user-defined functions can be invoked using `FUNCTION`.

- Stored procedures can be invoked using `StoredProcedureQuery` and `@NamedStoredProcedureQuery`.

Interceptors

- Associating interceptors using `InterceptorBinding` is now part of this specification, instead of CDI.

- `@AroundConstruct` designates an interceptor method that receives a callback when the target class constructor is invoked.

- Method-level interceptors can be extended to life-cycle callbacks, adding constructor-level interceptors.

- Priority ranges can be dedicated for ordering interceptors using interceptor binding.

Contexts and Dependency Injection

- Allows for automatic enabling of CDI for beans with a scope annotation, and EJBs, in Java EE.

- Supports global ordering and enabling of interceptors, decorators, and alternatives using the `@Priority` annotation.

- Adds the `@Vetoed` annotation, allowing easy programmatic disabling of classes.

Bean Validation

- Validation constraints can be applied to the parameters and return values of arbitrary methods and constructors.

- Integration points with CDI have been increased and reworked.

- The targeted group can be altered when validation cascading is happening.

Java Transaction

- `@Transactional` provides the application to declaratively control transaction boundaries on CDI-managed beans, as well as classes defined as managed beans by the Java EE specification, at both the class and method level where method-level annotations override those at the class level.

- `@TransactionScoped` is a new CDI scope that defines bean instances whose life cycle is scoped to the currently active JTA transaction.

JavaMail

- `@MailSessionDefinition` and `@MailSessionDefintions` defines `MailSession` to be registered with JNDI.

Java EE Connector Architecture

- Provides `@AdministeredObjectDefinition`, `@AdministeredObjectDefintions`, `@ConnectorFactoryDefinition`, and `@ConnectorFactoryDefini tions` to define a connector-administered object and factory to be registered in JNDI.

CHAPTER 2

Servlets

Servlets are defined as JSR 340, and the complete specification can be downloaded (*http://jcp.org/aboutJava/communityprocess/final/jsr340/index.html*).

A servlet is a web component hosted in a servlet container and generates dynamic content. The web clients interact with a servlet using a request/response pattern. The servlet container is responsible for the life cycle of the servlet, receives requests and sends responses, and performs any other encoding/decoding required as part of that.

WebServlet

A servlet is defined using the @WebServlet annotation on a POJO, and must extend the javax.servlet.http.HttpServlet class.

Here is a sample servlet definition:

```
@WebServlet("/account")
public class AccountServlet extends javax.servlet.http.HttpServlet {
  //. . .
}
```

The fully qualified class name is the default servlet name, and may be overridden using the name attribute of the annotation. The servlet may be deployed at multiple URLs:

```
@WebServlet(urlPatterns={"/account", "/accountServlet"})
public class AccountServlet extends javax.servlet.http.HttpServlet {
  //. . .
}
```

The @WebInitParam can be used to specify an initialization parameter:

```
@WebServlet(urlPatterns="/account",
            initParams={
                @WebInitParam(name="type", value="checking")
                      }
```

```
      )
public class AccountServlet extends javax.servlet.http.HttpServlet {
  //. . .
}
```

The HttpServlet interface has one do*XXX* method to handle each of HTTP GET, POST, PUT, DELETE, HEAD, OPTIONS, and TRACE requests. Typically the developer is concerned with overriding the doGet and doPost methods. The following code shows a servlet handling the GET request:

```
@WebServlet("/account")
public class AccountServlet
  extends javax.servlet.http.HttpServlet {
  @Override
  protected void doGet(
      HttpServletRequest request,
      HttpServletResponse response) {
    //. . .
  }
}
```

In this code:

- The HttpServletRequest and HttpServletResponse capture the request/response with the web client.

- The request parameters; HTTP headers; different parts of the path such as host, port, and context; and much more information is available from HttpServletRe quest.

The HTTP cookies can be sent and retrieved as well. The developer is responsible for populating the HttpServletResponse, and the container then transmits the captured HTTP headers and/or the message body to the client.

This code shows how an HTTP GET request received by a servlet displays a simple response to the client:

```
protected void doGet(HttpServletRequest request,
                     HttpServletResponse response) {
    try (PrintWriter out = response.getWriter()) {
        out.println("<html><head>");
        out.println("<title>MyServlet</title>");
        out.println("</head><body>");
        out.println("<h1>My First Servlet</h1>");
        //. . .
        out.println("</body></html>");
    } finally {
        //. . .
    }
}
```

Request parameters may be passed in GET and POST requests. In a GET request, these parameters are passed in the query string as name/value pairs. Here is a sample URL to invoke the servlet explained earlier with request parameters:

```
. . ./account?tx=10
```

In a POST request, the request parameters can also be passed in the posted data that is encoded in the body of the request. In both GET and POST requests, these parameters can be obtained from HttpServletRequest:

```
protected void doGet(HttpServletRequest request,
                     HttpServletResponse response) {
  String txValue = request.getParameter("tx");
  //. . .
}
```

Request parameters can differ for each request.

Initialization parameters, also known as *init params*, may be defined on a servlet to store startup and configuration information. As explained earlier, @WebInitParam is used to specify init params for a servlet:

```
String type = null;

@Override
public void init(ServletConfig config) throws ServletException {
  type = config.getInitParameter("type");
  //. . .
}
```

You can manipulate the default behavior of the servlet's life-cycle call methods by overriding the init, service, and destroy methods of the javax.servlet.Servlet interface. Typically, database connections are initialized in init and released in destroy.

You can also define a servlet using the servlet and servlet-mapping elements in the deployment descriptor of the web application, *web.xml*. You can define the Account Servlet using *web.xml*:

```
<?xml version="1.0" encoding="UTF-8"?>
<web-app version="3.1"
  xmlns="http://xmlns.jcp.org/xml/ns/javaee"
  xmlns:xsi="http://www.w3.org/2001/XMLSchema-instance"
  xsi:schemaLocation="http://xmlns.jcp.org/xml/ns/javaee
  http://xmlns.jcp.org/xml/ns/javaee/web-app_3_1.xsd">
  <servlet>
    <servlet-name>AccountServlet</servlet-name>
    <servlet-class>org.sample.AccountServlet</servlet-class>
  </servlet>
  <servlet-mapping>
    <servlet-name>AccountServlet</servlet-name>
    <url-pattern>/account</url-pattern>
```

```
        </servlet-mapping>
      </web-app>
```

The annotations cover most of the common cases, so *web.xml* is not required in those cases. But some cases, such as ordering of servlets, can only be done using *web.xml*.

If the `metadata-complete` element in *web.xml* is true, then the annotations in the class are not processed:

```
<web-app version="3.1"
  xmlns="http://xmlns.jcp.org/xml/ns/javaee"
  xmlns:xsi="http://www.w3.org/2001/XMLSchema-instance"
  xsi:schemaLocation="http://xmlns.jcp.org/xml/ns/javaee
  http://xmlns.jcp.org/xml/ns/javaee/web-app_3_1.xsd"
  metadata-complete="true">
  //. . .
</web-app>
```

The values defined in the deployment descriptor override the values defined using annotations.

A servlet is packaged in a web application in a *.war* file. Multiple servlets may be packaged together, and they all share a *servlet context*. The `ServletContext` provides detail about the execution environment of the servlets and is used to communicate with the container—for example, by reading a resource packaged in the web application, writing to a logfile, or dispatching a request.

The `ServletContext` can be obtained from `HttpServletRequest`:

```
protected void doGet(HttpServletRequest request,
                     HttpServletResponse response) {
  ServletContext context = request.getServletContext();
  //. . .
}
```

A servlet can send an HTTP cookie, named `JSESSIONID`, to the client for session tracking. This cookie may be marked as `HttpOnly`, which ensures that the cookie is not exposed to client-side scripting code, and thus helps mitigate certain kinds of cross-site scripting attacks:

```
SessionCookieConfig config = request.getServletContext().
                             getSessionCookieConfig();
config.setHttpOnly(true);
```

Alternatively, URL rewriting may be used by the servlet as a basis for session tracking. The `ServletContext.getSessionCookieConfig` method returns `SessionCookieConfig`, which can be used to configure different properties of the cookie.

The `HttpSession` interface can be used to view and manipulate information about a session such as the session identifier and creation time, and to bind objects to the session. A new session object may be created:

```
protected void doGet(HttpServletRequest request,
                     HttpServletResponse response) {
  HttpSession session = request.getSession(true);
  //. . .
}
```

The `session.setAttribute` and `session.getAttribute` methods are used to bind objects to the session.

A servlet may forward a request to another servlet if further processing is required. You can achieve this by dispatching the request to a different resource using `Reques tDispatcher`, which can be obtained from `HttpServletRequest.getRequestDispatch er` or `ServletContext.getRequestDispatcher`. The former can accept a relative path, whereas the latter can accept a path relative to the current context only:

```
protected void doGet(HttpServletRequest request,
                     HttpServletResponse response) {
  request.getRequestDispatcher("bank").forward(request, response);
  //. . .
}
```

In this code, `bank` is another servlet deployed in the same context.

The `ServletContext.getContext` method can be used to obtain `ServletContext` for foreign contexts. It can then be used to obtain a `RequestDispatcher`, which can dispatch requests in that context.

You can redirect a servlet response to another resource by calling the `HttpServletRes ponse.sendRedirect` method. This sends a temporary redirect response to the client, and the client issues a new request to the specified URL. Note that in this case, the original request object is not available to the redirected URL. The redirect may also be marginally slower because it entails two requests from the client, whereas `forward` is performed within the container:

```
protected void doGet(HttpServletRequest request,
                     HttpServletResponse response) {
  //. . .
  response.sendRedirect("http://example.com/SomeOtherServlet");
}
```

Here the response is redirected to the *http://example.com/SomeOtherServlet* URL. Note that this URL could be on a different host/port and may be relative or absolute to the container.

In addition to declaring servlets using `@WebServlet` and *web.xml*, you can define them programmatically using `ServletContext.addServlet` methods. You can do this from the `ServletContainerInitializer.onStartup` or `ServletContextListener.contex tInitialized` method. You can read more about this in "Event Listeners" on page 17.

The `ServletContainerInitializer.onStartup` method is invoked when the application is starting up for the given `ServletContext`. The `addServlet` method returns `ServletRegistration.Dynamic`, which can then be used to create URL mappings, set security roles, set initialization parameters, and manage other configuration items:

```
public class MyInitializer implements ServletContainerInitializer {
  @Override
  public void onStartup (Set<Class<?>> clazz, ServletContext context) {
    ServletRegistration.Dynamic reg =
        context.addServlet("MyServlet", "org.example.MyServlet");
    reg.addMapping("/myServlet");
  }
}
```

Servlet Filters

A servlet filter may be used to update the request and response payload and header information from and to the servlet. It is important to realize that filters do not create the response—they only modify or adapt the requests and responses. Authentication, logging, data compression, and encryption are some typical use cases for filters. The filters are packaged along with a servlet and act upon the dynamic or static content.

You can associate filters with a servlet or with a group of servlets and static content by specifying a URL pattern. You define a filter using the `@WebFilter` annotation:

```
@WebFilter("/*")
public class LoggingFilter implements javax.servlet.Filter {
  public void doFilter(HttpServletRequest request,
                       HttpServletResponse response) {
    //. . .
  }
}
```

In the code shown, the `LoggingFilter` is applied to all the servlets and static content pages in the web application.

The `@WebInitParam` may be used to specify initialization parameters here as well.

A filter and the target servlet always execute in the same invocation thread. Multiple filters may be arranged in a filter chain.

You can also define a filter using `<filter>` and `<filter-mapping>` elements in the deployment descriptor:

```
<filter>
  <filter-name>LoggingFilter</filter-name>
  <filter-class>org.sample.LoggingFilter</filter-class>
</filter>
    . . .
<filter-mapping>
  <filter-name>LoggingFilter</filter-name>
```

```
        <url-pattern>/*</url-pattern>
    </filter-mapping>
```

In addition to declaring filters using @WebFilter and *web.xml*, you can define them programmatically using ServletContext.addFilter methods. You can do this from the ServletContainerInitializer.onStartup method or the ServletContextLis tener.contextInitialized method. The addFilter method returns ServletRegis tration.Dynamic, which can then be used to add mapping for URL patterns, set initialization parameters, and handle other configuration items:

```
public class MyInitializer implements ServletContainerInitializer {
    public void onStartup (Set<Class<?>> clazz, ServletContext context) {
        FilterRegistration.Dynamic reg =
            context.addFilter("LoggingFilter",
                        "org.example.LoggingFilter");
        reg.addMappingForUrlPatterns(null, false, "/");
    }
}
```

Event Listeners

Event listeners provide life-cycle callback events for ServletContext, HttpSession, and ServletRequest objects. These listeners are classes that implement an interface that supports event notifications for state changes in these objects. Each class is annotated with @WebListener, declared in *web.xml*, or registered via one of the ServletCon text.addListener methods. A typical example of these listeners is where an additional servlet is registered programmatically without an explicit need for the programmer to do so, or a database connection is initialized and restored back at the application level.

There may be multiple listener classes listening to each event type, and they may be specified in the order in which the container invokes the listener beans for each event type. The listeners are notified in the reverse order during application shutdown.

Servlet context listeners listen to the events from resources in that context:

```
@WebListener
public class MyContextListener implements ServletContextListener {

    @Override
    public void contextInitialized(ServletContextEvent sce) {
        ServletContext context = sce.getServletContext();
        //. . .
    }

    @Override
    public void contextDestroyed(ServletContextEvent sce) {
        //. . .
    }
}
```

The `ServletContextAttributeListener` is used to listen for attribute changes in the context:

```java
public class MyServletContextAttributeListener
            implements ServletContextAttributeListener {

  @Override
  public void attributeAdded(ServletContextAttributeEvent event) {
    //. . . event.getName();
    //. . . event.getValue();
  }

  @Override
  public void attributeRemoved(ServletContextAttributeEvent event) {
    //. . .
  }

  @Override
  public void attributeReplaced(ServletContextAttributeEvent event) {
    //. . .
  }

}
```

The `HttpSessionListener` listens to events from resources in that session:

```java
@WebListener
public class MySessionListener implements HttpSessionListener {

  @Override
  public void sessionCreated(HttpSessionEvent hse) {
    HttpSession session = hse.getSession();
    //. . .
  }

  @Override
  public void sessionDestroyed(HttpSessionEvent hse) {
    //. . .
  }
}
```

The `HttpSessionActivationListener` is used to listen for events when the session is passivated or activated:

```java
public class MyHttpSessionActivationListener
            implements HttpSessionActivationListener {

  @Override
  public void sessionWillPassivate(HttpSessionEvent hse) {
    // ... hse.getSession();
  }

  @Override
```

```java
    public void sessionDidActivate(HttpSessionEvent hse) {
      // ...
    }
  }
```

The HttpSessionAttributeListener is used to listen for attribute changes in the session:

```java
public class MyHttpSessionAttributeListener
            implements HttpSessionAttributeListener {

  @Override
  public void attributeAdded(HttpSessionBindingEvent event) {
    HttpSession session = event.getSession();
    //. . . event.getName();
    //. . . event.getValue();
  }

  @Override
  public void attributeRemoved(HttpSessionBindingEvent event) {
    //. . .
  }

  @Override
  public void attributeReplaced(HttpSessionBindingEvent event) {
    //. . .
  }
}
```

The HttpSessionBindingListener is used to listen to events when an object is bound to or unbound from a session:

```java
public class MyHttpSessionBindingListener
            implements HttpSessionBindingListener {

  @Override
  public void valueBound(HttpSessionBindingEvent event) {
    HttpSession session = event.getSession();
    //. . . event.getName();
    //. . . event.getValue();
  }

  @Override
  public void valueUnbound(HttpSessionBindingEvent event) {
    //. . .
  }
}
```

The ServletRequestListener listens to the events from resources in that request:

```java
@WebListener
public class MyRequestListener implements ServletRequestListener {
  @Override
  public void requestDestroyed(ServletRequestEvent sre) {
```

```
      ServletRequest request = sre.getServletRequest();
      //. . .
    }

    @Override
    public void requestInitialized(ServletRequestEvent sre) {
      //. . .
    }
  }
```

The ServletRequestAttributeListener is used to listen for attribute changes in the request.

There is also AsyncListener, which is used to manage async events such as completed, timed out, or an error.

In addition to declaring listeners using @WebListener and *web.xml*, you can define them programmatically using ServletContext.addListener methods. You can do this from the ServletContainerInitializer.onStartup or ServletContextListener.con textInitialized method.

The ServletContainerInitializer.onStartup method is invoked when the application is starting up for the given ServletContext:

```
public class MyInitializer implements ServletContainerInitializer {
  public void onStartup(Set<Class<?>> clazz, ServletContext context) {
    context.addListener("org.example.MyContextListener");
  }
}
```

Asynchronous Support

Server resources are valuable and should be used conservatively. Consider a servlet that has to wait for a JDBC connection to be available from the pool, receiving a JMS message or reading a resource from the filesystem. Waiting for a "long-running" process to return completely blocks the thread—waiting, sitting, and doing nothing—which is not an optimal usage of your server resources. This is where the server can be asynchronously processed such that the control (or thread) is returned to the container to perform other tasks while waiting for the long-running process to complete. The request processing continues in the same thread after the response from the long-running process is returned, or may be dispatched to a new resource from within the long-running process. A typical use case for a long-running process is a chat application.

The asynchronous behavior needs to be explicitly enabled on a servlet. You achieve this by adding the asyncSupported attribute on @WebServlet:

```
@WebServlet(urlPatterns="/async", asyncSupported=true)
public class MyAsyncServlet extends HttpServlet {
```

```
//. . .
}
```

You can also enable the asynchronous behavior by setting the `<async-supported>` element to true in *web.xml* or calling `ServletRegistration.setAsyncSupported` (`true`) during programmatic registration.

You can then start the asynchronous processing in a separate thread using the `startA sync` method on the request. This method returns `AsyncContext`, which represents the execution context of the asynchronous request. Then you can complete the asynchronous request by calling `AsyncContext.complete` (explicit) or dispatching to another resource (implicit). The container completes the invocation of the asynchronous request in the latter case.

Let's say the long-running process is implemented:

```
class MyAsyncService implements Runnable {
  AsyncContext ac;

  public MyAsyncService(AsyncContext ac) {
    this.ac = ac;
  }

  @Override
  public void run() {
    //. . .
    ac.complete();
  }
}
```

This service may be invoked from the `doGet` method:

```
@Override
protected void doGet(HttpServletRequest request,
                     HttpServletResponse response) {
  AsyncContext ac = request.startAsync();
  ac.addListener(new AsyncListener() {
    public void onComplete(AsyncEvent event)
        throws IOException {
      //. . .
    }

    public void onTimeout(AsyncEvent event)
        throws IOException {
      //. . .
    }
    //. . .
  });

  ScheduledThreadPoolExecutor executor = new ScheduledThreadPoolExecutor(10);
  executor.execute(new MyAsyncService(ac));
}
```

In this code, the request is put into asynchronous mode. `AsyncListener` is registered to listen for events when the request processing is complete, has timed out, or resulted in an error. The long-running service is invoked in a separate thread and calls `Async Context.complete`, signalling the completion of request processing.

A request may be dispatched from an asynchronous servlet to synchronous, but the other way around is illegal.

The asynchronous behavior is available in the servlet filter as well.

Nonblocking I/O

Servlet 3.0 allowed asynchronous request processing but only permitted traditional I/O, which restricted the scalability of your applications. In a typical application, `Serv letInputStream` is read in a `while` loop:

```
protected void doGet(HttpServletRequest request, HttpServletResponse response)
    throws IOException, ServletException {
  ServletInputStream input = request.getInputStream();
  byte[] b = new byte[1024];
  int len = -1;
  while ((len = input.read(b)) != -1) {
    //. . .
  }
}
```

If the incoming data is blocking or streamed slower than the server can read, then the server thread is waiting for that data. The same can happen if the data is written to `ServletOutputStream`. This restricts the scalability of the Web Container.

Nonblocking I/O allows developers to read data as it becomes available or write data when it's possible to do so. This increases not only the scalability of the Web Container but also the number of connections that can be handled simultaneously. Nonblocking I/O only works with async request processing in Servlets, Filters, and Upgrade Processing.

Servlet 3.1 achieves nonblocking I/O by introducing two new interfaces: `ReadListen er` and `WriteListener`. These listeners have callback methods that are invoked when the content is available to be read or can be written without blocking.

The `doGet` method needs to be rewritten in this case:

```
AsyncContext context = request.startAsync();
ServletInputStream input = request.getInputStream();
input.setReadListener(new MyReadListener(input, context));
```

Invoking set*XXX*Listener methods indicates that nonblocking I/O is used instead of traditional.

`ReadListener` has three callback methods:

- The `onDataAvailable` callback method is called whenever data can be read without blocking.

- The `onAllDataRead` callback method is invoked whenever data for the current request is completely read.

- The `onError` callback is invoked if there is an error processing the request:

```
@Override
public void onDataAvailable() {
  try {
    StringBuilder sb = new StringBuilder();
    int len = -1;
    byte b[] = new byte[1024];
    while (input.isReady() && (len = input.read(b)) != -1) {
      String data = new String(b, 0, len);
    }
  } catch (IOException ex) {
    //. . .
  }
}

@Override
public void onAllDataRead() {
  context.complete();
}

@Override
public void onError(Throwable t) {
  t.printStackTrace();
  context.complete();
}
```

In this code, the `onDataAvailable` callback is invoked whenever data can be read without blocking. The `ServletInputStream.isReady` method is used to check if data can be read without blocking and then the data is read. `context.complete` is called in `onAllDataRead` and `onError` methods to signal the completion of data read. `ServletInputStream.isFinished` may be used to check the status of a nonblocking I/O read.

At most, one `ReadListener` can be registered on `ServletIntputStream`.

`WriteListener` has two callback methods:

- The `onWritePossible` callback method is called whenever data can be written without blocking.

- The `onError` callback is invoked if there is an error processing the response.

At most, one `WriteListener` can be registered on `ServletOutputStream`. `ServletOutputStream.canWrite` is a new method to check if data can be written without blocking.

Web Fragments

A web fragment is part or all of the *web.xml* file included in a library or framework JAR's *META-INF* directory. If this framework is bundled in the *WEB-INF/lib* directory, the container will pick up and configure the framework without requiring the developer to do it explicitly.

It can include almost all of the elements that can be specified in *web.xml*. However, the top-level element must be web-fragment and the corresponding *file* must be called *web-fragment.xml*. This allows logical partitioning of the web application:

```
<web-fragment>
  <filter>
    <filter-name>MyFilter</filter-name>
    <filter-class>org.example.MyFilter</filter-class>
    <init-param>
      <param-name>myInitParam</param-name>
      <param-value>...</param-value>
    </init-param>
  </filter>
  <filter-mapping>
    <filter-name>MyFilter</filter-name>
    <url-pattern>/*</url-pattern>
  </filter-mapping>
</web-fragment>
```

The developer can specify the order in which the resources specified in *web.xml* and *web-fragment.xml* need to be loaded. The <absolute-ordering> element in *web.xml* is used to specify the exact order in which the resources should be loaded, and the <ordering> element within *web-fragment.xml* is used to specify relative ordering. The two orders are mutually exclusive, and absolute ordering overrides relative.

The absolute ordering contains one or more <name> elements specifying the name of the resources and the order in which they need to be loaded. Specifying <others/> allows for the other resources not named in the ordering to be loaded:

```
<web-app>
  <name>MyApp</name>
  <absolute-ordering>
    <name>MyServlet</name>
    <name>MyFilter</name>
  </absolute-ordering>
</web-app>
```

In this code, the resources specified in *web.xml* are loaded first and followed by MyServlet and MyFilter.

Zero or one <before> and <after> elements in <ordering> are used to specify the resources that need to be loaded before and after the resource named in the web-fragment is loaded:

```
<web-fragment>
  <name>MyFilter</name>
  <ordering>
    <after>MyServlet</after>
  </ordering>
</web-fragment>
```

This code will require the container to load the resource `MyFilter` after the resource `MyServlet` (defined elsewhere) is loaded.

If *web.xml* has `metadata-complete` set to true, then the *web-fragment.xml* file is not processed. The *web.xml* file has the highest precedence when resolving conflicts between *web.xml* and *web-fragment.xml*.

If a *web-fragment.xml* file does not have an `<ordering>` element and *web.xml* does not have an `<absolute-ordering>` element, the resources are assumed to not have any ordering dependency.

Security

Servlets are typically accessed over the Internet, and thus having a security requirement is common. You can specify the servlet security model, including roles, access control, and authentication requirements, using annotations or in *web.xml*.

`@ServletSecurity` is used to specify security constraints on the servlet implementation class for all methods or a specific do*XXX* method. The container will enforce that the corresponding do*XXX* messages can be invoked by users in the specified roles:

```
@WebServlet("/account")
@ServletSecurity(
  value=@HttpConstraint(rolesAllowed = {"R1"}),
  httpMethodConstraints={
    @HttpMethodConstraint(value="GET",
                          rolesAllowed="R2"),
    @HttpMethodConstraint(value="POST",
                          rolesAllowed={"R3", "R4"})
  }
)
public class AccountServlet
            extends javax.servlet.http.HttpServlet {
  //. . .
}
```

In this code, `@HttpMethodConstraint` is used to specify that the `doGet` method can be invoked by users in the R2 role, and the `doPost` method can be invoked by users in the R3 and R4 roles. The `@HttpConstraint` specifies that all other methods can be invoked by users in the role R1. The roles are mapped to security principals or groups in the container.

The security constraints can also be specified using the `<security-constraint>` element in *web.xml*. Within it, a `<web-resource-collection>` element is used to specify constraints on HTTP operations and web resources, `<auth-constraint>` is used to specify the roles permitted to access the resource, and `<user-data-constraint>` indicates how data between the client and server should be protected by the subelement `<transport-guarantee>`:

```
<security-constraint>
  <web-resource-collection>
    <url-pattern>/account/*</url-pattern>
    <http-method>GET</http-method>
  </web-resource-collection>

  <auth-constraint>
    <role-name>manager</role-name>
  </auth-constraint>

  <user-data-constraint>
    <transport-guarantee>INTEGRITY</transport-guarantee>
  </user-data-constraint>
</security-constraint>
```

This deployment descriptor requires that only the GET method at the /account/* URL is protected. This method can only be accessed by a user in the manager role with a requirement for content integrity. All HTTP methods other than GET are unprotected.

If HTTP methods are not enumerated within a security-constraint, the protections defined by the constraint apply to the complete set of HTTP (extension) methods:

```
<security-constraint>
  <web-resource-collection>
    <url-pattern>/account/*</url-pattern>
  </web-resource-collection>

  . . .
</security-constraint>
```

In this code, all HTTP methods at the /account/* URL are protected.

Servlet 3.1 defines *uncovered* HTTP protocol methods as the methods that are not listed in the `<security-constraint>` and if at least one `<http-method>` is listed in `<security-constraint>`:

```
<security-constraint>
  <web-resource-collection>
    <url-pattern>/account/*</url-pattern>
    <http-method>GET</http-method>
  </web-resource-collection>
  . . .
</security-constraint>
```

In this code fragment, only the HTTP `GET` method is protected and all other HTTP protocols methods such as `POST` and `PUT` are uncovered.

The `<http-method-omission>` element can be used to specify the list of HTTP methods not protected by the constraint:

```
<security-constraint>
  <web-resource-collection>
    <url-pattern>/account/*</url-pattern>
    <http-method-omission>GET</http-method-omission>
  </web-resource-collection>

  . . .
</security-constraint>
```

In this code, only the HTTP `GET` method is not protected and all other HTTP protocol methods are protected.

The `<deny-uncovered-http-methods>` element, a new element in Servlet 3.1, can be used to deny an HTTP method request for an uncovered HTTP method. The denied request is returned with a 403 (`SC_FORBIDDEN`) status code:

```
<web-app xmlns="http://xmlns.jcp.org/xml/ns/javaee"
         xmlns:xsi="http://www.w3.org/2001/XMLSchema-instance"
         xsi:schemaLocation="http://xmlns.jcp.org/xml/ns/javaee
            http://xmlns.jcp.org/xml/ns/javaee/web-app_3_1.xsd"
         version="3.1">
  <deny-uncovered-http-methods/>
  <web-resource-collection>
    <url-pattern>/account/*</url-pattern>
    <http-method>GET</http-method>
  </web-resource-collection>
  . . .
</web-app>
```

In this code, the `<deny-uncovered-http-methods>` element ensures that HTTP `GET` is called with the required security credentials, and all other HTTP methods are denied with a 403 status code.

`@RolesAllowed`, `@DenyAll`, `@PermitAll`, and `@TransportProtected` provide an alternative set of annotations to specify security roles on a particular resource or a method of the resource:

```
@RolesAllowed("R2")
protected void doGet(HttpServletRequest request, HttpServletResponse response) {
  //. . .
}
```

If an annotation is specified on both the class and the method level, the one specified on the method overrides the one specified on the class.

Servlet 3.1 introduces two new predefined roles:

- * maps to any defined role.
- ** maps to any authenticated user independent of the role.

This allows you to specify security constraints at a higher level than a particular role.

At most, one of @RolesAllowed, @DenyAll, or @PermitAll may be specified on a target. The @TransportProtected annotation may occur in combination with either the @Ro lesAllowed or @PermitAll annotations.

The servlets can be configured for HTTP Basic, HTTP Digest, HTTPS Client, and form-based authentication:

```
<form method="POST" action="j_security_check">
  <input type="text" name="j_username">
  <input type="password" name="j_password" autocomplete="off">
  <input type="button" value="submit">
</form>
```

This code shows how form-based authentication can be achieved. The login form must contain fields for entering a username and a password. These fields must be named j_username and j_password, respectively. The action of the form is always j_securi ty_check.

Servlet 3.1 requires autocomplete="off" on the password form field, further strengthening the security of servlet-based forms.

The HttpServletRequest also provides programmatic security with the login, log out, and authenticate methods.

The login method validates the provided username and password in the password validation realm (specific to a container) configured for the ServletContext. This ensures that the getUserPrincipal, getRemoteUser, and getAuthType methods return valid values. The login method can be used as a replacement for form-based login.

The authenticate method uses the container login mechanism configured for the ServletContext to authenticate the user making this request.

Resource Packaging

You can access resources bundled in the *.war* file using the ServletContext.getRe source and .getResourceAsStream methods. The resource path is specified as a string with a leading "/." This path is resolved relative to the root of the context or relative to the *META-INF/resources* directory of the JAR files bundled in the *WEB-INF/lib* directory:

```
myApplication.war
  WEB-INF
```

```
    lib
        library.jar
```

library.jar has the following structure:

```
library.jar
  MyClass1.class
  MyClass2.class
  stylesheets
    common.css
  images
    header.png
    footer.png
```

Normally, if *stylesheets* and *image* directories need to be accessed in the servlet, you need to manually extract them in the root of the web application. Servlet 3.0 allows the library to package the resources in the *META-INF/resources* directory:

```
library.jar
  MyClass1.class
  MyClass2.class
  META-INF
    resources
      stylesheets
        common.css
      images
        header.png
        footer.png
```

In this case, the resources need not be extracted in the root of the application and can be accessed directly instead. This allows resources from third-party JARs bundled in *META-INF/resources* to be accessed directly instead of manually extracted.

The application always looks for resources in the root before scanning through the JARs bundled in the *WEB-INF/lib* directory. The order in which it scans JAR files in the *WEB-INF/lib* directory is undefined.

Error Mapping

An HTTP error code or an exception thrown by a serlvet can be mapped to a resource bundled with the application to customize the appearance of content when a servlet generates an error. This allows fine-grained mapping of errors from your web application to custom pages. These pages are defined via `<error-page>`:

```
<error-page>
  <error-code>404</error-code>
  <location>/error-404.jsp</location>
</error-page>
```

Adding the preceding fragment to *web.xml* will display the */error-404.jsp* page to a client attempting to access a nonexistent resource. You can easily implement this mapping for other HTTP status codes as well by adding other `<error-page>` elements.

The `<exception-type>` element is used to map an exception thrown by a servlet to a resource in the web application:

```
<error-page>
  <exception-type>org.example.MyException</exception-type>
  <location>/error.jsp</location>
</error-page>
```

Adding the preceding fragment to *web.xml* will display the */error.jsp* page to the client if the servlet throws the `org.example.MyException` exception. You can easily implement this mapping for other exceptions as well by adding other `<error-page>` elements.

The `<error-page>` declaration must be unique for each class name and HTTP status code.

Handling Multipart Requests

`@MultipartConfig` may be specified on a servlet, indicating that it expects a request of type `multipart/form-data`. The `HttpServletRequest.getParts` and `.getPart` methods then make the various parts of the multipart request available:

```
@WebServlet(urlPatterns = {"/FileUploadServlet"})
@MultipartConfig(location="/tmp")
public class FileUploadServlet extends HttpServlet {

  @Override
  protected void doPost(HttpServletRequest request,
                        HttpServletResponse response)
       throws ServletException, IOException {
    for (Part part : request.getParts()) {
      part.write("myFile");
    }
  }
}
```

In this code:

- `@MultipartConfig` is specified on the class, indicating that the `doPost` method will receive a request of type `multipart/form-data`.
- The `location` attribute is used to specify the directory location where the files are stored.
- The `getParts` method provides a `Collection` of parts for this multipart request.
- `part.write` is used to write this uploaded part to disk.

Servlet 3.1 adds a new method, `Part.getSubmittedFileName`, to get the filename specified by the client.

This servlet can be invoked from a JSP page:

```
<form action="FileUploadServlet"
      enctype="multipart/form-data"
      method="POST">
   <input type="file" name="myFile"><br>
   <input type="Submit" value="Upload File"><br>
</form>
```

In this code, the form is POSTed to `FileUploadServlet` with encoding `multipart/form-data`.

Upgrade Processing

Section 14.42 of HTTP 1.1 (RFC 2616 (*http://www.ietf.org/rfc/rfc2616.txt*)) defines an upgrade mechanism that allows you to transition from HTTP 1.1 to some other, incompatible protocol. The capabilities and nature of the application-layer communication after the protocol change are entirely dependent upon the new protocol chosen. After an upgrade is negotiated between the client and the server, the subsequent requests use the newly chosen protocol for message exchanges. A typical example is how the WebSocket protocol is upgraded from HTTP, as described in the Opening Handshake (*http://tools.ietf.org/html/rfc6455#section-1.3*) section of RFC 6455 (*http://tools.ietf.org/html/rfc6455*).

The servlet container provides an HTTP upgrade mechanism. However, the servlet container itself does not have any knowledge about the upgraded protocol. The protocol processing is encapsulated in the `HttpUpgradeHandler`. Data reading or writing between the servlet container and the `HttpUpgradeHandler` is in byte streams.

The decision to upgrade is made in the `Servlet.service` method. Upgrading is achieved by adding a new method, `HttpServletRequest.upgrade`, and two new interfaces, `javax.servlet.http.HttpUpgradeHandler` and `javax.servlet.http.WebConnection`:

```
if (request.getHeader("Upgrade").equals("echo")) {
    response.setStatus(HttpServletResponse.SC_SWITCHING_PROTOCOLS);
    response.setHeader("Connection", "Upgrade");
    response.setHeader("Upgrade", "echo");
    request.upgrade(MyProtocolHandler.class);
    System.out.println("Request upgraded to MyProtocolHandler");
}
```

The request looks for the `Upgrade` header and makes a decision based upon its value. In this case, the connection is upgraded if the `Upgrade` header is equal to `echo`. The correct response status and headers are set. The `upgrade` method is called on `HttpServ letRequest` by passing an instance of `HttpUpgradeHandler`.

After exiting the `service` method of the servlet, the servlet container completes the processing of all filters and marks the connection to be handled by the instance of `HttpUpgradeHandler`:

```java
public class MyProtocolHandler implements HttpUpgradeHandler {
  @Override
  public void init(WebConnection wc) {
    //. . .
  }

  @Override
  public void destroy() {
    //. . .
  }
}
```

This code shows an implementation of `HttpUpgradeHandler`. The servlet container calls the `HttpUpgradeHandler`'s `init` method, passing a `WebConnection` to allow the protocol handler access to the data streams. When the upgrade processing is done, `HttpUpgra deHandler.destroy` is invoked.

The servlet filters only process the initial HTTP request and response. They are not involved in subsequent communications.

CHAPTER 3

JavaServer Faces

JavaServer Faces (JSF) is defined as JSR 344, and the complete specification can be downloaded (*http://jcp.org/aboutJava/communityprocess/final/jsr344/index.html*).

JavaServer Faces is a server-side user interface (UI) framework for Java-based web applications. JSF allows you to:

- Create a web page with a set of reusable UI components following the Model-View-Controller (MVC) design pattern.
- Bind components to a server-side model. This allows a two-way migration of application data with the UI.
- Handle page navigation in response to UI events and model interactions.
- Manage UI component state across server requests.
- Provide a simple model for wiring client-generated events to server-side application code.
- Easily build and reuse custom UI components.

A JSF application consists of:

- A set of web pages in which the UI components are laid out.
- A set of managed beans. One set of beans binds components to a server-side model (typically CDI beans) and another set acts as controller (typically EJB or CDI beans).
- An optional deployment descriptor, *web.xml*.
- An optional configuration file, *faces-config.xml*.
- An optional set of custom objects such as converters and listeners, created by the application developer.

Facelets

Facelets is the *view declaration language* (aka view handler) for JSF. It is the replacement for JSP, which is now retained only for backward compatibility. New features introduced in version 2 of the JSF specification, such as composite components and Ajax, are only exposed to page authors using facelets. Key benefits of facelets include a powerful templating system, reuse and ease of development, better error reporting (including line numbers), and designer-friendliness.

Facelets pages are authored using XHTML 1.0 and Cascading Style Sheets (CSS). An XHTML 1.0 document is a reformulation of an HTML 4 document following the rules of XML 1.0. The pages must conform with the XHTML-1.0-Transitional DTD (*http://bit.ly/11q7IoK*).

You can define a simple Facelets page using XHTML:

```
<?xml version='1.0' encoding='UTF-8' ?>
<!DOCTYPE html
    PUBLIC "-//W3C//DTD XHTML 1.0 Transitional//EN"
 "http://www.w3.org/TR/xhtml1/DTD/xhtml1-transitional.dtd">
<html xmlns="http://www.w3.org/1999/xhtml"
      xmlns:h="http://xmlns.jcp.org/jsf/html">
  <h:head>
    <title>My Facelet Page Title</title>
  </h:head>
  <h:body>
    Hello from Facelets
  </h:body>
</html>
```

In this code, an XML prologue is followed by a document type declaration (DTD). The root element of the page is `html` in the namespace `http://www.w3.org/1999/xhtml`. An XML namespace is declared for the tag library used in the web page. Facelets HTML tags (those beginning with `h:`) and regular HTML tags are used to add components.

Table 3-1 shows the standard set of tag libraries supported by Facelets.

Table 3-1. Standard tag libraries supported by Facelets

Prefix	URI	Examples
h	*http://xmlns.jcp.org/jsf/html*	`h:head, h:inputText`
f	*http://xmlns.jcp.org/jsf/core*	`f:facet, f:actionListener`
c	*http://xmlns.jcp.org/jsp/jstl/core*	`c:forEach, c:if`
fn	*http://xmlns.jcp.org/jsp/jstl/functions*	`fn:toUpperCase, fn:contains`
ui	*http://xmlns.jcp.org/jsf/facelets*	`ui:component, ui:insert`

By convention, web pages built with XHTML have a *.xhtml* extension.

Facelets provides Expression Language (EL) integration. This allows two-way data binding between the backing beans and the UI:

```
Hello from Facelets, my name is #{name.value}!
```

In this code, #{name} is an EL that refers to the value field of a request-scoped CDI bean:

```
@Named
@RequestScoped
public class Name {
  private String value;

  //. . .
}
```

It's important to add @Named on a CDI bean to enable its injection in an EL.

In JSF 2.2, @javax.faces.bean.ManagedBean is targeted for deprecation in a future version, so it is highly recommended that you use @Named.

JSF 2.2 also introduces a new CDI scope: javax.faces.view.ViewScoped. Specifying this annotation on a bean binds it with the current view. javax.faces.bean.ViewSco ped is targeted for deprecation in a future version, so it is strongly recommended that you use the newly introduced scope.

Similarly, an EJB can be injected in an EL expression:

```
@Stateless
@Named
public class CustomerSessionBean {
  public List<Name> getCustomerNames() {
    //. . .
  }
}
```

This is a stateless session bean and has a business method that returns a list of customer names. @Named marks it for injection in an EL. It can be used in Facelets EL:

```
<h:dataTable value="#{customerSessionBean.customerNames}" var="c">
  <h:column>#{c.value}</h:column>
</h:dataTable>
```

In this code, the list of customer names returned is displayed in a table. Notice how the getCustomerNames method is available as a property in the EL.

Facelets also provides compile-time EL validation.

In addition, Facelets provides a powerful templating system that allows you to provide a consistent look and feel across multiple pages in a web application. A base page, called a *template*, is created via Facelets templating tags. This page defines a default structure for the page, including placeholders for the content that will be defined in the pages using the template. A *template client page* uses the template and provides actual content for the placeholders defined in the template.

Table 3-2 lists some of the common tags used in the template and template client pages.

Table 3-2. Common Facelets tags for a template

Tag	Description
ui:composition	Defines a page layout that optionally uses a template. If the template attribute is used, the children of this tag define the template layout. If not, it's just a group of elements—a composition—that can be inserted anywhere. Content outside of this tag is ignored.
ui:insert	Used in a template page and defines the placeholder for inserting content into a template. A matching ui:define tag in the template client page replaces the content.
ui:define	Used in a template client page; defines content that replaces the content defined in a template with a matching ui:insert tag.
ui:component	Inserts a new UI component into the JSF component tree. Any component or content fragment outside this tag is ignored.
ui:fragment	Similar to ui:component, but does not disregard content outside this tag.
ui:include	Includes the document pointed to by the src attribute as part of the current Facelets page.

A template page looks like:

```
<h:body>
  <div id="top">
    <ui:insert name="top">
      <h1>Facelets are Cool!</h1>
    </ui:insert>
  </div>

  <div id="content" class="center_content">
    <ui:insert name="content">Content</ui:insert>
  </div>

  <div id="bottom">
    <ui:insert name="bottom">
      <center>Powered by GlassFish</center>
    </ui:insert>
  </div>

</h:body>
```

In this code, the page defines the structure using <div> and CSS (not shown here). ui:insert defines the content that gets replaced by a template client page.

A template client page looks like:

```
<html xmlns="http://www.w3.org/1999/xhtml"
      xmlns:ui="http://xmlns.jcp.org/jsf/facelets"
      xmlns:h="http://xmlns.jcp.org/jsf/html">
  <body>
```

```
<ui:composition template="./template.xhtml">
  <ui:define name="content">
    <h:dataTable
      value="#{customerSessionBean.customerNames}"
      var="c">
    <h:column>#{c.value}</h:column>
      </h:dataTable>
    </ui:define>

  </ui:composition>
  </body>
</html>
```

In this code, `ui:insert` with `top` and `bottom` names is not defined, so those sections are used from the template page. There is a `ui:define` element with a name matching the `ui:insert` element in the template, so the contents are replaced.

Resource Handling

JSF defines a standard way of handling resources, such as images, CSS, or JavaScript files. These resources are required by a component to be rendered properly.

Such resources can be packaged in the */resources* directory in the web application or in */META-INF/resources* in the classpath. The resources may also be localized, versioned, and collected into libraries.

A resource can be referenced in EL:

```
<a href="#{resource['header.jpg']}">click here</a>
```

In this code, *header.jpg* is bundled in the standard *resources* directory.

If a resource is bundled in a library *corp* (a folder at the location where resources are packaged), then you can access it using the `library` attribute:

```
<h:graphicImage library="corp" name="header.jpg" />
```

JavaScript may be included:

```
<h:outputScript
    name="myScript.js"
    library="scripts"
    target="head"/>
```

In this code, *myScript.js* is a JavaScript resource packaged in the *scripts* directory in the standard *resources* directory.

A CSS stylesheet can be included:

```
<h:outputStylesheet name="myCSS.css" library="css" />
```

The `ResourceHandler` API provides a programmatic way to serve these resources as well.

Composite Components

Using features of Facelets and resource handling, JSF defines a *composite component* as a component that consists of one or more JSF components defined in a Facelets markup file. This *.xhtml* file resides inside of a resource library. This allows you to create a reusable component from an arbitrary region of a page.

The composite component is defined in the *defining page* and used in the *using page*. The defining page defines the metadata (or parameters) using `<cc:interface>` and the implementation using `<cc:implementation>`, where `cc` is the prefix for the `http://xmlns.jcp.org/jsf/composite/` namespace. Future versions of the JSF specification may relax the requirement to specify metadata, as it can be derived from the implementation itself.

You can define a composite component using JSF 1.2 as well, but it requires a much deeper understanding of the JSF life cycle and also authoring multiple files. JSF2 really simplifies the authoring of composite components using just an XHTML file.

Let's say a Facelet has the following code fragment to display a login form:

```
<h:form>
  <h:panelGrid columns="3">
    <h:outputText value="Name:" />
    <h:inputText value="#{user.name}" id="name"/>
    <h:message for="name" style="color: red" />
    <h:outputText value="Password:" />
    <h:inputText value="#{user.password}"
                    id="password"/>
    <h:message for="password" style="color: red" />
  </h:panelGrid>

  <h:commandButton actionListener="#{userService.register}"
    id="loginButton"
    action="status"
    value="submit"/>
</h:form>
```

This code renders a table with two rows and three columns, as shown in Figure 3-1.

Figure 3-1. JSF Facelets page output in a browser

The first column displays a prompt for the field to be entered; the second column displays an input text box where the data can be entered; and the third column (which is empty to begin with) is for displaying a message for the corresponding field. The first row binds the input value to the User.name field, and the second row binds the input value to the User.password field. There is also a command button, and clicking the button invokes the register method of the UserService bean.

If this login form is to be displayed in multiple pages, then instead of repeating this code everywhere, it is beneficial to convert this fragment into a composite component. This requires the code fragment to be copied to an *.xhtml* file, and the file itself is copied in a library in the standard *resources* directory. Via convention-over-configuration, the fragment is then automatically assigned a namespace and a tag name.

If the fragment shown earlier is copied to *login.xhtml* in the *resources/mycomp* directory, the defining page looks like:

```
<?xml version='1.0' encoding='UTF-8' ?>
<!DOCTYPE html
    PUBLIC "-//W3C//DTD XHTML 1.0 Transitional//EN"
 "http://www.w3.org/TR/xhtml1/DTD/xhtml1-transitional.dtd">
<html xmlns="http://www.w3.org/1999/xhtml"
      xmlns:cc="http://xmlns.jcp.org/jsf/composite"
      xmlns:h="http://xmlns.jcp.org/jsf/html">

<!-- INTERFACE -->
<cc:interface>
</cc:interface>

<!-- IMPLEMENTATION -->
<cc:implementation>
  <h:form>
    <h:panelGrid columns="3">
      <h:outputText value="Name:" />
      <h:inputText value="#{user.name}" id="name"/>

    <!-- . . . -->

  </h:form>
</cc:implementation>
</html>
```

In this code, cc:interface defines metadata that describes the characteristics of the component, such as supported attributes, facets, and attach points for event listeners. cc:implementation contains the markup substituted for the composite component.

The namespace of the composite component is constructed by concatenating http:// xmlns.jcp.org/jsf/composite/ and mycomp. The tag name is the filename without the *.xhtml* suffix in the using page:

```
<html xmlns="http://www.w3.org/1999/xhtml"
      xmlns:mc="http://xmlns.jcp.org/jsf/composite/mycomp"

   <!-- . . . -->
   <mc:login/>

</html>
```

Let's say that the code fragment needs to pass different value expressions (instead of #{user.name}) and invoke a different method (instead of #{userService.register}) when the submit button is clicked in a different using page. The defining page can then pass the values:

```
<!-- INTERFACE -->
<cc:interface>
  <cc:attribute name="name"/>
  <cc:attribute name="password"/>
  <cc:attribute name="actionListener"
      method-signature=
          "void action(javax.faces.event.Event)"
      targets="ccForm:loginButton"/>
</cc:interface>

<!-- IMPLEMENTATION -->
<cc:implementation>
  <h:form id="ccForm">
  <h:panelGrid columns="3">
    <h:outputText value="Name:" />
    <h:inputText value="#{cc.attrs.name}" id="name"/>
    <h:message for="name" style="color: red" />
    <h:outputText value="Password:" />
    <h:inputText value="#{cc.attrs.password}"
         id="password"/>
    <h:message for="password" style="color: red" />
  </h:panelGrid>

  <h:commandButton id="loginButton"
                   action="status"
                   value="submit"/>
  </h:form>
</cc:implementation>
```

In this code, all the parameters are explicitly specified in cc:interface for clarity. The third parameter has a targets attribute referring to ccForm:loginButton.

In cc:implementation:

- The h:form has an id attribute. This is required so that the button within the form can be explicitly referenced.

- h:inputText is now using #{cc.attrs.xxx} instead of #{user.xxx}. #{cc.attrs} is a default EL expression that is available for composite component authors and provides access to attributes of the current composite component. In this case, `#{cc.attrs}` has `name` and `password` defined as attributes.

- `actionListener` is an attach point for an event listener. It is defined as a `method-signature` and describes the signature of the method.

- `h:commandButton` has an `id` attribute so that it can be clearly identified within the `h:form`.

The `user`, `password`, and `actionListener` are then passed as required attributes in the using page:

```
<ez:login
    name="#{user.name}"
    password="#{user.password}"
    actionListener="#{userService.register}"/>
```

Now the using page can pass different backing beans, and different business methods can be invoked when the submit button is clicked.

Overall, the composite component provides the following benefits:

- Follows the Don't Repeat Yourself (DRY) design pattern and allows you to keep code that can be repeated at multiple places in a single file.

- Allows developers to author new components without any Java code or XML configuration.

Request Processing Life-Cycle Phases

JSF defines standard request processing life-cycle phases. Application developers don't necessarily need to know the details of the life cycle, but it helps those who need to know information such as when validations, conversions, and events are usually handled and what they can do to change how and when they are handled.

A JSF page is represented by a tree of UI components, called a *view*. When a client makes a request for the page, the life cycle starts. During the life cycle, the JavaServer Faces implementation must build the view while considering the state saved from a previous submission of the page. When the client submits a page, the JavaServer Faces implementation must perform several tasks, such as validating the data input of components in the view, converting input data to types specified on the server side, and binding data to the backing beans. The JavaServer Faces implementation performs all these tasks as a series of steps in the life cycle.

The different components of the application go through the following well-defined request processing life-cycle *phases*:

Restore view

Restores and creates a server-side component tree to represent the UI information from a client.

If the request is made to a URL for the first time, then a new View object is created and rendered to the client. This view is also stored in the current FacesContext instance. If the view state is already found in FacesContext, then it is restored and displayed.

Any custom converters, validators, renderers, if attached for the UI components, are restored in this phase. If the UI component values are directly mapped to the property defined in a *managed bean*, then the value for the property is restored and it is associated with the view. Most of the work is handled by the ViewHandler.re storeView method.

Apply request values

This phase updates the server-side components with request parameters, headers, cookies, and so on from the client.

More specifically, the UIComponent.processDecodes method is called on all components. The outcome of this phase may either end in *the process validations phase* or the *render response phase*. If any of the conversions or the validations fail, then the current processing is terminated and the control directly goes to the *render response* for rendering the conversion or the validation errors to the client.

Process validations

This phase will process any validations and data type conversions configured for UIComponents.

In this phase, the UIComponent.processValidators method is called on all components. If any conversion or validation error happens here, then the current process is terminated and the control is directed to the *render response* phase for reporting any errors.

Update model values

Reaching this phase means that the request values are syntactically valid.

The values from UIComponents are synchronized with the model objects, which are usually backing beans. In this phase, the UIComponent.processUpdates method is called on all components. Setting the request value to the model object may also result in events being queued and fired.

Invoke application

Invokes application logic and performs navigation processing.

All the listeners that are registered for the `UIComponents` are invoked. For example, all action components, like the command button or the hyperlink, have *default action listeners* that are invoked in this phase.

Render response
Renders the response back to the client application.

Before rendering the response, the application stores the state of `View` in the cache by calling the `UIViewRoot.saveState` method.

Ajax

JSF provides native support for adding Ajax capabilities to web pages. It allows *partial view processing*, where only some components from the view are used for processing the response. It also enables *partial page rendering*, where selective components from the page, as opposed to the complete page, are rendered.

There are two ways this support can be enabled:

- Programmatically using JavaScript resources
- Declaratively using `f:ajax`

Programmatic Ajax integration is enabled through the resource handling mechanism. *jsf.js* is a predefined resource in the `javax.faces` library. This resource contains the JavaScript API that facilitates Ajax interaction with JSF pages. You can make it available in pages using the `outputScript` tag:

```
<h:body>
<!-- . . . -->
<h:outputScript
    name="jsf.js"
    library="javax.faces"
    target="body"/>
<!-- . . . -->
</h:body>
```

You can also make an asynchronous request to the server:

```
<h:form prependId="false">
  <h:inputText value="#{user.name}" id="name"/>
  <h:inputText value="#{user.password}" id="password"/>
  <h:commandButton value="Login"
                   type="button"
                   actionListener="#{user.login}"
     onclick="jsf.ajax.request(this, event, {execute:
'name password', render: 'status'}); return false;"/>

  <h:outputText value="#{user.status}" id="status"/>
</h:form>
```

In this code:

- Two input text fields accept the username and password, and the third output field displays the status (whether the user is logged in or not).

- The form has prependId set to false to ensure that the id of each element is preserved as mentioned in the form. Otherwise, JSF prepends the form's id to the id of its children.

- The command button has an actionListener identifying the method in the backing bean to be invoked when the button is clicked. Instead of the usual response rendering and displaying a different page, jsf.ajax.request sends an asynchronous request to the server. This request is made on the command button's onclick event. execute and render provide a space-separated identifier of the components. execute is the list of input components whose bean setters are invoked, and render is the list of components that needs to be rendered after the asynchronous response is received.

The ability to process only part of the view (name and password elements in this case) is referred to as *partial view processing*. Similarly, rendering only part of the output page (the status element in this case) is referred to as *partial output rendering*.

Table 3-3 lists the possible values of the render attribute.

Table 3-3. Values for the render attribute in f:ajax

Value	Description
@all	All components on the page
@none	No components on the page; this is the default value
@this	Element that triggered the request
@form	All components within the enclosing form
IDs	Space-separated identifiers of the components
EL expression	EL expression that resolves to a collection of strings

The execute attribute takes a similar set of values, but the default value for the execute attribute is @this.

- The User bean has fields, setters/getters, and a simple business method:

```
@Named
@SessionScoped
public class User implements Serializable {
    private String name;
    private String password;
    private String status;

    . . .
```

```
        public void login(ActionEvent evt) {
            if (name.equals(password))
                status = "Login successful";
            else
                status = "Login failed";
        }
    }
```

Note the signature of the login method. It must return void and take javax.
faces.event.ActionEvent as the only parameter.

Declarative Ajax integration is enabled via f:ajax. This tag may be nested within a single component (enabling Ajax for a single component), or it may be "wrapped" around multiple components (enabling Ajax for many components).

The preceding code can be updated to use this style of Ajax:

```
<h:form prependId="false">
    <h:inputText value="#{user.name}"
                 id="name"/>
    <h:inputText value="#{user.password}"
                 id="password"/>
    <h:commandButton value="Login"
                     type="button"
                     actionListener="#{user.login}">
        <f:ajax execute="name password"
                render="status"/>
    </h:commandButton>

    <h:outputText value="#{user.status}"
                  id="status"/>
</h:form>
```

In this code, we use f:ajax to specify the list of input elements using the execute attribute, and the output elements to be rendered using the render attribute. By default, if f:ajax is nested within a single component and no event is specified, the asynchronous request is fired based upon the default event for the parent component (the on click event in the case of a command button).

A delay attribute may be specified on the f:ajax tag. This attribute takes a value in milliseconds. If multiple requests are issued before the *delay* time elapses, then only the most recent request is sent and all others are discarded.

```
<f:ajax delay="200" ...>
  . . .
</f:ajax>
```

This code fragment sets the delay to 200 milliseconds. The default value is 300 milliseconds, but you could also specify the special value of none to disable this mechanism.

The f:ajax tag may be wrapped around multiple components:

```
<f:ajax listener="#{user.checkFormat}">
    <h:inputText value="#{user.name}" id="name"/>
    <h:inputText value="#{user.password}" id="password"/>
</f:ajax>
```

In this code, `f:ajax` has a `listener` attribute and the corresponding Java method:

```
public void checkFormat(AjaxBehaviorEvent evt) {
    //. . .
}
```

This listener method is invoked for the default event for the child elements (the `value Change` event for `h:inputText`, in this case). You can specify additional Ajax functionality on the child elements using a nested `f:ajax`.

HTTP GET

JSF provides support for mapping URL parameters in HTTP `GET` requests to an EL. It also provides support to generate `GET`-friendly URLs.

View parameters can be used to map URL parameters in `GET` requests to an EL. You can do so by adding the following fragment to a Facelets page:

```
<f:metadata>
    <f:viewParam name="name" value="#{user.name}"/>
</f:metadata>
```

Accessing a web application at *index.xhtml?name=jack* will:

- Get the request parameter by the name `name`.
- Convert and validate if necessary. This is achieved by way of a nested `f:convert er` and `f:validator`, just like with any `h:inputText`, and can be done as shown:

```
<f:metadata>
    <f:viewParam name="name" value="#{user.name}">
        <f:validateLength minimum="1" maximum="5"/>
    </f:viewParam>
</f:metadata>
```

- If successful, bind it to #{user.name}.

You can postprocess the view parameters before the page is rendered using `f:event`:

```
<f:metadata>
  <f:viewParam name="name" value="#{user.name}">
    <f:validateLength minimum="1" maximum="5"/>
  </f:viewParam>
  <f:event type="preRenderView" listener="#{user.process}"/>
</f:metadata>
```

In this code, the method identified by #{user.process} can be used to perform any initialization required prior to rendering the page.

You can generate GET-friendly URLs using h:link and h:button. You specify the desired Facelets page instead of manually constructing the URL:

```
<h:link value="Login" outcome="login"/>
```

This is translated to the following HTML tag:

```
<a href=".../faces/login.xhtml">Login</a>
```

View parameters can be easily specified:

```
<h:link value="Login" outcome="login">
    <f:param name="name" value="#{user.name}"/>
</h:link>
```

In this code, if #{user.name} is bound to "Jack," then this fragment is translated to the following HTML tag:

```
<a href=".../faces/login.xhtml?name=Jack">Login</a>
```

Similarly, h:button can be used to specify the outcome:

```
<h:button value="login"/>
```

This code will generate the following HTML tag:

```
<input
    type="button"
    onclick="window.location.href='/JSFSample/faces/index.xhtml'; return false;"
    value="login" />
```

Server and Client Extension Points

Converters, validators, and listeners are server-side *attached objects* that add more functionality to the components on a page. Behaviors are client-side extension points that can enhance a component's rendered content with behavior-defined scripts.

A converter converts the data entered in a component from one format to another (e.g., string to number). JSF provides several built-in converters such as f:convertNumber and f:convertDateTime. They can be applied to any editable component:

```
<h:form>
    Age: <h:inputText value="#{user.age}" id="age">
        <f:convertNumber integerOnly="true"/>
    </h:inputText>
    <h:commandButton value="Submit"/>
</h:form>
```

In this code, the text entered in the text box will be converted to an integer if possible. An error message is thrown if the text cannot be converted.

A custom converter can be easily created:

```
@FacesConverter("myConverter")
public class MyConverter implements Converter {

    @Override
    public Object getAsObject(
            FacesContext context,
            UIComponent component,
            String value) {
        //. . .
    }

    @Override
    public String getAsString(
            FacesContext context,
            UIComponent component,
            Object value) {
        //. . .
    }
}
```

In this code, the methods `getAsObject` and `getAsString` perform object-to-string and string-to-object conversions between model data objects and a string representation of those objects that is suitable for rendering. The POJO implements the `Converter` interface and is also marked with `@FacesConverter`. This converter can then be used in a JSF page:

```
<h:inputText value="#{user.age}" id="age">
  <f:converter converterId="myConverter"/>
</h:inputText>
```

The `value` attribute of `@FacesConverter` must match the value of the `converterId` attribute here.

A validator is used to validate data that is received from the input components. JSF provides several built-in validators such as `f:validateLength` and `f:validateDou bleRange`. These validators can be applied to any editable component:

```
<h:inputText value="#{user.name}" id="name">
  <f:validateLength min="1" maximum="10"/>
</h:inputText>
```

In this code, the length of the entered text is validated to be between 1 and 10 characters. An error message is thrown if the length is outside the specified range.

A custom validator can be easily created:

```
@FacesValidator("nameValidator")
public class NameValidator implements Validator {

    @Override
    public void validate(
        FacesContext context,
        UIComponent component,
```

```
      Object value)
      throws ValidatorException {
    //. . .
  }

}
```

In this code, the method `validate` returns if the value is successfully validated. Otherwise, a `ValidatorException` is thrown. This validator can be applied to any editable component:

```
<h:inputText value="#{user.name}" id="name">
  <f:validator id="nameValidator"/>
</h:inputText>
```

The `value` attribute of `@FacesValidator` must match the value of the `id` attribute of `f:validator` here.

JSF also provides built-in integration with constraints defined using Bean Validation. Other than placing annotation constraints on the bean, no additional work is required by the developer. Any error message because of constraint violation is automatically converted to a `FacesMessage` and displayed to the end user. `f:validateBean` may be used to specify `validationGroups` to indicate which validation groups should be taken into consideration when validating a particular component. This is explained in detail in Chapter 11.

A listener listens for events on a component. The event can be a change of value, a click of a button, a click on a link, or something else. A listener can be a method in a managed bean or a class by itself.

A `ValueChangeListener` can be registered on any editable component:

```
<h:inputText value="#{user.age}"
             id="age"
             valueChangeListener="#{user.nameUpdated}">
```

In this code, the `nameUpdated` method in the `User` bean is called when the associated form is submitted. You can create a class-level listener by implementing the `ValueChangeListener` interface and specify it in the page using the `f:valueChangeListener` tag.

Unlike converters, validators, and listeners, a behavior enhances the client-side functionality of a component by declaratively attaching scripts to it. For example, `f:ajax` is defined as a client-side behavior. Client-side behavior also allows you to perform client-side validation and client-side logging, show tooltips, and other similar functionality.

You can define custom behaviors by extending `ClientBehaviorBase` and marking with `@FacesBehavior`.

Validating Data

In addition to using built-in and creating custom JSF validators, you can specify constraints defined on a backing bean using Bean Validation.

Consider a simple web application that has one page with several text fields inside of a form:

```
<h:form>
  Name: <h:inputText value="#{myBean.name}"/>
  Age: <h:inputText value="#{myBean.age}"/>
  Zip: <h:inputText value="#{myBean.zip}"/>
  <h:commandButton value="Submit"/>
</h:form>
```

Assume that every text field is bound to a managed bean property that has at least one Bean Validation constraint annotation attached to it:

```
@Named
@SessionScoped
public class MyBean implements Serializable {

  @Size(min = 3, message = "At least 3 characters")
  private String name;

  @Min(18)
  @Max(25)
  private int age;

  @Pattern(regexp = "[0-9]{5}")
  private String zip;

  //. . .
}
```

Every h:inputText element that is backed by a UIInput component has an instance of Validator with id javax.faces.Bean attached to it. The validate method of this Validator is called for the user-specified validation constraints during the *process validations* phase.

The javax.faces.Bean standard validator also ensures that every ConstraintViolation that resulted in attempting to validate the model data is wrapped in a FacesMessage and added to the FacesContext as with every other kind of validator. This message is then displayed to the user as other validator messages are handled.

One or more validation groups can be associated with an input tag:

```
Name:
<h:inputText value="#{person.name}" id="name">
  <f:validateBean validationGroups=
    "org.sample.Page1Group, org.sample.OtherGroup"/>
```

```
    </h:inputText>
    <h:commandButton action="index2" value="Next >"/>
```

which can also be used to create validation across multiple pages.

The validation groups can also be associated with a group of input tags:

```
<f:validateBean validationGroups="org.sample.MyGroup">
    <h:inputText value="#{person.name}"/>
    <h:inputText value="#{person.age}"/>
</f:validateBean>
```

In this code, the constraints are validated for the fields identified by `#{person.name}` and `#{person.age}`.

Navigation Rules

JSF defines implicit and explicit navigation rules.

Implicit navigation rules look for the outcome of an action (e.g., a click on a link or a button). If a Facelets page matching the action outcome is found, that page is then rendered:

```
<h:commandButton action="login" value="Login"/>
```

In this code, clicking the button will render the page *login.xhtml* in the same directory.

You can specify explicit navigation using `<navigation-rule>` in *faces-config.xml*, and you can specify conditional navigation using `<if>`:

```
<navigation-rule>
  <from-view-id>/index.xhtml</from-view-id>
  <navigation-case>
    <from-outcome>success</from-outcome>
    <to-view-id>/login.xhtml</to-view-id>
    <if>#{user.isPremium}</if>
  </navigation-case>
</navigation-rule>
```

In this code, the page navigation from *index.xhtml* to *login.xhtml* only occurs if the user is a premium customer.

Faces Flow

JSF 2.2 introduces Faces Flow. This feature borrows core concepts from ADF Task Flows, Spring Web Flow, and Apache MyFaces CODI to provide a modular approach for defining control flow in an application and standardizes them as part of JSF 2.2.

Faces Flow provides an encapsulation of related pages and corresponding backing beans as a module. This module has well-defined entry and exit points assigned by the application developer. Usually the objects in a faces flow are designed to allow the user to accomplish a task that requires input over a number of different views. An application thus becomes a collection of flows instead of just views.

Imagine a multipage shopping cart with one page for selecting the items, a second page for choosing shipping options, a third page for entering credit card details, and a fourth page for confirming the order. You can use managed beans to capture the data, session scope variables to pass information between pages, button clicks to invoke the business logic in backing EJBs, and (conditional) navigation rules to go from one page to another. There are a few issues with this approach:

- This flow of sequence will typically be part of a bigger application. This application, typically with several pages, is one large flow and everything has global visibility with no logical partitioning.

- The flow of pages or views cannot be encapsulated as a logical unit and thus cannot be reused—that is, incorporated into another bigger application or flow easily.

- The same flow cannot be opened in multiple windows because session scoped variables are used to pass information between pages. CDI defines `@ConversationSco ped`, but that is only part of the solution.

- A request-based scope is for a particular request. A session-based scope is more than a request scope, but becomes invalid after the browser is closed. We require a scope of something in between that can span multiple pages per the application logic. This is what is missing.

- The lowest logical granularity is a page. The only way to invoke application logic is to tie it to a UI component activated by the user in a page. Business logic cannot be invoked without any user-initiated action.

Faces Flow provides a solution to these issues:

- The application is broken into a series of modular flows that can call one another.

- The flow of pages can be packaged as a module that can be reused within the same or an entirely different application.

- Shared memory scope (for example, flow scope) enables data to be passed between views within the task flow.

- A new CDI scope, `@FlowScoped`, can be specified on a bean. This allows automatic activation/passivation of the bean as the scope is entered/exited.

- Business logic can be invoked from anywhere in the page based upon the flow definition.

The flow of application is no longer restricted to flow between pages but instead is defined as flow between "nodes." There are five different types of nodes:

View

Any JSF page in the application.

Method call

Invoke application logic from the flow graph via an EL.

Switch

Navigation decisions in the flow graph based on Boolean EL.

Flow call

Call another flow with parameters and receive return values.

Flow return

Return to the calling flow.

These nodes define the entry and exit points of a flow.

The newly introduced CDI scope `@FlowScoped` defines the scope of a bean in the specified flow. This enables automatic activation/passivation of the bean when the scope is entered/exited:

```
@FlowScoped("flow1")
public class MyFlow1Bean {
  String address;
  String creditCard;
  //. . .
}
```

In this code, the bean has two flow-scoped variables: `address` and `creditCard`. The bean is defined for the flow `flow1`.

A new EL object for flow storage, `#{flowScope}`, is also introduced. This maps to `facesContext.getApplication().getFlowHandler().getCurrentFlowScope()`:

```
value: <h:inputText id="input" value="#{flowScope.value}" />
```

In this code, the value entered in the text box is bound to `#{flowScope.value}`. This EL expression can be used in other pages in the flow to access the value.

You can define flows declaratively using `<flow-definition>`, or programmatically using the fluent `FlowBuilder` API. The two mechanisms are mutually exclusive.

Flows can be packaged in JAR files or in directories. JAR packaging requires flows to be explicitly declared in *META-INF/faces-config.xml* in the JAR file. Flow nodes are packaged in *META-INF/flows/<flowname>* where *<flowname>* is a JAR directory entry whose name is identical to that of a flow `id` in the corresponding `FlowDefinition` classes. If `@FlowScoped` beans and a flow defined via `FlowBuilder` are packaged in the JAR file, they must be accompanied by *META-INF/beans.xml*:

```
META-INF/faces-config.xml
META-INF/flows/flow1/entry.xhtml
```

```
META-INF/flows/flow1/next.xhtml
META-INF/flows/flow1/end.xhtml
META-INF/flows/flow2/start.xhtml
META-INF/flows/flow2/next.xhtml
META-INF/flows/flow2/end.xhtml
META-INF/beans.xml
org/glassfish/sample/MyFlow1Bean.class
org/glassfish/sample/MyFlow2Bean.class
org/glassfish/sample/MyFlow1Defintion.class
org/glassfish/sample/MyFlow2Defintion.class
```

In this JAR packaging:

- There are two flows, flow1 and flow2.

- *META-INF/beans.xml* is required to enable CDI. It may be implicitly enabled if bean-defining annotations are used in the archive.

- MyFlow1Bean and MyFlow2Bean are the flow-scoped beans. These beans are used to store any flow-local data.

- MyFlow1Definition defines the entry and exit points of a flow, inbound parameter name and value coming from another flow, outbound parameter name and value for another flow, and navigation to other nodes:

```
public class MyFlow1Definition {

  @Produces @FlowDefinition
  public Flow defineFlow(@FlowBuilderParameter FlowBuilder flowBuilder) {
    String flowId = "flow1";
    flowBuilder.id("unique", flowId);
    flowBuilder.viewNode(flowId, "/" + flowId + "/" + flowId + ".xhtml")
               .markAsStartNode();

    flowBuilder.returnNode("goHome").
      fromOutcome("#{flow1Bean.homeValue}");

    flowBuilder.inboundParameter("param1FromFlow2", "#{flowScope.param1Value}");

    flowBuilder.flowCallNode("call2").flowReference("", "flow2").
      outboundParameter("param1FromFlow1", "param1 flow1 value");

    return flowBuilder.getFlow();
  }
}
```

In this code:

— Flow is defined programmatically via the CDI producer. @FlowDefinition is a class-level annotation that allows the flow to be defined via the fluent Flow Builder API.

— A `FlowBuilder` instance is injected as a parameter via the `@FlowBuilderPara meter` and is used to define the flow.

— `flow1` is defined as the flow identifier and *flow1.xhtml* is marked as the starting node.

— The `returnNode` method is used to define an exit point from the flow. In this case, the flow is directed to */index* for the action `goHome`. The node value can be specified as an EL expression as well—for example, "may be bound to a bean."

— Named inbound parameters are named parameters from another flow and are defined via the `inboundParameter` method. The method's value is populated elsewhere with a corresponding `outboundParameter` element. The value is stored in the flow local storage via `#{flowScope}`.

— `flowCallNode` method is used to define an exit point from the flow. In this case, `flow2` flow is called. A named outbound parameter and its value are set via the `outboundParameter` method.

Similarly `MyFlow2Definition` class defines `flow2`.

Flows packaged in directories use convention-over-configuration. The conventions are:

• Every View Declaration Language file, defined by an *.xhtml* page, in that directory is a view node of that flow.

• The start node of the flow is the view whose name is the same as the name of the flow.

• Navigation among any of the views in the directory is considered to be within the flow.

• Navigation to a view outside of that directory is considered to be an exit of the flow.

• An optional *<flowname>-flow.xml* file represents the flow definition. The rules in this file override the conventions just described:

```
flow1/flow1.xhtml
flow1/flow1a.xhtml
flow1/flow1b.xhtml
flow2/flow2-flow.xml
flow2/flow2.xhtml
flow2/flow2a.xhtml
flow2/flow2b.xhtml
WEB-INF/...
```

Following the conventions just defined, in this directory:

• *flow1.xhtml* is the starting node of flow `flow1`, and `flow1a` and `flow1b` are two other nodes in the same flow.

- flow2 is the starting node of flow flow2, and flow2a and flow2b are two other nodes in the same flow. *flow2/flow2-flow.xml* defines declarative navigation of the flow flow2. It defines the entry and exit points of a flow, inbound parameter name and value coming from another flow, outbound parameter name and value for another flow, and navigation to other nodes:

```
<faces-config version="2.2"
               xmlns="http://xmlns.jcp.org/xml/ns/javaee"
               xmlns:xsi="http://www.w3.org/2001/XMLSchema-instance"
               xsi:schemaLocation="
               http://xmlns.jcp.org/xml/ns/javaee
               http://xmlns.jcp.org/xml/ns/javaee/web-facesconfig_2_2.xsd">

  <flow-definition id="flow1">
    <flow-return id="goHome">
      <from-outcome>/index</from-outcome>
    </flow-return>

    <inbound-parameter>
      <name>param1FromFlow1</name>
      <value>#{flowScope.param1Value}</value>
    </inbound-parameter>

    <flow-call id="callFlow2">
      <flow-reference>
        <flow-id>flow2</flow-id>
      </flow-reference>
      <outbound-parameter>
        <name>param1FromFlow1</name>
        <value>param1 flow1 value</value>
      </outbound-parameter>
    </flow-call>
  </flow-definition>
</faces-config>
```

In this fragment:

— <flow-definition> defines flow for flow1, identified by the id attribute.

— <flow-return> defines an exit point from the flow. In this case, the flow is directed to */index* for the action goHome. The node value can be specified as an EL expression—for example, "may be bound to a bean."

— A named inbound parameter is defined via <inbound-parameter>. Its value is populated elsewhere with a corresponding <outbound-parameter> element. The value is stored in the flow local storage via #{flowScope}.

— <flow-call> defines an exit point from the flow. In this case, flow2 flow is called. A named outbound parameter and its value are set via <outbound-parameter>.

- The *WEB-INF* directory will contain other resources required by the pages, such as backing beans.

Resource Library Contracts

JSF 2 introduced Facelets as the default View Declaration Language. Facelets allows you to create templates using XHTML and CSS that can then be used to provide a consistent look and feel across different pages of an application. JSF 2.2 defines *Resource Library Contracts*, a library of templates and associated resources that can be applied to an entire application in a reusable and interchangeable manner. A configurable set of views in the application will be able to declare themselves as template-clients of any template in the resource library contract.

Resource library contracts reside in the *contracts* directory of the web application's root:

```
index.xhtml
new/index.xhtml
contracts/blue/layout.css
contracts/blue/template.xhtml
contracts/blue/footer.png
contracts/red
contracts/red/layout.css
contracts/red/template.xhtml
contracts/red/logo.png
WEB-INF/faces-config.xml
```

In this code:

- The application also has two pages: *index.xhtml* and *new/index.xhtml*. These are template client pages.

- All contracts reside in the *contracts* directory of the WAR. All templates and resources for a contract are in their own directory. For example, the preceding structure has two defined contracts, blue and red.

- Each contract has a *template.xhtml* file, a CSS, and an image. Each template is called as a *declared template*. In the template, it is recommended that you refer to the stylesheets using h:outputStylesheet so that they are resolved appropriately.

- The *template.xhtml* file has <ui:insert> tags called as *declared insertion points*.

- CSS, images, and other resources bundled in the directory are *declared resources*.

- The declared template, declared insertion points, and declared resources together define the resource library contract. A template client needs to know the value of all three in order to use the contract. The client pages will use the contract by referring to the template:

```
<ui:composition template="/template.xhtml">
  <ui:define name="content">
```

```
       . . .
    </ui:define>
  </ui:composition>
```

- *WEB-INF/faces-config.xml* defines the usage of the contract:

```
<application>
  <resource-library-contracts>
    <contract-mapping>
      <url-pattern>/new/*</url-pattern>
      <contracts>blue</contracts>
    </contract-mapping>
    <contract-mapping>
      <url-pattern>*</url-pattern>
      <contracts>red</contracts>
    </contract-mapping>
  </resource-library-contracts>
</application>
```

A contract is applied based upon the URL pattern invoked. Based upon the configuration specified here, the `red` contract will be applied to *faces/index.xhtml* and the `blue` contract will be applied to *faces/new/index.xhtml*.

The contracts can be packaged in the *META-INF/contracts* entry of a JAR file. Each contract in the JAR file must have a marker file. The filename is given by the value of the symbolic constant `javax.faces.application.ResourceHandler.RESOURCE_CON` `TRACT_XML`:

```
META-INF/contracts/blue/javax.faces.contract.xml
META-INF/contracts/blue/layout.css
META-INF/contracts/blue/template.xhtml
META-INF/contracts/blue/footer.png
META-INF/contracts/red/javax.faces.contract.xml
META-INF/contracts/red/layout.css
META-INF/contracts/red/template.xhtml
META-INF/contracts/red/logo.png
```

The contents of the *contracts* directory from our application can be packaged in the *META-INF/contracts* entry of a JAR file, say *layout.jar*. This JAR can then be packaged into *WEB-INF/lib*, and the declared templates can be used in the application:

```
index.xhtml
new/index.xhtml
WEB-INF/lib/layout.jar
```

You can use a new *layout.jar* file, providing a similar set of declared insertion points and resources (likely with a different CSS), to change the look and feel of the application.

You can change the template of the page dynamically as well by enclosing the template client page `ui:composition` in an `f:view`:

```
<f:view contracts="#{contractsBean.contract}">
  <ui:composition template="/template.xhtml">
```

```
<ui:define name="content">
  . . .
  <h:form>
    <h:selectOneRadio value="#{contractsBean.contract}">
      <f:selectItem itemValue="red" itemLabel="red"/>
      <f:selectItem itemValue="blue" itemLabel="blue"/>
    </h:selectOneRadio>
    <h:commandButton value="Apply" action="index" />
  </h:form>
</ui:define>
  </ui:composition>
</f:view>
```

In this code:

- f:view has an attribute, contracts, that binds to an EL.
- The value of this EL is populated from the radio button in the form inside ui:de fine.
- The radio button values match the contract names.
- Clicking on the Apply command button will apply the chosen template to this page.

The backing bean definition is trivial:

```
@Named
@SessionScoped
public class ContractsBean implements Serializable {
  String contract = "red";

  // getter & setter
}
```

Passthrough Attributes and HTML5-Friendly Markup

HTML5 adds a series of new attributes for existing elements. These attributes include the type attribute for input elements, which supports values such as email, url, tel, number, range, and date:

```
<input type="email" name="myEmail"/>
```

This code fragment allows the browser to check whether the entered text is in email format.

In addition, custom data attributes, also known as *data-** attributes, can be defined to store custom data private to the page or application. Every HTML element may have any number of custom data attributes specified, with any value:

```
<input id="myData" type="text" data-length="3"/>
```

This code fragment introduces data-length as a custom data attribute.

These attributes are not rendered but can be read by JavaScript. This attribute can be accessed in JavaScript as:

```
document.getElementById("myData").dataset.length;
```

Prior to JSF 2.2, by default, these newly introduced types and data-* attributes were not supported by the components. The set of available attributes supported by a JSF component is determined by the combination of the UIComponent and Renderer for that tag. In some cases, the value of the attribute is interpreted by the UIComponent or Renderer (for example, the columns attribute of h:panelGrid), and in others, the value is passed straight through to the user agent (for example, the lang attribute of h:input Text). In both cases, the UIComponent/Renderer has a prior knowledge of the set of allowable attributes.

JSF 2.2 introduces *passthrough attributes*, which allow us to list arbitrary name/value pairs in a component that are passed straight through to the user agent without interpretation by the UIComponent or Renderer. The passthrough attributes can be specified in three different ways:

- Prefixing the attribute with the shortname assigned to the http://xmlns.jcp.org/jsf/passThrough XML namespace:

  ```
  <h:inputText p:type="email" value="#{user.email}"/>
  ```

  In this code, p is the shortname for the namespace.

- Nesting the <f:passThroughAttribute> tag within a component:

  ```
  <h:inputText value="#{user.email}">
    <f:passThroughAttribute name="type" value="email"/>
  </h:inputText>
  ```

  In this code, a type attribute of value email is marked as a passthrough attribute.

- Nesting the <f:passThroughAttributes> tag within a component:

  ```
  <h:inputText value="#{user.data}">
    <f:passThroughAttributes value="#{user.myAttributes}"/>
  </h:inputText>
  ```

  #{user.myAttributes} must point to a Map<String, Object> where the values can be either literals or a value expression.

This mechanism can be applied to any JSF component and is not restricted to just HTML5 elements.

Component Tags

JSF 2 defines a variety of component tags. Each component is backed by a UICompo nent class. These component tags are rendered as an HTML element via the HTML RenderKit Renderer.

Here are sme commonly used components:

h:commandButton

- Usage:

```
<h:commandButton
  value="Next"
  action="next"/>
```

- HTML:

```
<input
  type="submit"
  name="j_idt8"
  value="Next" />
```

h:commandLink

- Usage:

```
<h:commandLink
  value="myLink"
  action="next"/>
```

- HTML:

```
<script
  type="text/javascript"
  src="/components/faces/javax.faces.resource/jsf.js?
      ln=javax.faces&amp;stage=Development">
</script>
<a
  href="#"
  onclick="mojarra.jsfcljs(document.getElementById('j_idt6'),
          {'j_idt10':'j_idt10'},'');return false">
  myLink
</a>
```

h:dataTable

- Usage:

```
<h:dataTable
  value="#{myBean.list}"
  var="p">
  <h:column>
    <f:facet name="header">Id</f:facet>
    #{p.id}
  </h:column>
  <h:column>
    <f:facet name="header">Name</f:facet>
    #{p.name}
  </h:column>
</h:dataTable>
```

- HTML:

```
<table>
  <thead>
    <tr>
      <th scope="col">Id</th>
      <th scope="col">Name</th>
    </tr>
  </thead>
  <tbody>
    <tr>
      <td> 1 </td>
      <td> Penny </td>
    </tr>
    <tr>
      <td> 2 </td>
      <td> Leonard </td>
    </tr>
    <tr>
      <td> 3 </td>
      <td> Sheldon </td>
    </tr>
  </tbody>
</table>
```

h:form

- Usage:

```
<h:form> ... </h:form>
```

- HTML:

```
<form
  id="j_idt6"
  name="j_idt6"
  method="post"
  action="/components/faces/index.xhtml"
  enctype="application/x-www-form-urlencoded">
  ...
</form>
```

h:graphicImage

- Usage:

```
<h:graphicImage
  value="/images/glassfish.png"/>
```

- HTML:

```
<img
  src="/components/images/glassfish.png" />
```

h:inputHidden

- Usage:

```
<h:inputHidden
  value="myHiddenValue"/>
```

- HTML:

```
<input
  type="hidden"
  name="j_idt22"
  value="myHiddenValue" />
```

h:inputSecret
- Usage:

```
<h:inputSecret
  value="#{myBean.password}"/>
```

- HTML:

```
<input
  type="password"
  name="j_idt24"
  value="" />
```

h:inputText
- Usage:

```
<h:inputText
  id="myInputText"
  value="#{myBean.inputText}"/>
```

- HTML:

```
<input
  id="myInputText"
  type="text"
  name="myInputText" />
```

h:inputTextArea
- Usage:

```
<h:inputTextarea
  value="#{myBean.inputTextarea}"/>
```

- HTML:

```
<textarea
  name="j_idt27">
</textarea>
```

h:button
- Usage:

```
<h:button
  value="myButton"
  outcome="next"/>
```

- HTML:

```
<input
  type="button"
  onclick="window.location.href='/components/faces/next.xhtml';
           return false;"
  value="myButton" />
```

h:link

- Usage:

```
<h:link
  value="Next"
  outcome="next">
  <f:param
    name="foo"
    value="bar"/>
</h:link>
```

- HTML:

```
<a
  href="/components/faces/next.xhtml?foo=bar">
  Next
</a>
```

h:body

- Usage:

```
<h:body>
  This is body
</h:body>
```

- HTML:

```
<body>
  This is body
</body>
```

h:outputFormat

- Usage:

```
<h:outputFormat
  value="Hello {0}">
  <f:param value="Duke"/>
</h:outputFormat>
```

- HTML:

```
Hello Duke
```

h:outputLabel

- Usage:

```
<label
  for="inputTextId">
```

```
      myLabel
    </label>
    <input
      id="inputTextId"
      type="text"
      name="inputTextId"
      value="myInputText" />
```

- HTML:

```
    <h:outputLabel
      for="inputTextId"
      value="myLabel"/>
    <h:inputText
      id="inputTextId"
      value="myInputText"/>
```

h:outputLink
- Usage:

```
    <h:outputLink
      value="next.xhtml">
      myOutput
    </h:outputLink>
```

- HTML:

```
    <a href="next.xhtml">
      myOutput
    </a>
```

h:outputText
- Usage:

```
    <h:outputText
      value="myOutputText"/>
```

- HTML:

```
    myOutputText
```

h:outputScript
- Usage:

```
    <h:outputScript
      library="scripts"
      name="main.js"/>
```

- HTML:

```
    <script
      type="text/javascript"
      src="/components/faces/javax.faces.resource/main.js">
```

h:outputStylesheet

- Usage:

```
<h:outputStylesheet
  library="stylesheets"
  name="main.css"/>
```

- HTML:

```
<link
  type="text/css"
  rel="stylesheet"
  href ="/components/faces/javax.faces.resource/main.css?
        ln=stylesheets"/>
```

h:panelGrid

- Usage:

```
<h:panelGrid
  columns="2">
  <h:outputLabel
    for="inputText1"
    value="myLabel1"/>
  <h:inputText
    id="inputText1"
    value="#{myBean.inputText}"/>
  <h:outputLabel
    for="inputText2"
    value="myLabel2"/>
  <h:inputText
    id="inputText2"
    value="#{myBean.inputText}"/>
</h:panelGrid>
```

- HTML:

```
<table>
  <tbody>
    <tr>
      <td>
        <label for="inputText1">myLabel1</label>
      </td>
      <td>
        <input
          id="inputText1"
          type="text"
          name="inputText1" />
      </td>
    </tr>
    <tr>
      <td>
        <label for="inputText2">myLabel2</label>
      </td>
      <td>
```

```
            <input
              id="inputText2"
              type="text"
              name="inputText2" />
          </td>
        </tr>
      </tbody>
    </table>
```

h:selectBooleanCheckbox

- Usage:

```
<h:selectBooleanCheckbox
  value="#{myBean.selectBooleanCheckbox}"/>
```

- HTML:

```
<input
  type="checkbox"
  name="j_idt52" />
```

h:selectOneRadio

- Usage:

```
<h:selectOneRadio
  value="#{myBean.selectBooleanCheckbox}">
  <f:selectItem
    itemValue="red"
    itemLabel="Red"/>
  <f:selectItem
    itemValue="green"
    itemLabel="Green"/>
  <f:selectItem
    itemValue="blue"
    itemLabel="Blue"/>
</h:selectOneRadio>
```

- HTML:

```
<table>
  <tr>
    <td>
      <input
        type="radio"
        checked="checked"
        name="j_idt54"
        id="j_idt54:0"
        value="red" />
      <label for="j_idt54:0"> Red</label>
    </td>
    <td>
      <input
        type="radio"
        checked="checked"
```

```
            name="j_idt54"
            id="j_idt54:1"
            value="green" />
          <label for="j_idt54:1"> Green</label>
      </td>
      <td>
        <input
          type="radio"
          checked="checked"
          name="j_idt54"
          id="j_idt54:2"
          value="blue" />
        <label for="j_idt54:2"> Blue</label>
      </td>
    </tr>
  </table>
```

h:selectOneListbox

- Usage:

```
<h:selectOneListbox
  value="#{myBean.selectBooleanCheckbox}">
  <f:selectItem
    itemValue="red"
    itemLabel="Red"/>
  <f:selectItem
    itemValue="green"
    itemLabel="Green"/>
  <f:selectItem
    itemValue="blue"
    itemLabel="Blue"/>
</h:selectOneListbox>
```

- HTML:

```
<select name="j_idt59" size="3">
  <option
    value="red"
    selected="selected">Red</option>
  <option
    value="green"
    selected="selected">Green</option>
  <option
    value="blue"
    selected="selected">Blue</option>
</select>
```

h:selectOneMenu

- Usage:

```
<h:selectOneMenu
  value="#{myBean.selectBooleanCheckbox}">
  <f:selectItem
```

```
        itemValue="red"
        itemLabel="Red"/>
      <f:selectItem
        itemValue="green"
        itemLabel="Green"/>
      <f:selectItem
        itemValue="blue"
        itemLabel="Blue"/>
    </h:selectOneMenu>
```

- HTML:

```
<select name="j_idt64" size="1">
  <option
    value="red"
    selected="selected">Red</option>
  <option
    value="green"
    selected="selected">Green</option>
  <option
    value="blue"
    selected="selected">Blue</option>
</select>
```

h:selectManyCheckbox

- Usage:

```
<h:selectManyCheckbox
  value="#{myBean.selectManyCheckbox}">
  <f:selectItem
    itemValue="red"
    itemLabel="Red"/>
  <f:selectItem
    itemValue="green"
    itemLabel="Green"/>
  <f:selectItem
    itemValue="blue"
    itemLabel="Blue"/>
</h:selectManyCheckbox>
```

- HTML:

```
<table>
  <tr>
    <td>
      <input
        name="j_idt69"
        id="j_idt69:0"
        value="red"
        type="checkbox" />
      <label
        for="j_idt69:0"
        class=""> Red</label>
    </td>
```

```
      <td>
        <input
          name="j_idt69"
          id="j_idt69:1"
          value="green"
          type="checkbox" />
        <label
          for="j_idt69:1"
          class=""> Green</label>
      </td>
      <td>
        <input
          name="j_idt69"
          id="j_idt69:2"
          value="blue"
          type="checkbox" />
        <label
          for="j_idt69:2"
          class=""> Blue</label>
      </td>
    </tr>
  </table>
```

h:selectManyListbox

- Usage:

```
<h:selectManyListbox
  value="#{myBean.selectBooleanCheckbox}"
  size="2">
  <f:selectItem
    itemValue="red"
    itemLabel="Red"/>
  <f:selectItem
    itemValue="green"
    itemLabel="Green"/>
  <f:selectItem
    itemValue="blue"
    itemLabel="Blue"/>
</h:selectManyListbox>
```

- HTML:

```
<select name="j_idt74" size="2">
  <option
    value="red"
    selected="selected">Red</option>
  <option
    value="green"
    selected="selected">Green</option>
  <option
    value="blue"
```

```
              selected="selected">Blue</option>
          </select>
```

h:selectManyMenu
- Usage:
```
<h:selectManyMenu
  value="#{myBean.selectBooleanCheckbox}">
  <f:selectItem
    itemValue="red"
    itemLabel="Red"/>
  <f:selectItem
    itemValue="green"
    itemLabel="Green"/>
  <f:selectItem
    itemValue="blue"
    itemLabel="Blue"/>
</h:selectManyMenu>
```

- HTML:
```
<select name="j_idt81" multiple="multiple" size="1">
  <option value="red">Red</option>
  <option value="green">Green</option>
  <option value="blue">Blue</option>
</select>
<input
  type="hidden"
  name="javax.faces.ViewState"
  id="j_id1:javax.faces.ViewState:0"
  value="-6389029500114305749:3536902027553202703"
  autocomplete="off" />
```

h:inputFile is a new component added in JSF 2.2. This component allows a file to be
uploaded. This component can be used inside an h:form and bound to a bean that has
a field of the type javax.servlet.http.Part:

```
<h:form enctype="multipart/form-data">
  <h:inputFile value="#{fileUploadBean.file}"/><br/>

  <h:commandButton value="Upload"/><p/>
</h:form>
```

In this code:

- An HTML form is created via the h:form element. The form must have multipart/
  form-data as the value of enctype. This is a standard MIME type that should be
  used for submitting forms that contain files, non-ASCII data, and binary data.

- The value attribute of h:inputFile is bound to a bean:
```
@Named
@RequestScoped
```

```
public class FileUploadBean {
  private Part file;

  public Part getFile() {
    return file;
  }

  public setFile(Part file) {
    this.file = file;
  }
}
```

- The file is uploaded when the Upload button is clicked.

The file upload can also be wrapped in a <f:ajax> tag:

```
<h:form enctype="multipart/form-data" prependId="false">
  <h:inputFile value="#{fileUploadBean.file}"/><br/>

  <h:commandButton value="Upload">
    <f:ajax onevent="statusUpdate"/>
  </h:commandButton>
</h:form>
<textarea id="status" cols="40" rows="10" readonly="readonly"/>
```

This code is similar to that previously shown with the following differences:

- The <textarea> outside h:form is a placeholder for displaying the status of the file upload.

- h:commandButton has a nested <f:ajax> tag. This tag invokes the statusUpdate method defined separately in JavaScript:

```
var statusUpdate = function statusUpdate(data) {
  var statusArea = document.getElementById("status");
  var text = statusArea.value;
  text = text + "Name: " + data.source.id;
  if (data.type === "event") {
    text = text + " Event: " + data.status + " ";
  }
  statusArea.value = text;
}
```

This code prints the event source and name as the Ajax request goes through the JSF Ajax life cycle and receives the standard life-cycle events.

CHAPTER 4

RESTful Web Services

RESTful Web Services are defined as JSR 339, and the complete specification can be downloaded (*http://jcp.org/aboutJava/communityprocess/final/jsr339/index.html*).

REST is an architectural style of services that utilizes web standards. Web services designed using REST are called RESTful web services, and their main principles are:

- Everything can be identified as a resource, and each resource can be uniquely identified by a URI.

- A resource can be represented in multiple formats, defined by a media type. The media type will provide enough information on how the requested format needs to be generated. Standard methods are defined for the client and server to negotiate on the content type of the resource.

- Use standard HTTP methods to interact with the resource: GET to retrieve a resource, POST to create a resource, PUT to update a resource, and DELETE to remove a resource.

- Communication between the client and the endpoint is stateless. All the associated state required by the server is passed by the client in each invocation.

Java API for RESTful web services (JAX-RS) defines a standard annotation-driven API that helps developers build a RESTful web service in Java and invoke it. The standard principles of REST, such as identifying a resource as a URI, a well-defined set of methods to access the resource, and multiple representation formats of a resource, can be easily marked in a POJO via annotations.

Resources

A simple RESTful web service can be defined as a resource using @Path:

```
@Path("orders")
public class OrderResource {
  @GET
  public List<Order> getAll() {
    //. . .
  }

  @GET
  @Path("{oid}")
  public Order getOrder(@PathParam("oid")int id) {
    //. . .
  }
}

@XmlRootElement
public class Order {
  int id;
  //. . .
}
```

In this code:

- OrderResource is a POJO class and is published as a RESTful resource at the or ders path when we add the class-level @Path annotation.

- The Order class is marked with the @XmlRootElement annotation, allowing a conversion between Java and XML.

- The getAll resource method, which provides a list of all orders, is invoked when we access this resource using the HTTP GET method; we identify it by specifying the @GET annotation on the method.

- The @Path annotation on the getOrder resource method marks it as a subresource that is accessible at orders/{oid}.

- The curly braces around oid identify it as a template parameter and bind its value at runtime to the id parameter of the getOrder resource method.

- The @PathParam can also be used to bind template parameters to a resource class field.

Typically, a RESTful resource is bundled in a *.war* file along with other classes and resources. The Application class and @ApplicationPath annotation are used to specify the base path for all the RESTful resources in the packaged archive. The Application class also provides additional metadata about the application.

Let's say this POJO is packaged in the *store.war* file, deployed at localhost:8080, and the Application class is defined:

```
@ApplicationPath("webresources")
public class ApplicationConfig extends Application {
}
```

You can access a list of all the orders by issuing a GET request to:

```
http://localhost:8080/store/webresources/orders
```

You can obtain a specific order by issuing a GET request to:

```
http://localhost:8080/store/webresources/orders/1
```

Here, the value 1 will be passed to getOrder's method parameter id. The resource method will locate the order with the correct order number and return back the Order class. The @XmlRootElement annotation ensures that an automatic mapping from Java to XML occurs following JAXB mapping and an XML representation of the resource is returned.

A URI may pass HTTP query parameters using name/value pairs. You can map these to resource method parameters or fields using the @QueryParam annotation. If the resource method getAll is updated such that the returned results start from a specific order number, the number of orders returned can also be specified:

```
public List<Order> getAll(@QueryParam("start")int from,
                          @QueryParam("page")int page) {
  //. . .
}
```

And the resource is accessed as:

```
http://localhost:8080/store/webresources/orders?start=10&page=20
```

Then 10 is mapped to the from parameter and 20 is mapped to the page parameter.

By default, a resource method is required to wait and produce a response before returning to the JAX-RS implementation, which then returns control to the client. JAX-RS 2 allows for an asynchronous endpoint that informs the JAX-RS implementation that a response is not readily available upon return but will be produced at a future time. It achieves this by first *suspending* the client connection and later *resuming* when the response is available:

```
@Path("orders")
public class OrderResource {
  @GET
  public void getAll(@Suspended final AsyncResponse ar) {
    executor.submit(new Runnable() {

      @Override
      public void run() {
        List<Order> response = new ArrayList<>();
        //. . .
        ar.resume(response);
      }
    });
  }
}
```

In this code:

- The `getAll` method is marked to produce an asynchronous response. We identify this by injecting a method parameter of the class `AsyncResponse` using the new annotation `@Suspended`. The return type of this method is `void`.

- This method returns immediately after forking a new thread, likely using `ManagedExecutorService` as defined by Concurrency Utilities for Java EE. The client connection is *suspended* at this time.

- The new thread executes the long-running operation and *resumes* the connection by calling `resume` when the response is ready.

You can receive request processing completion events by registering an implementation of `CompletionCallback`:

```
public class OrderResource {
  public void getAll(@Suspended final AsyncResponse ar) {
    ar.register(new MyCompletionCallback());
  }

  class MyCompletionCallback implements CompletionCallback {

    @Override
    public void onComplete(Throwable t) {
      //. . .
    }
  }
}
```

In this code, the `onComplete` method is invoked when the request processing is finished, after a response is processed and is sent back to the client, or when an unmapped throwable has been propagated to the hosting I/O container.

You can receive connection-related life-cycle events by registering an implementation of `ConnectionCallback`:

```
public class OrderResource {
  public void getAll(@Suspended final AsyncResponse ar) {
    ar.register(new MyCompletionCallback());
  }

  class MyCompletionCallback implements CompletionCallback {

    @Override
    public void onDisconnect(AsyncResponse ar) {
      //. . .
    }
  }
}
```

In this code, the onDisconnect method is invoked in case the container detects that the remote client connection associated with the asynchronous response has been disconnected.

Binding HTTP Methods

JAX-RS provides support for binding standard HTTP GET, POST, PUT, DELETE, HEAD, and OPTIONS methods using the corresponding annotations described in Table 4-1.

Table 4-1. HTTP methods supported by JAX-RS

HTTP method	JAX-RS annotation
GET	@GET
POST	@POST
PUT	@PUT
DELETE	@DELETE
HEAD	@HEAD
OPTIONS	@OPTIONS

Let's take a look at how @POST is used. Consider the following HTML form, which takes the order identifier and customer name and creates an order by posting the form to *webresources/orders/create*:

```
<form method="post" action="webresources/orders/create">
  Order Number: <input type="text" name="id"/><br/>
  Customer Name: <input type="text" name="name"/><br/>
  <input type="submit" value="Create Order"/>
</form>
```

The updated resource definition uses the following annotations:

```
@POST
@Path("create")
@Consumes("application/x-www-form-urlencoded")
public Order createOrder(@FormParam("id")int id,
                         @FormParam("name")String name) {
  Order order = new Order();
  order.setId(id);
  order.setName(name);
  return order;
}
```

The @FormParam annotation binds the value of an HTML form parameter to a resource method parameter or a field. The name attribute in the HTML form and the value of the @FormParam annotation are exactly the same to ensure the binding. Clicking the submit button in this form will return the XML representation of the created Order. A Re sponse object may be used to create a custom response.

The following code shows how @PUT is used:

```
@PUT
@Path("{id}")
@Consumes("*/xml")
public Order putXml(@PathParam("id")int id,
                    String content) {
  Order order = findOrder(id);
  // update order from "content"
  . . .
  return order;
}
```

The resource method is marked as a subresource, and {id} is bound to the resource method parameter id. The contents of the body can be any XML media type as defined by @Consumes and are bound to the content method parameter. A PUT request to this resource may be issued as:

```
curl -i -X PUT -d "New Order"
    http://localhost:8080/store/webresources/orders/1
```

The content method parameter will have the value New Order.

Similarly, an @DELETE resource method can be defined as follows:

```
@DELETE
@Path("{id}")
public void putXml(@PathParam("id")int id) {
  Order order = findOrder(id);
  // delete order
}
```

The resource method is marked as a subresource, and {id} is bound to the resource method parameter id. A DELETE request to this resource may be issued as:

```
curl -i -X DELETE
    http://localhost:8080/store/webresources/orders/1
```

The content method parameter will have the value New Order.

The HEAD and OPTIONS methods receive automated support from JAX-RS.

The HTTP HEAD method is identical to GET except that no response body is returned. This method is typically used to obtain metainformation about the resource without requesting the body. The set of HTTP headers in response to a HEAD request is identical to the information sent in response to a GET request. If no method is marked with @HEAD, an equivalent @GET method is called, and the response body is discarded. The @HEAD annotation is used to mark a method serving HEAD requests:

```
@HEAD
@Path("{id}")
public void headOrder(@PathParam("id")int id) {
```

```
    System.out.println("HEAD");
}
```

This method is often used for testing hypertext links for validity, accessibility, and recent modification. A HEAD request to this resource may be issued as:

```
curl -i -X HEAD
    http://localhost:8080/store/webresources/orders/1
```

The HTTP response header contains HTTP/1.1 204 No Content and no content body.

The HTTP OPTIONS method requests the communication options available on the request/response identified by the URI. If no method is designated with @OPTIONS, the JAX-RS runtime generates an automatic response using the annotations on the matching resource class and methods. The default response typically works in most cases. @OPTIONS may be used to customize the response to the OPTIONS request:

```
@OPTIONS
@Path("{id}")
  public Response options() {
  // create a custom Response and return
}
```

An OPTIONS request to this resource may be issued as:

```
curl -i -X OPTIONS
    http://localhost:8080/store/webresources/orders/1
```

The HTTP Allow response header provides information about the HTTP operations permitted. The Content-Type header is used to specify the media type of the body, if any is included.

In addition to the standard set of methods supported with corresponding annotations, HttpMethod may be used to build extensions such as WebDAV.

Multiple Resource Representations

By default, a RESTful resource is published or consumed with the */* MIME type. A RESTful resource can restrict the media types supported by request and response using the @Consumes and @Produces annotations, respectively. These annotations may be specified on the resource class or a resource method. The annotation specified on the method overrides any on the resource class.

Here is an example showing how Order can be published using multiple MIME types:

```
@GET
@Path("{oid}")
@Produces({"application/xml", "application/json"})
public Order getOrder(@PathParam("oid")int id) { . . . }
```

The resource method can generate an XML or JSON representation of `Order`. The exact return type of the response is determined by the HTTP `Accept` header in the request.

Wildcard pattern matching is supported as well. The following resource method will be dispatched if the HTTP `Accept` header specifies any `application` MIME type such as `application/xml`, `application/json`, or any other media type:

```
@GET
@Path("{oid}")
@Produces("application/*")
public Order getOrder(@PathParam("oid")int id) { . . . }
```

Here is an example of how multiple MIME types may be consumed by a resource method:

```
@POST
@Path("{oid}")
@Consumes({"application/xml", "application/json"})
public Order getOrder(@PathParam("oid")int id) { . . . }
```

The resource method invoked is determined by the HTTP `Content-Type` header of the request.

JAX-RS 2.0 allows you to indicate a media preference on the server side using the qs (short for "quality on server") parameter.

qs is a floating-point number with a value in the range of 0.000 through 1.000 and indicates the relative quality of a representation compared to the others available, independent of the client's capabilities. A representation with a qs value of 0.000 will never be chosen. A representation with no qs parameter value is given a qs factor of 1.0:

```
@POST
@Path("{oid}")
@Consumes({"application/xml; qs=0.75", "application/json; qs=1"})
public Order getOrder(@PathParam("oid")int id) { . . . }
```

If a client issues a request with no preference for a particular representation or with an `Accept` header of `application/*;`, then the server will select a representation with a higher qs value—`application/json` in this case.

qs values are relative and, as such, are only comparable to other qs values within the same `@Produces` annotation instance.

You can define a mapping between a custom representation and a corresponding Java type by implementing the `MessageBodyReader` and `MessageBodyWriter` interfaces and annotating with `@Provider`.

Binding a Request to a Resource

By default, a new resource is created for each request to access a resource. The resource method parameters, fields, or bean properties are bound by way of *xxx*Param annotations added during object creation time. In addition to @PathParam and @QueryParam, the following annotations can be used to bind different parts of the request to a resource method parameter, field, or bean property:

- @CookieParam binds the value of a cookie:

```
public Order getOrder(
    @CookieParam("JSESSIONID")String sessionid) {
        //. . .
}
```

  This code binds the value of the "JSESSIONID" cookie to the resource method parameter sessionid.

- @HeaderParam binds the value of an HTTP header:

```
public Order getOrder(
    @HeaderParam("Accept")String accept) {
    //. . .
}
```

- @FormParam binds the value of a form parameter contained within a request entity body. Its usage is displayed in "Binding HTTP Methods" on page 77.

- @MatrixParam binds the name/value parameters in the URI path:

```
public List<Order> getAll(
    @MatrixParam("start")int from,
    @MatrixParam("page")int page) {
    //. . .
}
```

  And the resource is accessed as:

```
http://localhost:8080/store/webresources/orders;
start=10;
page=20
```

  Then 10 is mapped to the from parameter and 20 is mapped to the page parameter.

You can obtain more details about the application deployment context and the context of individual requests using the @Context annotation.

Here is an updated resource definition where more details about the request context are displayed before the method is invoked:

```
@Path("orders")
public class OrderResource {

  @Context Application app;
```

```
@Context UriInfo uri;
@Context HttpHeaders headers;
@Context Request request;

@Context SecurityContext security;
@Context Providers providers;

@GET
@Produces("application/xml")
public List<Order> getAll(@QueryParam("start")int from,
                          @QueryParam("end")int to) {
    //. . .(app.getClasses());
    //. . .(uri.getPath());
    //. . .(headers.getRequestHeader(HttpHeaders.ACCEPT));
    //. . .(headers.getCookies());
    //. . .(request.getMethod());
    //. . .(security.isSecure());
    //. . .
}
}
```

In this code:

- `UriInfo` provides access to application and request URI information.
- `Application` provides access to application configuration information.
- `HttpHeaders` provides access to HTTP header information either as a `Map` or as convenience methods. Note that `@HeaderParam` can also be used to bind an HTTP header to a resource method parameter, field, or bean property.
- `Request` provides a helper to request processing and is typically used with `Response` to dynamically build the response.
- `SecurityContext` provides access to security-related information about the current request.
- `Providers` supplies information about runtime lookup of provider instances based on a set of search criteria.

Entity Providers

JAX-RS defines *entity providers* that supply mapping services between on-the-wire representations and their associated Java types. The entities, also known as "message payload" or "payload," represent the main part of an HTTP message. These are specified as method parameters and return types of resource methods. Several standard Java types —such as `String`, `byte[]`, `javax.xml.bind.JAXBElement`, `java.io.InputStream`, `java.io.File`, and others—have a predefined mapping and are required by the specification. Applications may provide their own mapping to custom types using the `Mes` sageBodyReader and MessageBodyWriter interfaces. This allows us to extend the JAX-RS runtime easily to support our own custom entity providers.

The MessageBodyReader interface defines the contract for a provider that supports the conversion of a stream to a Java type. Conversely, the MessageBodyWriter interface defines the contract for a provider that supports the conversion of a Java type to a stream.

If we do not specify @XmlRootElement on OrderResource, then we need to define the mapping between XML to Java and vice versa. Java API for XML Processing can be used to define the mapping between the Java type to XML and vice versa. Similarly, Java API for JSON Processing can be used to define the two-way mapping between Java and JSON:

```
@Provider
@Produces("application/json")
public class OrderReader implements MessageBodyReader<Order> {
  //. . .

  @Override
  public void writeTo(Order o,
                      Class<?> type,
                      Type t,
                      Annotation[] as,
                      MediaType mt,
                      MultivaluedMap<String, Object> mm,
                      OutputStream out)
          throws IOException, WebApplicationException {
    JsonGeneratorFactory factory = Json.createGeneratorFactory();
    JsonGenerator gen = factory.createGenerator(out);
    gen.writeStartObject()
       .write("id", o.getId())
       .writeEnd();
  }
}
```

This code shows the implementation of the MessageBodyWriter.writeTo method, which is responsible for writing the object to an HTTP response. The method is using the Streaming API defined by Java API for JSON Processing to write Order o to the underlying OutputStream out for the HTTP entity. The implementation class needs to be marked with @Provider to make it discoverable by the JAX-RS runtime on the server side. The providers need to be explicitly registered on the client side. @Produces ensures that this entity provider will only support the specified media type:

```
@Provider
@Consumes("application/json")
public class OrderReader implements MessageBodyReader<Order> {
  //. . .

  @Override
  public Order readFrom(Class<Order> type,
```

```
                        Type t,
                        Annotation[] as,
                        MediaType mt,
                        MultivaluedMap<String, String> mm,
                        InputStream in)
            throws IOException, WebApplicationException {
    Order o = new Order();
    JsonParser parser = Json.createParser(in);
    while (parser.hasNext()) {
      switch (parser.next()) {
        case KEY_NAME:
          String key = parser.getString();
          parser.next();
          switch (key) {
            case "id":
              o.setId(parser.getIntValue());
              break;
            default:
              break;
          }
          break;
        default:
          break;
      }
    }

    return o;
  }
}
```

This code shows the implementation of the MessageBodyReader.readFrom method, which is responsible for reading the object from the HTTP request. This method is using the Streaming API defined by Java API for JSON Processing to read Order o from the InputStream in for the HTTP entity. The implementation class needs to be marked with @Provider to make it discoverable by the JAX-RS runtime. The providers need to be explicitly registered on the client side. @Consumes ensures that this entity provider will only support the specified media type.

Client API

JAX-RS 2 adds a new Client API that can be used to access web resources and provides integration with JAX-RS providers. Without this API, users must use a low-level HttpUrlConnection to access the REST endpoint:

```
Client client = ClientBuilder.newClient();
Order order = client
  .target("http://localhost:8080/store/webresources/orders")
  .path("{oid}")
  .resolveTemplate("oid", 1)
```

```
      .request()
      .get(Order.class);
```

This code uses the fluent builder pattern and works as follows:

- **ClientBuilder** is the entry point to the client API. It is used to obtain an instance of **Client** that uses method chaining to build and execute client requests in order to consume the responses returned.

  Clients are heavyweight objects that manage the client-side communication infrastructure. Initialization as well as disposal of a **Client** instance may be a rather expensive operation. It is therefore recommended that you construct only a small number of **Client** instances in the application.

- We create **WebTarget** by specifying the URI of the web resource. We then use these targets to prepare client request invocation by resolving the URI template, using the **resolveTemplate** method for different names. We can specify additional query or matrix parameters here using the **queryParam** and **matrixParam** methods, respectively.

- We build the client request by invoking the **request** method.

- We invoke the HTTP **GET** method by calling the **get** method. The Java type of the response entity is specified as the parameter to the invoked method.

The fluency of the API hides its complexity, but a better understanding of the flow allows us to write better code.

We can make HTTP **POST** or **PUT** requests by using the **post** or **put** methods, respectively:

```
Order order =
  client
    .target(...)
    .request()
    .post(Entity.entity(new Order(1), "application/json"),
      Order.class);
```

In this code, a new message entity is created with the specified media type, a **POST** request is created, and a response of type **Order** is expected. There are other variations of the **Entity.entity** method that would allow us to manipulate the request. The **Entity** class defines variants of the most popular media types. It also allows us to **POST** an HTML form using the **form** method.

We can make an HTTP **DELETE** request by identifying the resource with the URI and using the **delete** method:

```
client
  .target("...")
  .target("{oid}")
  .resolveTemplate("oid", 1)
```

```
        .request()
        .delete();
```

We need to explicity register entity providers using the `register` method:

```
Order o = client
            .register(OrderReader.class)
            .register(OrderWriter.class)
            .target(...)
            .request()
            .get(Order.class);
```

By default, the client is invoked synchronously but can be invoked asynchronously if we call the `async` method as part of the fluent builder API and (optionally) register an instance of `InvocationCallback`:

```
Future<Order> f = client
    .target("http://localhost:8080/store/webresources/orders")
    .path("{oid}")
    .resolveTemplate("oid", 1)
    .request()
    .async()
    .get();
//. . .
Order o = f.get();
```

In this code, the call to `get` after `async` is called returns immediately without blocking the caller's thread. The response is a `Future` instance that can be used to monitor or cancel asynchronous invocation or retrieve results.

Optionally, `InvocationCallback` can be registered to receive the events from the asynchronous invocation processing:

```
client
    .target("http://localhost:8080/store/webresources/orders/{oid}")
    .resolveTemplate("oid", 1)
    .request()
    .async()
    .get(new InvocationCallback<Order>() {

      @Override
      public void completed(Order o) {
        //. . .
      }

      @Override
      public void failed(Throwable t) {
        //. . .
      }
    });
```

The `completed` method is called on successful completion of invocation, and the response data is made available in the parameter o. The `failed` method is called when the invocation is failed for any reason, and the parameter t contains failure details.

A more generic client request can be prepared and executed at a later time. This enables a separation of concerns between the creator and the submitter:

```
Invocation i1 = client.target(...).request().buildGet();
Invocation i2 = client
                .target(...)
                .request()
                .post(Entity.entity(new Order(1),
                    "application/json"));
//. . .
Response r = i1.invoke();
Order o = i2.invoke(Order.class);
```

In this code, a GET request is prepared and stored as i1, and a POST request is prepared and stored as i2. These requests are then executed at a later time via the `invoke` method and the result retrieved. In the first case, a more generic `Response` is returned, which can then be used to extract the result and other metadata about it. In the second case, an `Order` instance is returned because of the type specified before.

You can submit these as asynchronous requests using the `submit` method:

```
Future<Response> f1 = i1.submit();
Future<Order> f2 = i2.submit(Order.class);
//. . .
Response r1 = f1.get();
Order r11 = r1.readEntity(Order.class);
Order r2 = f2.get();
```

In this code, we submit the `Invocations` for asynchronous execution using the `submit` method. A `Future` response object is returned in both cases. After waiting for some time, we can obtain the first result by calling the `get` method on the returned `Future`. In the first case, we need to extract the exact result by calling the `readEntity` method. In the second case, an `Order` response is returned directly because of the type specified during the `submit` invocation.

Mapping Exceptions

An application-specific exception may be thrown from within the resource method and propagated to the client. The application can supply checked or exception mapping to an instance of the `Response` class. Let's say the application throws the following exception if an order is not found:

```
public class OrderNotFoundException
    extends RuntimeException {
```

```
  public OrderNotFoundException(int id) {
    super(id + " order not found");
  }

}
```

The method `getOrder` may look like:

```
@Path("{id}")
public Order getOrder(@PathParam("id")int id) {
  Order order = null;
  if (order == null) {
    throw new OrderNotFoundException(id);
  }
  //. . .
  return order;
}
```

The exception mapper will look like:

```
@Provider
public class OrderNotFoundExceptionMapper
    implements ExceptionMapper<OrderNotFoundException> {

  @Override
  public Response toResponse(
OrderNotFoundException exception) {
    return Response
      .status(Response.Status.PRECONDITION_FAILED)
      .entity("Response not found")
      .build();
  }

}
```

This ensures that the client receives a formatted response instead of just the exception being propagated from the resource.

Filters and Entity Interceptors

JAX-RS 2 defines extension points to customize the request/response processing on both the client and server side. These are used to extend an implementation in order to provide capabilities such as logging, confidentiality, and authentication. The two kinds of extension points are: filters and entity interceptors.

Filters are mainly used to modify or process incoming and outgoing request or response headers. Entity interceptors are mainly concerned with marshaling and unmarshaling of HTTP message bodies.

Filters can be configured on the client and server, giving us four extension points for filters, defined by four interfaces:

- `ClientRequestFilter`
- `ClientResponseFilter`
- `ContainerRequestFilter`
- `ContainerResponseFilter`

As the names indicate, `ClientRequestFilter` and `ClientResponseFilter` are client-side filters, and `ContainerRequestFilter` and `ContainerResponseFilter` are server-side filters. Similarly, `ClientRequestFilter` and `ContainerRequestFilter` operate on the request, and `ContainerResponseFilter` and `ClientResponseFilter` operate on the response.

The client-side or server-side filters may be implemented by the same class or different classes:

```
public class ClientLoggingFilter implements ClientRequestFilter,
                                            ClientResponseFilter {
  @Override
  public void filter(ClientRequestContext crc) throws IOException {
    String method = crc.getMethod();
    String uri = crc.getUri();
    for (Entry e : crc.getHeaders().entrySet()) {
      ... = e.getKey();
      ... = e.getValue();
    }
  }

  @Override
  public void filter(ClientRequestContext crc, ClientResponseContext crc1)
              throws IOException {
    for (Entry e : crc1.getHeaders().entrySet()) {
      ... = e.getKey();
      ... = e.getValue();
    }
  }
}
```

This code shows a simple client-side filter that will log the headers sent as part of the request and received in the response message. `ClientRequestContext` provides request-specific information for the filter, such as the request URI, message headers, and message entity or request-scoped properties. `ClientResponseContext` provides response-specific information for the filter, such as message headers, the message entity, or response-scoped properties.

On the client side, you can register this filter using the client-side API:

```
Client client = ClientBuilder.newClient();
client.register(ClientLoggingFilter.class);
WebTarget target = client.target(...);
```

A server-side filter that will log the headers received as part of the request and sent in the response message can be implemented similarly:

```
@Provider
public class ServerLoggingFilter implements ContainerRequestFilter,
                                            ContainerResponseFilter {
  @Override
  public void filter(ContainerRequestContext crc) throws IOException {
    String method = crc.getMethod();
    String uri = crc.getUriInfo().getAbsolutePath();
    for (String key : crc.getHeaders().keySet()) {
      ... = key;
      ... = crc.getHeaders().get(key);
    }
  }

  @Override
  public void filter(ContainerRequestContext crc, ContainerResponseContext crc1)
              throws IOException {
    for (String key : crc1.getHeaders().keySet()) {
      ...  = key;
      .... = crc1.getHeaders().get(key);
    }
  }
}
```

In this code, the filter is a provider class and thus must be marked with @Provider. This ensures that the filters are automatically discovered. If the filter is not marked with @Provider, it needs to be explicitly registered in the Application class:

```
@ApplicationPath("webresources")
public class MyApplication extends Application {
  @Override
  public Set<Class<?>> getClasses() {
    Set<Class<?>> resources = new java.util.HashSet<>();
    resources.add(org.sample.filter.ServerLoggingFilter.class);
    return resources;
  }
}
```

ContainerRequestFilter comes in two flavors: *pre-match* and *post-match*. A pre-match filter is applied globally on all resources before the resource is matched with the incoming HTTP request. A pre-match filter is typically used to update the HTTP method in the request and is capable of altering the matching algorithm. A post-match filter is applied after the resource method has been matched. You can convert any Contain erRequestFilter to a pre-match filter by adding the @PreMatching annotation.

On the server side, the filters can be registered in four different ways:

Globally bound to all resources and all methods in them

By default, if no annotation is specified on the filter, then it is globally bound—that is, it all applies to methods on all resources in an application.

Globally bound to all resources and methods via the meta-annotation `@NameBinding`

The annotation may be specified on the `Application` class and then the filter becomes globally enabled on all methods for all resources:

```
@ApplicationPath("webresources")
@ServerLogged
public class MyApplication extends Application {
  //. . .
}
```

Statically bound to a specific resource/method via the meta-annotation `@NameBinding`

A filter may be statically targeted to a resource class or method via the meta-annotation `@NameBinding` as follows:

```
@NameBinding
@Target({ElementType.TYPE, ElementType.METHOD})
@Retention(value = RetentionPolicy.RUNTIME)
public @interface ServerLogged {}
```

This annotation then needs to be specified on the filter implementation and the resource class and/or method:

```
@Provider
@ServerLogged
public class ServerLoggingFilter implements ContainerRequestFilter,
                                            ContainerResponseFilter {
  //. . .
}

@Path("orders")
@ServerLogged
public class MyResource {
  //. . .
}
```

If the annotation is specified on a resource, then the filter is applied to all methods of the resource. If the annotation is specified on a specific resource method, then the filter is applied only when that particular method is invoked.

`@NameBinding` annotation is ignored on filters marked with `@PreMatch`.

Dynamically bound to a specific resource/method via `DynamicFeature`

A non−globally bound filter (i.e., a filter annotated with `@NameBinding`) can be dynamically bound to a resource or a method within a resource via `DynamicFeature`. For example, the following feature binds all resource methods in `MyResource` that are annotated with `@GET`:

```
@Provider
public class DynamicServerLogggingFilterFeature implements DynamicFeature {
  @Override
  public void configure(ResourceInfo ri, Configurable c) {
    if (MyResource.class.isAssignableFrom(ri.getResourceClass())
        && ri.getResourceMethod().isAnnotationPresent(GET.class)) {
      c.register(new ServerLoggingFilter());
    }
  }
}
```

In this code, `ServerLoggingFilter` is configured on the methods of `MyResource` marked with the `GET` annotation. This feature is marked with `@Provider` and is thus automatically discovered by the JAX-RS runtime. Dynamic binding is ignored on filters marked with `@PreMatch`.

Multiple filters may be implemented at each extension point and arranged in *filter chains*. Filters in a chain are sorted based on their priorities and are executed in order. Priorities are defined through the `@javax.annotation.Priority` annotation and represented by integer numbers. The `Priorities` class defines built-in priorities for security, decoders/encoders, and more. The default binding priority is `Priorities.USER`.

The priorities for `ClientRequestFilter` and `ContainerRequestFilter` are sorted in ascending order; the lower the number, the higher the priority. The priorities for `ContainerResponseFilter` and `ClientResponseFilter` are sorted in descending order; the higher the number, the higher the priority. These rules ensure that response filters are executed in reverse order of request filters.

The priority of `ClientLoggingFilter` defined previously can be changed as shown:

```
@Provider
@Priority(Priorities.HEADER_DECORATOR)
public class ClientLoggingFilter implements ClientRequestFilter,
                                            ClientResponseFilter {
  //. . .
}
```

Filters are executed without method invocation wrapping (i.e., filters execute in their own silos and do not directly invoke the next filter in the chain). The JAX-RS runtime decides whether to invoke the next filter or not.

`ClientRequestFilter` and `ContainerRequestFilter` can stop the execution of their corresponding chains by calling `abortWith(Response)`.

Entity interceptors are mainly concerned with marshaling and unmarshaling of HTTP message bodies. They implement `ReaderInterceptor` or `WriterInterceptor`, or both.

`WriterInterceptor` operates on the outbound request on the client side and on the outbound response on the server side:

```
public class MyWriterInterceptor implements WriterInterceptor {

  @Override
  public void aroundWriteTo(WriterInterceptorContext wic)
               throws IOException, WebApplicationException {

    wic.setOutputStream(new FilterOutputStream(wic.getOutputStream()) {

      final ByteArrayOutputStream baos = new ByteArrayOutputStream();

      @Override
      public void write(int b) throws IOException {
        baos.write(b);
        super.write(b);
      }

      @Override
      public void close() throws IOException {
        System.out.println("MyClientWriterInterceptor --> " + baos.toString());
        super.close();
      }
    });
    wic.proceed();
  }
}
```

ReaderInterceptor operates on the outbound response on the client side and on the
inbound request on the server side:

```
public class MyReaderInterceptor implements ReaderInterceptor {

  @Override
  public Object aroundReadFrom(ReaderInterceptorContext ric)
                 throws IOException, WebApplicationException {
    final InputStream old = ric.getInputStream();
    ByteArrayOutputStream baos = new ByteArrayOutputStream();
    int c;
    while ((c = old.read()) != -1) {
      baos.write(c);
    }
    ... = baos.toString();

    ric.setInputStream(new ByteArrayInputStream(baos.toByteArray()));

    return ric.proceed();
  }
}
```

As with filters, there is an *interceptor chain* for each kind of entity interceptor. Entity
interceptors in a chain are sorted based on their priorities and are executed in order.
Priorities are defined via the @javax.annotation.Priority annotation and represented by integer numbers. The Priorities class defines built-in priorities for security,

decoders/encoders, and more. The default binding priority is `Priorities.USER`. The priorities are sorted in ascending order; the lower the number, the higher the priority.

Filters and entity interceptors may be specified on a client and resource. Figure 4-1 shows the invocation sequence on both client and server.

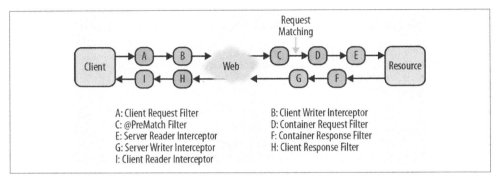

A: Client Request Filter   B: Client Writer Interceptor
C: @PreMatch Filter   D: Container Request Filter
E: Server Reader Interceptor F: Container Response Filter
G: Server Writer Interceptor H: Client Response Filter
I: Client Reader Interceptor

Figure 4-1. JAX-RS filters and interceptors sequencing

Validation of Resources

Bean Validation 1.1 allows declarative validation of resources. The constraints can be specified in any location in which the JAX-RS binding annotations are allowed, with the exception of constructors and property setters:

```
@Path("/names")
public class NameResource {
  @NotNull
  @Size(min=1)
  @FormParam("firstName")
  private String firstName;

  @NotNull
  @Size(min=1)
  @FormParam("lastName")
  private String lastName;

  @FormParam("email")
  public void setEmail(String email) {
    this.email = email;
  }

  @Email
  public String getEmail() {
    return email;
  }
```

```
  //. . .
}
```

In this code:

- firstName and lastName are fields initialized via injection. These fields cannot be null and must be at least one character.

- email is a resource class property, and the constraint annotation is specified on the corresponding getter.

You can specify cross-field and cross-property constraints by declaring annotations on the class:

```
@NotNullAndNonEmptyNames
public class NameResource {
  @FormParam("firstName")
  private String firstName;

  @FormParam("lastName")
  private String lastName;

  //. . .
}
```

In this code, @NotNullAndNonEmptyNames is a custom constraint that requires the first and last name to be not null and both the names to be at least one character long.

You can map request entity bodies to resource method parameters and validate them by specifying the constraint on the resource method parameter:

```
public class NameResource {
  @POST
  @Consumes("application/json")
  public void addAge(@NotNull @Min(16) @Max(25)int age) {
    //. . .
  }
}
```

In this code, the request entity body is mapped to the age parameter and must be not null and between the values of 16 and 25.

Alternatively, if the request entity is mapped to a bean that is decorated with constraint annotations already, then @Valid can be used to trigger the validation:

```
public class NameResource {
  @POST
  @Consumes
  public void addName(@Valid Name name) {
    //. . .
  }
}
```

JAX-RS constraint validations are carried out in the Default validation group only. Processing other validation groups is not required.

CHAPTER 5
SOAP-Based Web Services

SOAP-Based Web Services are defined as JSR 224, and the complete specification can be downloaded (*http://jcp.org/aboutJava/communityprocess/mrel/jsr224/index4.html*).

SOAP is an XML-based messaging protocol used as a data format for exchanging information over web services. The SOAP specification defines an envelope that represents the contents of a SOAP message and encoding rules for data types. It also defines how SOAP messages may be sent over different transport protocols, such as exchanging messages as the payload of HTTP POST. The SOAP protocol provides a way to communicate among applications running on different operating systems, with different technologies, and different programming languages.

Java API for XML-Based Web Services (JAX-WS) hides the complexity of the SOAP protocol and provides a simple API for development and deployment of web service endpoints and clients. The developer writes a web service endpoint as a Java class. The JAX-WS runtime publishes the web service and its capabilities using Web Services Description Language (WSDL). Tools provided by a JAX-WS implementation, such as wscompile by the JAX-WS Reference Implementation, are used to generate a proxy to the service and invoke methods on it from the client code. The JAX-WS runtime converts the API calls to and from SOAP messages and sends them over HTTP, as shown in Figure 5-1.

In addition to sending SOAP messages over HTTP, JAX-WS provides XML-over-HTTP protocol binding and is extensible to other protocols and transports. The XML-over-HTTP binding use case is better served by JAX-RS and will not be discussed here.

Data mapping between Java and XML is defined through the Java API for XML Binding (JAXB).

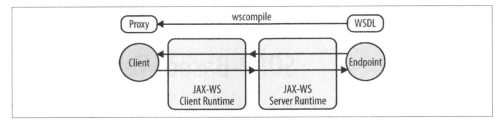

Figure 5-1. JAX-WS client and server

The JAX-WS specification defines mapping from WSDL 1.1 to Java. This mapping defines how different WSDL constructs such as `wsdl:service`, `wsdl:portType`, and `wsdl:operation` are mapped to Java. This mapping is used when web service interfaces for clients and endpoints are generated from a WSDL 1.1 description.

Java to WSDL 1.1 mapping is also defined by this specification. This mapping defines how Java packages, classes, interfaces, methods, parameters, and other parts of a web service endpoint are mapped to WSDL 1.1 constructs. This mapping is used when web service endpoints are generated from existing Java interfaces.

JAX-WS uses technologies defined by the W3C: HTTP, SOAP, and WSDL. It also requires compliance with the WS-I Basic Profile, the WS-I Simple SOAP Binding Profile, and the WS-I Attachments Profile, which promotes interoperability between web services. This allows a JAX-WS endpoint to be invoked by a client on another operating system written in another programming language and vice versa.

JAX-WS also facilitates, using a nonstandard programming model, the publishing and invoking of a web service that uses WS-* specifications such as WS-Security, WS-Secure Conversation, and WS-Reliable Messaging. Some of these specifications are already implemented in the JAX-WS implementation bundled as part of GlassFish. However, this particular usage of JAX-WS will not be discussed here. More details about it can be found at *http://metro.java.net*.

Web Service Endpoints

You can convert a POJO to a SOAP-based web service endpoint by adding the `@WebSer` `vice` annotation:

```
@WebService
public class SimpleWebService {

    public String sayHello(String name) {
        return "Hello " + name;
    }
}
```

All `public` methods of the class are exposed as web service operations.

This is called a Service Endpoint Interface (SEI)–based endpoint. Even though the name contains the word *interface*, an interface is not required for building a JAX-WS endpoint. The web service implementation class implicitly defines an SEI. This approach of starting with a POJO is also called the *code-first approach*. The other approach—in which you start with a WSDL and generate Java classes from it—is called the *contract-first approach*.

There are reasonable defaults for `wsdl:service` name, `wsdl:portType` name, `wsdl:port` name, and other elements in the generated WSDL. The `@WebService` annotation has several attributes to override the defaults, as defined in Table 5-1.

Table 5-1. @WebService attributes

Attributes	Description
endpointInterface	Fully qualified class name of the service endpoint interface defining the service's abstract web service contract
name	Name of the web service (`wsdl:portType`)
portName	Port name of the web service (`wsdl:port`)
serviceName	Service name of the web service (`wsdl:service`)
targetNamespace	Namespace for the web service (`targetNamespace`)
wsdlLocation	Location of a predefined WSDL describing the service

The `@WebMethod` annotation can be used on each method to override the corresponding default values:

```
@WebMethod(operationName="hello")
public String sayHello(String name) {
    return "Hello " + name;
}
```

Specifying this annotation overrides the default name of the `wsdl:operation` matching this method.

Additionally, if any method is annotated with `@WebMethod`, all other methods of the class are implicitly not available at the SEI endpoint. Any additional methods are required to be annotated.

If there are multiple methods in the POJO and a particular method needs to be excluded from the web service description, the `exclude` attribute can be used:

```
@WebMethod(exclude=true)
public String sayHello(String name) {
    return "Hello " + name;
}
```

You can customize the mapping of an individual parameter of a method to WSDL using `@WebParam`, and the mapping of the return value using `@WebResult`.

The mapping of Java programming language types to and from XML definitions is delegated to JAXB. It follows the default Java-to-XML and XML-to-Java mapping for each method parameter and return type. The usual JAXB annotations can be used to customize the mapping to the generated schema:

```
@WebService
public class ShoppingCart {
    public void purchase(List<Item> items) {
        //. . .
    }
    //. . .
}

@XmlRootElement
class Item {
    private String name;
    //. . .
}
```

In this code, @XmlRootElement allows the Item class to be converted to XML and vice versa.

By default, the generated WSDL uses the document/literal style of binding. You can change this by specifying the @SOAPBinding annotation on the class:

```
@WebService
@SOAPBinding(style= SOAPBinding.Style.RPC)
public class SimpleWebService {
    //. . .
}
```

The business methods can throw a service-specific exception:

```
@WebMethod
public String sayHello(String name) throws InvalidNameException {
    //. . .
}

public class InvalidNameException extends Exception {
    //. . .
}
```

If this exception is thrown in the business method on the server side, it is propagated to the client side. If the exception is declared as an unchecked exception, it is mapped to SOAPFaultException on the client side. The @WebFault annotation may be used to customize the mapping of wsdl:fault in the generated WSDL.

By default, a message follows the *request/response* design pattern where a response is received for each request. A method may follow the *fire-and-forget* design pattern by specifying the @Oneway annotation on it so that a request can be sent from the message but no response is received. Such a method must have a void return type and must not throw any checked exceptions:

```
@Oneway
public void doSomething() {
    //. . .
}
```

A WebServiceContext may be injected in an endpoint implementation class:

```
@Resource
WebServiceContext context;
```

This provides information about message context (via the getMessageContext method) and security information (via the getUserPrincipal and isUserInRole methods) relative to a request being served.

Provider-Based Dynamic Endpoints

A Provider-based endpoint provides a dynamic alternative to the SEI-based endpoint. Instead of just the mapped Java types, the complete protocol message or protocol message payload is available as Source, DataSource, or SOAPMessage at the endpoint. The response message also needs to be prepared using these APIs.

The endpoint needs to implement the Provider<Source>, Provider<SOAPMessage>, or Provider<DataSource> interface:

```
@WebServiceProvider
public class MyProvider implements Provider<Source> {

  @Override
  public Source invoke(Source request) {
    //. . .
  }

}
```

In this code, the SOAP body payload is available as a Source. @WebServiceProvider is used to associate the class with a wsdl:service and a wsdl:port element in the WSDL document.

Table 5-2 describes the attributes that can be used to provide additional information about the mapping.

Table 5-2. @WebServiceProvider attributes

Attribute	Description
portName	Port name
serviceName	Service name
targetNamespace	Target namespace for the service
wsdlLocation	Location of the WSDL for the service

By default, only the message payload (i.e., the SOAP body in the case of the SOAP protocol) is received at the endpoint and sent in a response. The `ServiceMode` annotation can be used to override this if the provider endpoint wishes to send and receive the entire protocol message:

```
@ServiceMode(ServiceMode.Mode.MESSAGE)
public class MyProvider implements Provider<Source> {
    //. . .
}
```

In this code, the complete SOAP message is received and sent from the endpoint.

`Provider<Source>` is the most commonly used `Provider`-based endpoint. A `Provider<SOAP message>` in PAYLOAD mode is not valid because the entire SOAP message is received, not just the payload that corresponds to the body of the SOAP message.

The runtime catches the exception thrown by a `Provider` endpoint and converts it to a protocol-specific exception (e.g., `SOAPFaultException` for the SOAP protocol).

Endpoint-Based Endpoints

An `Endpoint`-based endpoint offers a lightweight alternative for creating and publishing an endpoint. This is a convenient way of deploying a JAX-WS-based web service endpoint from Java SE applications.

A code-first endpoint can be published:

```
@WebService
public class SimpleWebService {

    public String sayHello(String name) {
        return "Hello " + name;
    }
}

//. . .

Endpoint endpoint =
    Endpoint.publish("http://localhost:8080" +
                        "/example/SimpleWebService",
                     new SimpleWebService());
```

In this code, a POJO annotated with @WebService is used as the endpoint implementation. The address of the endpoint is passed as an argument to Endpoint.publish. This method call publishes the endpoint and starts accepting incoming requests.

The endpoint can be taken down and stop receiving incoming requests:

```
endpoint.stop();
```

The endpoint implementation can be a Provider-based endpoint as well.

A mapped WSDL is automatically generated by the underlying runtime in this case.

You can publish a contract-first endpoint by packaging the WSDL and specifying the wsdl:port and wsdl:service as part of the configuration:

```
Endpoint endpoint = Endpoint.create
(new SimpleWebService());

List<Source> metadata = new ArrayList<Source>();
Source source = new StreamSource(new InputStream(...));
metadata.add(source);
endpoint.setMetadata(metadata);

Map<String, Object> props = new HashMap<String, Object>();
props.put(Endpoint.WSDL_PORT, new QName(...));
props.put(Endpoint.WSDL_SERVICE, new QName(...));
endpoint.setProperties(props);

endpoint.publish("http://localhost:8080" +
                 "/example.com/SimpleWebService");
```

An Executor may be set on the endpoint to gain better control over the threads used to dispatch incoming requests:

```
ThreadPoolExecutor executor = new
ThreadPoolExecutor(4, 10, 100,
    TimeUnit.MILLISECONDS, new PriorityBlockingQueue());
endpoint.setExecutor(executor);
```

EndpointContext allows multiple endpoints in an application to share any information.

Web Service Client

The contract between the web service endpoint and a client is defined through WSDL. As with an SEI-based web service endpoint, you can easily generate a high-level web service client by importing the WSDL. Such tools follow the WSDL-to-Java mapping defined by the JAX-WS specification and generate the corresponding classes.

Table 5-3 describes the mapped Java artifact names generated for some of the WSDL elements.

Table 5-3. WSDL-to-Java mappings

WSDL element	Java class
wsdl:service	Service class extending javax.xml.ws.Service; provides the client view of a web service
wsdl:portType	Service endpoint interface
wsdl:operation	Java method in the corresponding SEI
wsdl:input	Wrapper- or nonwrapper-style Java method parameters
wsdl:output	Wrapper- or nonwrapper-style Java method return value
wsdl:fault	Service-specific exception
XML schema elements in wsdl:types	As defined by XML-to-Java mapping in the JAXB specification

You can generate a new instance of the proxy by calling one of the getPort methods on the generated Service class:

```
@WebServiceClient(name="...",
                  targetNamespace="...",
                  wsdlLocation="...")
public class SimpleWebServiceService
    extends Service {

    URL wsdlLocation = ...
    QName serviceQName = ...

    public SimpleWebServiceService() {
        super(wsdlLocation, serviceQName);
    }

    //. . .

    public SimpleWebService getSimpleWebServicePort() {
        return super.getPort(portQName,
                             SimpleWebService.class);
    }
}
```

A client will then invoke a business method on the web service:

```
SimpleWebServiceService service = new SimpleWebServiceService();
SimpleWebService port = service.getSimpleWebServicePort();
port.sayHello("Duke");
```

A more generic getPort method may be used to obtain the endpoint:

```
SimpleWebServiceService service = new SimpleWebServiceService();
SimpleWebService port = service.getPort(SimpleWebService.class);
port.sayHello("Duke");
```

Each generated proxy implements the `BindingProvider` interface. Table 5-4 describes the properties that may be set on the provider.

Table 5-4. BindingProvider properties

Property name	Description
ENDPOINT_ADDRESS_PROPERTY	Target service endpoint address
USERNAME_PROPERTY	Username for HTTP basic authentication
PASSWORD_PROPERTY	Password for HTTP basic authentication
SESSION_MAINTAIN_PROPERTY	Boolean property to indicate whether the client is participating in a session with service endpoint
SOAPACTION_USE_PROPERTY	Controls whether SOAPAction HTTP header is used in SOAP/HTTP requests; default value is false
SOAPACTION_URI_PROPERTY	Value of SOAPAction HTTP header; default value is empty string

Typically, a generated client has an endpoint address preconfigured based upon the value of the `soap:address` element in the WSDL. The `ENDPOINT_ADDRESS_PROPERTY` can be used to target the client to a different endpoint:

```
BindingProvider provider = (BindingProvider)port;
port.getRequestContext().put(
        BindingProvider.ENDPOINT_ADDRESS_PROPERTY,
        "http://example.com/NewWebServiceEndpoint");
```

Dispatch-Based Dynamic Client

A `Dispatch`-based endpoint provides a dynamic alternative to the generated proxy-based client. Instead of just the mapped Java types, the complete protocol message or protocol message payload is prepared by way of XML APIs.

The client can be implemented via `Dispatch<Source>`, `Dispatch<SOAPMessage>`, `Dispatch<DataSource>`, or `Dispatch<JAXB Object>`:

```
QName serviceQName = new QName("http://example.com",
                              "SimpleWebServiceService");
Service service = Service.create(serviceQName);

QName portQName = new QName("http://example.com",
                           "SimpleWebService");
Dispatch<Source> dispatch = service.createDispatch(
                                   portQName,
                                   Source.class,
                                   Service.Mode.PAYLOAD);
//. . .
Source source = new StreamSource(...);
Source response = dispatch.invoke(source);
```

In this code, we create a Service by specifying the fully qualified QName, a port is created from the service, a Dispatch<Source> is created, and the web service endpoint is invoked. The business method invoked on the service endpoint is dispatched based upon the received SOAP message.

A pregenerated Service object, generated by a tool following WSDL-to-Java mapping, may be used to create the Dispatch client as well.

A Dispatch<SOAPMessage> can be created:

```
Dispatch<SOAPMessage> dispatch =
    service.createDispatch(portQName,
                         SOAPMessage.class,
                         Service.Mode.MESSAGE);
```

The value of Service.Mode must be MESSAGE for Dispatch<SOAPMessage>.

JAXB objects generated from XML-to-Java mapping may be used to create and manipulate XML representations. Such a Dispatch client can be created:

```
Dispatch<Object> dispatch =
    service.create(portQName,
                 jaxbContext,
                 Service.Mode.MESSAGE);
```

In this code, jaxbContext is the JAXBContext used to marshal and unmarshal messages or message payloads.

A Dispatch client can also be invoked asynchronously:

```
Response<Source> response = dispatch.invoke(...);
```

The Response object can then be used to query (via the isDone method), cancel (via the cancel method), or obtain the results from (via get methods) the method invocation. You can convert the asynchronous invocation into a blocking request by invoking re sponse.get right after obtaining the response object.

You can make an asynchronous request using a callback:

```
Future<?> response =
    dispatch.invokeAsync(source, new MyAsyncHandler());

//. . .

class MyAsyncHandler implements AysnchHandler<Source> {
    @Override
    public void handleResponse(Response<Source> res) {
        //. . .
    }
}
```

A new class, MyAsyncHandler, registers a callback class that receives control when the response is received from the endpoint. The response can be used to check if the web service invocation has completed, wait for its completion, or retrieve the result. The handleResponse method of the callback is used to process the response received.

A one-way request using a Dispatch-based client may be made:

```
dispatch.invokeOneWay(source);
```

Handlers

Handlers are well-defined extension points that perform additional processing of the request and response messages. They can be easily plugged into the JAX-WS runtime. There are two types of handlers:

Logical handler

Logical handlers are protocol-agnostic and cannot change any protocol-specific parts of a message (such as headers). Logical handlers act only on the payload of the message.

Protocol handler

Protocol handlers are specific to a protocol and may access or change the protocol-specific aspects of a message.

You can write logical handlers by implementing LogicalHandler:

```
public class MyLogicalHandler implements LogicalHandler {
    @Override
    public boolean handleMessage(MessageContext context) {
        Source source =
            ((LogicalMessageContext)context)
            .getMessage()
            .getPayload();
        //. . .
        return true;
    }

    @Override
    public boolean handleFault(MessageContext context) {
        //. . .
    }

    @Override
    public void close(MessageContext context) {
        //. . .
    }
}
```

In this code, the handler has implemented the handleMessage, handleFault, and close methods. The handleMessage method is called for inbound and outbound message processing, and the handleFault method is invoked for fault processing. The handle

`Message` and `handleFault` messages return `true` to continue further processing, and `false` to block processing.

`MessageContext` provides a context about the message that is currently being processed by the handler instance. It provides a predefined set of properties that can be used to communicate among different handlers. Properties are scoped to `APPLICATION` or `HANDLER`.

The message payload may be obtained as a JAXB object:

```
LogicalMessage message = context.getMessage();
Object jaxbObject = message.getPayload(jaxbContext);
// Update the JAXB Object
message.setPayload(modifiedJaxbObject,jaxbContext);
```

In this code, `jaxbObject` is obtained as the payload, updated, and then sent back explicitly as the payload on the message.

Protocol handlers, specific to the SOAP protocol, are called by the SOAP handler:

```
public class MySOAPHandler implements SOAPHandler {

    @Override
    public Set getHeaders() {
        //. . .
    }

    @Override
    public boolean handleMessage(MessageContext context) {
        SOAPMessage message = ((SOAPMessageContext) context).getMessage();
        //. . .
        return true;
    }

    @Override
    public boolean handleFault(MessageContext context) {
        //. . .
    }

    @Override
    public void close(MessageContext context) { }
}
```

In this code, the handler has implemented the `handleMessage`, `handleFault`, `close`, and `getHeaders` methods. SOAP handlers are generally used to process SOAP-specific information, such as SOAP headers. The `getHeaders` method returns the set of SOAP headers processed by this handler instance.

Handlers can be organized in a *handler chain*. The handlers within a handler chain are invoked each time a message is sent or received. Inbound messages are processed by handlers prior to dispatching a request to the service endpoint or returning a response to the client. Outbound messages are processed by handlers after a request is sent from the client or a response is returned from the service endpoint.

During runtime, the handler chain is reordered such that logical handlers are executed before the SOAP handlers on an outbound message and SOAP handlers are executed before logical handlers on an inbound message.

The sequence of logical and SOAP handlers during a request and response is shown in Figure 5-2.

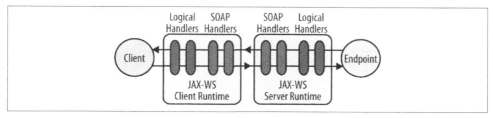

Figure 5-2. JAX-WS logical and SOAP handlers

CHAPTER 6

JSON Processing

JSON Processing is defined as the Java API for JSON Processing in JSR 353, and the complete specification can be downloaded (*http://jcp.org/aboutJava/communitypro cess/final/jsr353/index.html*).

JSON (JavaScript Object Notation) is a lightweight data-interchange format. The format is easy for humans and machines to read and write. JSON was based on a subset of JavaScript and is commonly used with it, but it is a language-independent data format. A JSON structure can be built as either of the following:

- A collection of name/value pairs, generally realized as dictionary, hash table, or associative array
- An ordered list of values, generally realized as an array, list, or sequence

The following example shows the JSON representation of an object that describes a movie:

```
{
  "name": "The Matrix",
  "actors": [
    "Keanu Reeves",
    "Laurence Fishburne",
    "Carrie-Ann Moss"
  ],
  "year": 1999
}
```

The object has three name/value pairs. The first name is name with a string value for the movie name, the second name is actors with an array value for the actors in the movie, and the third name is year with a number value for the year the movie was released.

JSON is quickly becoming the primary choice for developers for consuming and creating web services. Currently, Java applications use different implementation libraries to produce/consume JSON. These libraries are bundled along with the application, thereby increasing the overall size of the deployed archive. Java API for JSON Processing will provide a standard API to parse and generate JSON so that the applications that use the API are smaller and portable. The goals of the API are to:

- Produce/consume JSON text in a streaming fashion (similar to StAX API for XML)
- Build a Java object model for JSON text (similar to DOM API for XML)

Binding of JSON text to Java objects is outside the scope of this API.

Streaming API

The Streaming API provides a way to parse and generate JSON text in a streaming fashion. The API provides an event-based parser and allows an application developer to ask for the next event (i.e., pull the event), rather than handling the event in a callback. This gives a developer more procedural control over processing of the JSON. Parser events can be processed or discarded, or the next event may be generated.

The streaming model is adequate for local processing where only specific parts of the JSON structure need to be accessed, and random access to other parts of the data is not required. The streaming API is a low-level API designed to process large amounts of JSON data efficiently. Other JSON frameworks (such as JSON binding) can be implemented with this API.

The streaming API is similar to the StAX API for XML and consists of the interfaces JsonParser for consuming JSON and JsonGenerator for producing JSON.

Consuming JSON Using the Streaming API

JsonParser contains methods to parse JSON data using the streaming model. Json Parser provides forward, read-only access to JSON data using the pull parsing programming model. In this model, the application code controls the thread and calls methods in the parser interface to move the parser forward or to obtain JSON data from the current state of the parser.

JsonParser can be created from an InputStream:

```
JsonParser parser = Json.createParser(new FileInputStream(...));
```

This code shows how to create a parser from an InputStream obtained from a new FileInputStream.

JsonParser can also be created from a Reader:

```
JsonParser parser = Json.createParser(new StringReader(...));
```

This code shows how to create a parser from a StringReader.

You can create multiple parser instances using `JsonParserFactory`:

```
JsonParserFactory factory = Json.createParserFactory(null);
JsonParser parser1 = factory.createParser(...);
JsonParser parser2 = factory.createParser(...);
```

The factory can be configured with the specified map of provider-specific configuration properties. Any unsupported configuration properties specified in the map are ignored. In this case, `null` properties are passed during the creation of the parser factory.

The pull-parsing programming model is used to to parse the JSON. The `next` method returns the event for the next parsing state, which could be any of the following types:

- START_ARRAY
- END_ARRAY
- START_OBJECT
- END_OBJECT
- KEY_NAME
- VALUE_STRING
- VALUE_NUMBER
- VALUE_TRUE
- VALUE_FALSE
- VALUE_NULL

The parser generates `START_OBJECT` and `END_OBJECT` events for an empty JSON object `{ }`.

For an object with two name/value pairs:

```
{
  "apple":"red",
  "banana":"yellow"
}
```

The events generated are shown in bold:

```
{START_OBJECT
  "apple"KEY_NAME:"red"VALUE_STRING,
  "banana"KEY_NAME:"yellow"VALUE_STRING
}
```

The events generated for an array with two JSON objects are shown in bold:

```
[START_ARRAY
  {START_OBJECT "apple"KEY_NAME:"red"VALUE_STRING }END_OBJECT,
  {START_OBJECT "banana"KEY_NAME:"yellow"VALUE_STRING }END_OBJECT
]END_ARRAY
```

The events generated for a nested structure are shown in bold:

```
{START_OBJECT
  "title"KEY_NAME:"The Matrix"VALUE_STRING,
  "year"KEY_NAME:1999VALUE_NUMBER,
  "cast"KEY_NAME:[START_ARRAY
    "Keanu Reeves"VALUE_STRING,
    "Laurence Fishburne"VALUE_STRING,
    "Carrie-Anne Moss"VALUE_STRING
  ]END_ARRAY
}END_OBJECT
```

Producing JSON Using the Streaming API

The Streaming API provides a way to generate well-formed JSON to a stream by writing one event at a time.

JsonGenerator contains write*XXX* methods to write name/value pairs in JSON objects and values in JSON arrays:

```
JsonGeneratorFactory factory = Json.createGeneratorFactory(null);
JsonGenerator gen = factory.createGenerator(System.out);
gen.writeStartObject().writeEnd();
```

In this code:

- A JsonGenerator is obtained from JsonGeneratorFactory and configured to write the output to System.out.

  The factory can be configured with the specified map of provider-specific configuration properties. Any unsupported configuration properties specified in the map are ignored. In this case, null properties are passed during the creation of the generator factory.

- An empty object, with no name/value pairs, is created and written to the configured output stream. An object is started when the writeStartObject method is called, and ended with the writeEnd method.

JsonGenerator may be configured to write to a Writer as well.

The generated JSON structure is:

```
{ }
```

An object with two name/value pairs can be generated:

```
gen.writeStartObject()
    .write("apple", "red")
    .write("banana", "yellow")
  .writeEnd();
```

A name/value pair is written via the `write` method, which takes a name as the first parameter and a value as the second parameter. The value can be `BigDecimal`, `BigInteger`, `boolean`, `double`, `int`, `long`, `String`, and `JsonValue`.

The generated JSON structure is:

```
{
  "apple":"red",
  "banana":"yellow"
}
```

An array with two objects with each object with a name/value pair can be generated:

```
gen.writeStartArray()
    .writeStartObject()
      .write("apple", "red")
    .writeEnd()
    .writeStartObject()
      .write("banana", "yellow")
    .writeEnd()
.writeEnd();
```

A new array is started when the `writeStartArray` method is called and ended when the `writeEnd` method is called. An object within an array is written via the `writeStartObject` and `writeEnd` methods. The generated JSON structure is:

```
[
  { "apple":"red" },
  { "banana":"yellow" }
]
```

A nested structure with two name/value pairs and a named array can be generated:

```
gen.writeStartObject()
    .write("title", "The Matrix")
    .write("year", 1999)
    .writeStartArray("cast")
      .write("Keanu Reeves")
      .write("Laurence Fishburne")
      .write("Carrie-Anne Moss")
    .writeEnd()
  .writeEnd();
```

A named array is started via `writeStartArray`. Each element of the array is written via the `write` method, which can take values of the type `BigDecimal`, `BigInteger`, `boolean`, `double`, `int`, `long`, `String`, and `JsonValue`.

The generated JSON structure is:

```
{
  "title":"The Matrix",
  "year":1999,
  "cast":[
    "Keanu Reeves",
```

```
        "Laurence Fishburne",
        "Carrie-Anne Moss"
    ]
}
```

Object Model API

The Object Model API is a high-level API that provides immutable object models for JSON object and array structures. These JSON structures are represented as object models via the Java types `JsonObject` and `JsonArray`. `JsonObject` provides a `Map` view to access the unordered collection of zero or more name/value pairs from the model. Similarly, `JsonArray` provides a `List` view to access the ordered sequence of zero or more values from the model.

This programming model is most flexible and enables processing that requires random access to the complete contents of the tree. However, it is often not as efficient as the streaming model and requires more memory.

The Object Model API is similar to the DOM API for XML and uses builder patterns to create these object models. It consists of the interfaces `JsonReader` (for consuming JSON) and `JsonObjectBuilder` and `JsonArrayBuilder` (for producing JSON).

Consuming JSON Using the Object Model API

`JsonReader` contains methods to read JSON data using the object model from an input source.

`JsonReader` can be created from `InputStream`:

```
JsonReader reader = Json.createReader(new FileInputStream(...));
```

This code shows how to create a new parser from an `InputStream` obtained from a new `FileInputStream`.

`JsonReader` can also be created from `Reader`:

```
JsonParser parser = Json.createParser(new StringReader(...));
```

This code shows how to create a parser from a `StringReader`.

You can create multiple parser instances using `JsonReaderFactory`:

```
JsonReaderFactory factory = Json.createReaderFactory(null);
JsonReader parser1 = factory.createReader(...);
JsonReader parser2 = factory.createReader(...);
```

The factory can be configured with the specified map of provider-specific configuration properties. Any unsupported configuration properties specified in the map are ignored. In this case, `null` properties are passed during the creation of the reader factory.

An empty JSON object can be read as:

```
JsonReader jsonReader = Json.createReader(new StringReader("{}"));
JsonObject json = jsonReader.readObject();
```

In this code, a `JsonReader` is initialized via `StringReader`, which reads the empty JSON object. Calling the `readObject` method returns an instance of `JsonObject`.

An object with two name/value pairs can be read as:

```
jsonReader = Json.createReader(new StringReader("{"
                + "  \"apple\":\"red\","
                + "  \"banana\":\"yellow\""
                + "}"));
JsonObject json = jsonReader.readObject();
json.getString("apple");
json.getString("banana");
```

In this code, the `getString` method returns the string value for the specific key in the object. Other `getXXX` methods can be used to access the value based upon the data type.

An array with two objects with each object with a name/value pair can be read as:

```
jsonReader = Json.createReader(new StringReader("["
                + "  { \"apple\":\"red\" },"
                + "  { \"banana\":\"yellow\" }"
                + "]"));
JsonArray jsonArray = jsonReader.readArray();
```

In this code, calling the `readArray` method returns an instance of the `JsonArray` interface. This interface has convenience methods to get `boolean`, `integer`, and `String` values at a specific index. This interface extends from `java.util.List`, so usually the list operations are available as well.

A nested structure can be read as:

```
jsonReader = Json.createReader(new StringReader("{"
                + "  \"title\":\"The Matrix\","
                + "  \"year\":1999,"
                + "  \"cast\":["
                + "    \"Keanu Reeves\","
                + "    \"Laurence Fishburne\","
                + "    \"Carrie-Anne Moss\""
                + "  ]"
                + "}"));
json = jsonReader.readObject();
```

Producing JSON Using the Object Model API

`JsonObjectBuilder` can be used to create models that represent JSON objects. The resulting model is of type `JsonObject`. Similarly, `JsonArrayBuilder` can be used to create models that represent JSON arrays where the resulting model is of type JsonArray:

```
JsonObject jsonObject = Json.createObjectBuilder().build();
```

In this code, a `JsonObjectBuilder` is used to create an empty object. An empty object, with no name/value pairs, is created. The generated JSON structure is:

```
{ }
```

Multiple builder instances can be created via `JsonBuilderFactory`:

```
JsonBuilderFactory factory = Json.createBuilderFactory(null);
JsonArrayBuilder arrayBuilder = factory.createArrayBuilder();
JsonObjectBuilder objectBuilder = factory.createObjectBuilder();
```

The factory can be configured with the specified map of provider-specific configuration properties. Any unsupported configuration properties specified in the map are ignored. In this case, `null` properties are passed during the creation of the reader factory.

The generated `JsonObject` can be written to an output stream via `JsonWriter`:

```
Json.createWriter(System.out).writeObject(jsonObject);
```

In this code, a new `JsonWriter` instance is created and configured to write to `System.out`. The previously created `jsonObject` is then written when the `writeObject` method is called.

`JsonWriter` may be configured to write to a `Writer` as well.

An object with two name/value pairs can be generated:

```
Json.createObjectBuilder()
  .add("apple", "red")
  .add("banana", "yellow")
.build();
```

A name/value pair is written via the `add` method, which takes a name as the first parameter and a value as the second parameter. The value can be `BigDecimal`, `BigInteger`, `boolean`, `double`, `int`, `long`, `String`, `JsonValue`, `JsonObjectBuilder`, or `JsonArrayBuilder`. Specifying the value as `JsonObjectBuilder` and `JsonArrayBuilder` allows us to create nested objects and arrays.

The generated JSON structure is:

```
{
  "apple":"red",
  "banana":"yellow"
}
```

An array with two objects with each object with a name/value pair can be generated:

```
JsonArray jsonArray = Json.createArrayBuilder()
  .add(Json.createObjectBuilder().add("apple","red"))
```

```
        .add(Json.createObjectBuilder().add("banana","yellow"))
        .build();
```

You start a new array by creating a `JsonArrayBuilder`. You write an object within an array by calling the add method and creating a new object using the `JsonObjectBuild er` method. The generated JSON structure is:

```
[
  { "apple":"red" },
  { "banana":"yellow" }
]
```

The `JsonWriter.writeArray` method is called to write an array to the configured output stream.

A nested structure with two name/value pairs and a named array can be generated:

```
jsonArray = Json.createArrayBuilder()
            .add(Json.createObjectBuilder()
              .add("title", "The Matrix")
              .add("year", 1999)
              .add("cast", Json.createArrayBuilder()
                .add("Keanu Reaves")
                .add("Laurence Fishburne")
                .add("Carrie-Anne Moss")))
            .build();
```

You start a named array by calling the add method, passing the name of the array, and creating a new array by calling the `Json.createArrayBuilder` method. Each element of the array is written via the add method, which can take values of the type `BigDeci mal`, `BigInteger`, boolean, double, `int`, `long`, `String`, `JsonValue`, `JsonObjectBuild er`, and `JsonArrayBuilder`.

The generated JSON structure is:

```
{
  "title":"The Matrix",
  "year":1999,
  "cast":[
    "Keanu Reeves",
    "Laurence Fishburne",
    "Carrie-Anne Moss"
  ]
}
```

CHAPTER 7

WebSocket

The Java API for WebSocket is defined as JSR 356, and the complete specification can be downloaded (*http://jcp.org/aboutJava/communityprocess/final/jsr356/index.html*).

WebSocket provides a full-duplex and bidirectional communication protocol over a single TCP connection. Full-duplex means a client and server can send messages independent of each other. Bidirectional means a client can send a message to the server and vice versa. WebSocket is a combination of the IETF RFC 6455 Protocol (*http:// tools.ietf.org/html/rfc6455*) and the W3C JavaScript API (*http://www.w3.org/TR/ websockets/*). The protocol defines an opening handshake and basic message framing, layered over TCP. The API enables web pages to use the WebSocket protocol for two-way communication with the remote host.

Unlike HTTP, there is no need to create a new TCP connection and send a message chock-full of headers for every exchange between client and server. Once the initial handshake happens via HTTP Upgrade (defined in RFC 2616 (*http://www.ietf.org/rfc/ rfc2616.txt*), section 14.42), the client and server can send messages to each other, independent of the other. There are no predefined message exchange patterns of request/ response or one-way between client and server. These need to be explicitly defined over the basic protocol.

The communication between client and server is pretty symmetric, but there are two differences:

- A client initiates a connection to a server that is listening for a WebSocket request.
- A client connects to one server using a URI. A server may listen to requests from multiple clients on the same URI.

Other than these two differences, the client and server behave symmetrically after the opening handshake. In that sense, they are considered *peers*. After a successful handshake, clients and servers transfer data back and forth in conceptual units referred to as *messages*. On the wire, a message is composed of one or more *frames*. Application frames carry a payload intended for the application and can be text or binary data. Control frames carry data intended for protocol-level signaling.

Java API for WebSocket defines a standard API for building WebSocket applications and will provide support for:

- Creating a WebSocket client and server endpoint using annotations and an interface
- Creating and consuming WebSocket text, binary, and control messages
- Initiating and intercepting WebSocket life-cycle events
- Configuring and managing WebSocket sessions, like timeouts, retries, cookies, and connection pooling
- Specifying how the WebSocket application will work within the Java EE security model

Annotated Server Endpoint

You can convert a Plain Old Java Object (POJO) into a WebSocket server endpoint by using @ServerEndpoint. Such an endpoint is also called an *annotated endpoint*:

```
@ServerEndpoint("/chat")
public class ChatServer {
  @OnMessage
  public String receiveMessage(String message) {
    //. . .
  }
}
```

In this code:

- @ServerEndpoint decorates the class as a WebSocket endpoint published at the URI mentioned as a value of the annotation. The annotated class must have a public no-arg constructor. The annotation can have the attributes specified in Table 7-1.

Table 7-1. @ServerEndpoint attributes

Attribute	Value
value	Required URI or URI template where the endpoint will be deployed.
encoders	Optional ordered array of encoders used by this endpoint.
decoders	Optional ordered array of decoders used by this endpoint.
subprotocols	Optional ordered array of WebSocket protocols supported by this endpoint.
configurator	Optional custom configurator class used to further configure new instances of this endpoint. This will be an implementation of ServerEndpointConfig.Configurator.

- @OnMessage decorates a Java method that receives the incoming WebSocket message. This message can process text, binary, and pong messages. The text and binary messages contain the payload generated by the application. A pong message is a WebSocket control message and is generally not dealt with at the application layer.

The method can have the following parameters:

— Each method can process text, binary, or pong messages.

If the method is handling text messages:

— Use a String to receive the whole text message:

```
public void receiveMessage(String s) {
  //. . .
}
```

— Use a Java primitive or class equivalent to receive the whole message converted to that type:

```
public void receiveMessage(int i) {
  //. . .
}
```

— Use a String and a boolean pair to receive the message in parts:

```
public void receiveBigText(String message, boolean last) {
  //. . .
}
```

The Boolean parameter is true if the part received is the last part, and false otherwise.

— Use a Reader to receive the whole text message as a blocking stream:

```
@OnMessage
public void processReader(Reader reader) {
  //. . .
}
```

— Use any object parameter for which the endpoint has a text decoder (Decoder.Text or Decoder.TextStream)—more on this later.

If the method is handling binary messages:

— Use byte[] or ByteBuffer to receive the whole binary message:

```
public void receiveMessage(ByteBuffer b) {
  //. . .
}
```

— Use byte[] and a boolean pair, or ByteBuffer and a boolean pair, to receive the message in parts:

```
public void receiveBigBinary(ByteBuffer buf, boolean last) {
  //. . .
}
```

The Boolean parameter is `true` if the part received is the last part, and `false` otherwise.

— Use `InputStream` to receive the whole binary message as a blocking stream:

```
public void processStream(InputStream stream) {
  //. . .
}
```

— Use any object parameter for which the endpoint has a binary decoder (`Decoder.Binary` or `Decoder.BinaryStream`)—more on this later.

If the method is handling pong messages:

— Use `PongMessage` to receive the pong message:

```
public void processPong(PongMessage pong) {
  //. . .
}
```

— Use a 0..n `String` or Java primitive parameters annotated with `@PathParam` for server endpoints:

```
@ServerEndpoint("/chat/{room}")
public class MyEndpoint {
  @OnMessage
  public void receiveMessage(String message,
                    @PathParam("room")String room) {
    //. . .
  }
}
```

`@PathParam` is used to annotate the `room` method parameter on a server endpoint where a URI template has been used in the path mapping of the `ServerEnd point` annotation. The method parameter may be of type `String`, any Java primitive type, or any boxed version thereof. If a client URI matches the URI template, but the requested path parameter cannot be decoded, then the WebSocket's error handler will be called.

— Use an optional `Session` parameter:

```
public void receiveMessage(String message, Session session) {
  //. . .
}
```

`Session` indicates a conversation between two WebSocket endpoints and represents the other end of the connection. In this case, a response to the client may be returned:

```
public void receiveMessage(String message, Session session) {
  session.getBasicRemote().sendText(...);
}
```

The parameters may be listed in any order.

The method may have a void return type. Such a message is consumed at the endpoint without returning a response.

The method may have String, ByteBuffer, byte[], any Java primitive or class equivalent, and any other class for which there is an encoder as the return value. If a return type is specified, then a response is returned to the client.

The maxMessageSize attribute may be used to define the maximum size of the message in bytes that this method will be able to process:

```
@Message(maxMessageSize=6)
public void receiveMessage(String s) {
  //. . .
}
```

In this code, if a message of more than 6 bytes is received, then an error is reported and the connection is closed. You can receive the exact error code and message by intercepting the life-cycle callback using @OnClose. The default value is -1 to indicate that there is no maximum.

The maxMessageSize attribute only applies when the annotation is used to process whole messages, not to those methods that process messages in parts or use a stream or reader parameter to handle the incoming message.

Encoders provide a way to convert custom Java objects into WebSocket messages and can be specified via the encoders attribute. Decoders provide a way to convert WebSocket messages to custom Java objects and can be specified via the decoders attribute. (More on this later.)

An optional configurator attribute can be used to specify a custom configuration class for configuring new instances of this endpoint:

```
public class MyConfigurator extends ServerEndpointConfig.Configurator {
  @Override
  public void modifyHandshake(ServerEndpointConfig sec,
                              HandshakeRequest request,
                              HandshakeResponse response) {
    //. . .
  }
}

@ServerEndpoint(value="/websocket", configurator = MyConfigurator.class)
public class MyEndpoint {

  @OnMessage
  public void receiveMessage(String name) {
    //. . .
  }
}
```

In this code:

- The `MyConfigurator` class provides an implementation of `ServerEndpointConfig.Configurator`. This abstract class offers several methods to configure the endpoint, such as providing custom configuration algorithms and intercepting the opening handshake.

- The `modifyHandshake` method is called when a handshake response resulting from a well-defined handshake request is prepared. `ServerEndpointConfig` is the endpoint configuration object used to configure this endpoint. `HandshakeRequest` provides information about the WebSocket defined HTTP `GET` request for the opening handshake. This class provides access to data such as the list of HTTP headers that came with the request or the `HttpSession` that the handshake request was part of. `HandshakeResponse` identifies the HTTP handshake response prepared by the container.

- The `configurator` attribute is used to specify the custom configurator class as part of `@ServerEndpoint`.

`@OnOpen` can be used to decorate a method to be called when a new connection from a peer is received. Similarly, `@OnClose` can be used to decorate a method to be called when a connection is closed from the peer. `@OnError` may be used to decorate a method to be called when an error is received.

These methods may take any of the following parameters:

- Optional `Session` parameter
- Optional `EndpointConfig` for `@OnOpen`, `CloseReason` for `@OnClose`, or `Throwable` for `@OnError` parameter
- `0..n` `String` parameters annotated with `@PathParam`:

```
@OnOpen
public void open(Session s) {
  //. . .
}

@OnClose
public void close(CloseReason c) {
  //. . .
}

@OnError
public void error(Throwable t) {
  //. . .
}
```

In this code:

- The open method is called when a new connection is established with this endpoint. The parameter s provides more details about other end of the connection.
- The close method is called when the connection is terminated. The parameter c provides more details about why a WebSocket connection was closed.
- The error method is called when there is an error in the connection. The parameter t provides more details about the error.

For endpoints deployed in the Java EE platform, full dependency injection support as described in the CDI specification is available. Field, method, and constructor injection is available in all WebSocket endpoint classes. Interceptors may be enabled for these classes using the standard mechanism:

```
@ServerEndpoint("/chat")
public class ChatServer {
  @Inject User user;
  //. . .
}
```

In this code, the User bean is injected using the standard injection mechanism.

The WebSocket annotation behaviors are not passed down the Java class inheritance hierarchy. They apply only to the Java class on which they are marked. For example, a Java class that inherits from a Java class annotated with a class-level @ServerEndpoint annotation does not itself become an annotated endpoint, unless it itself is annotated with a class-level @ServerEndpoint annotation:

```
@ServerEndpoint("/chat")
public class ChatServer {
}

public class CustomChatServer extends ChatServer {
  //. . .
}
```

In this code, the ChatServer class is identified as a WebSocket endpoint; however, CustomChatServer is not. If it needs to be recognized as a WebSocket endpoint, then it must be explicitly marked with a class-level @ServerEndpoint annotation.

Subclasses of an annotated endpoint may not use method-level WebSocket annotations unless they themselves use a class-level WebSocket annotation. Subclasses that override methods annotated with WebSocket method annotations do not obtain WebSocket callbacks unless those subclass methods themselves are marked with a method-level WebSocket annotation.

Programmatic Server Endpoint

You can create a WebSocket server endpoint by extending the `Endpoint` class. Such an endpoint is also called a *programmatic endpoint*:

```
public class MyEndpoint extends Endpoint {
  @Override
  public void onOpen(final Session session, EndpointConfig ec) {
    //. . .
  }
}
```

In this code, the onOpen method is called when a new connection is initiated. `Endpoint Config` identifies the configuration object used to configure this endpoint.

Multiple `MessageHandlers` may be registered in this method to process incoming text, binary, and pong messages. However, only one `MessageHandler` per text, binary, or pong message may be registered per `Endpoint`:

```
session.addMessageHandler(new MessageHandler.Whole<String>() {

  @Override
  public void onMessage(String s) {
    //. . .
  }
});

session.addMessageHandler(new MessageHandler.Whole<ByteBuffer>() {

  @Override
  public void onMessage(ByteBuffer b) {
    //. . .
  }
});

session.addMessageHandler(new MessageHandler.Whole<PongMessage>() {

  @Override
  public void onMessage(PongMessage p) {
    //. . .
  }
});
```

In this code:

- `MessageHandler.Whole<String>` handler is registered to handle the incoming text messages. The onMessage method of the handler is invoked when the message is received. The parameter s is bound to the payload of the message.

- The `MessageHandler.Whole<ByteBuffer>` handler is registered to handle the incoming binary messages. The `onMessage` method of the handler is invoked when the message is received. The parameter `b` is bound to the payload of the message.
- The `MessageHandler.Whole<PongMessage>` handler is registered to handle the incoming `PongMessage`. The `onMessage` method of the handler is invoked when the message is received. The parameter `p` is bound to the payload of the message.

Although not required, a response can be sent to the other end of the connection synchronously:

```
session.addMessageHandler(new MessageHandler.Whole<String>() {

  @Override
  public void onMessage(String s) {
    try {
      session.getBasicRemote().sendText(s);
    } catch (IOException ex) {
      //. . .
    }
  }
});
```

A response may be returned asynchronously as well. The `Session.getAsyncRemote` method returns an instance of `RemoteEndpoint.Async` that can be used to send messages asynchronously. Two variations are possible:

```
@Override
public void onMessage(String data) {
  session.getAsyncRemote().sendText(data, new SendHandler() {

    @Override
    public void onResult(SendResult sr) {
      //. . .
    }
  });
}
```

In the first variation, a callback handler `SendHandler` is registered. The `onResult` method of the registered handler is called once the message has been transmitted. The parameter `sr` indicates whether the message was sent successfully, and if not, it carries an exception to indicate what the problem was.

In the second variation, an instance of `Future` is returned:

```
@Override
public void onMessage(String data) {
  Future f = session.getAsyncRemote().sendText(data);
  //. . .
  if (f.isDone()) {
    Object o = f.get();
```

```
    }
  }
```

The `sendXXX` method returns before the message is transmitted. The returned `Future` object is used to track the progress of the transmission. The `Future`'s `get` method returns `null` upon successful completion. Errors in transmission are wrapped in the `Execu tionException` thrown when the `Future` object is queried.

The `Endpoint.onClose` and `onError` methods can be overridden to invoke other life-cycle callbacks:

```
public class MyEndpoint extends Endpoint {
  //. . .

  @Override
  public void onClose(Session session, CloseReason c) {
    //. . .
  }

  @Override
  public void onError(Session session, Throwable t) {
    //. . .
  }
}
```

In the `onClose` method, the `c` parameter provides more details about why the WebSocket connection was closed. Likewise, the `t` parameter provides more details about the error received.

You receive a multipart message by overriding `MessageHandler.Partial<T>`, where `T` is a `String` for text messages, and `ByteBuffer` or `byte[]` is for binary messages:

```
session.addMessageHandler(new MessageHandler.Partial<String>() {

  @Override
  public void onMessage(String name, boolean part) {
    //. . .
  }
});
```

The Boolean parameter is `true` if the part received is the last part, and `false` otherwise.

You configure programmatic endpoints by implementing the `ServerApplicationCon fig` interface. This interface provides methods to specify the WebSocket endpoints within an archive that must be deployed:

```
public class MyApplicationConfig implements ServerApplicationConfig {
  @Override
  public Set<ServerEndpointConfig> getEndpointConfigs(
        Set<Class<? extends Endpoint>> set) {
    return new HashSet<ServerEndpointConfig>() {
      add(ServerEndpointConfig
```

```
                    .Builder
                    .create(MyEndpoint.class, "/chat")
                    .build());
            }
        };
    }

    //. . .
}
```

In this code:

- The `MyApplicationConfig` class implements the `ServerApplicationConfig` interface.
- The `getEndpointConfig` method provides a list of `ServerEndpointConfig` that is used to deploy the programmatic endpoints. The URI of the endpoint is specified here as well.

You can configure the endpoint with custom configuration algorithms by providing an instance of `ServerEndpointConfig.Configurator`:

```
@Override
public Set<ServerEndpointConfig> getEndpointConfigs(
        Set<Class<? extends Endpoint>> set) {
    return new HashSet<ServerEndpointConfig>() {{
        add(ServerEndpointConfig.Builder
            .create(MyEndpoint.class, "/websocket")
            .configurator(new ServerEndpointConfig.Configurator() {

                @Override
                public void modifyHandshake(ServerEndpointConfig sec,
                                            HandshakeRequest request,
                                            HandshakeResponse response) {
                    //. . .
                }

            })
            .build());
    }};
}
```

In this code:

- The `ServerEndpointConfig.Configurator` abstract class offers several methods to configure the endpoint such as providing custom configuration algorithms, intercepting the opening handshake, or providing arbitrary methods and algorithms that can be accessed from each endpoint instance configured with this configurator.
- The `modifyHandshake` method is used to intercept the opening handshake. `ServerEndpointConfig` is the endpoint configuration object used to configure this

endpoint. `HandshakeRequest` provides information about the WebSocket-defined HTTP `GET` request for the opening handshake. This class provides access to data such as the list of HTTP headers that came with the request or the `HttpSession` that the handshake request was part of. `HandshakeResponse` identifies the HTTP handshake response prepared by the container.

You may override other methods of `ServerEndpointConfig.Configurator` to customize the endpoint behavior. For example, you can specify the list of extensions supported by the endpoint by overriding the `getNegotiatedExtensions` method, and specify the list of subprotocols supported by the endpoint by overriding the `getNegotiatedSubprotocol` method.

For endpoints deployed in the Java EE platform, full dependency injection support as described in the CDI specification is available. Field, method, and constructor injection is available in all WebSocket endpoint classes. Interceptors may be enabled for these classes via the standard mechanism:

```
public class MyEndpoint extends Endpoint {
  @Inject MyBean bean;
  //. . .
}
```

In this code, the `MyBean` bean is injected via the standard injection mechanism.

Annotated Client Endpoint

You can convert a POJO to a WebSocket client endpoint by using `@ClientEndpoint`:

```
@ClientEndpoint
public class MyClientEndpoint {
  //. . .
}
```

The `@ClientEndpoint` decorates the class as a WebSocket client endpoint. The annotation can have the attributes described in Table 7-2.

Table 7-2. @ClientEndpoint attributes

Attribute	Value
configurator	An optional custom configurator class used to provide custom configuration of new instances of this endpoint. This will be an implementation of `ClientEndpointConfig.Configurator`.
encoders	Optional ordered array of encoders used by this endpoint.
decoders	Optional ordered array of decoders used by this endpoint.
subprotocols	Optional ordered array of WebSocket protocols supported by this endpoint.

You can intercept life-cycle events by specifying `@OnOpen`, `@OnClose`, and `@OnError` annotations on methods:

```
@ClientEndpoint
public class MyClientEndpoint {
  @OnOpen
  public void open(Session s) {
    //. . .
  }

  @OnClose
  public void close(CloseReason c) {
    //. . .
  }

  @OnError
  public void error(Throwable t) {
    //. . .
  }
}
```

In this code:

- The open method is called when a new connection is established with this endpoint. The parameter s provides more details about the other end of the connection.
- The close method is called when the connection is terminated. The parameter c provides more details about why a WebSocket connection was closed.
- The error method is called when there is an error in the connection. The parameter t provides more details about the error.

A new outbound message from the client to the endpoint can be sent during the connection initiation—for example, in the open method:

```
@OnOpen
public void onOpen(Session session) {
  try {
    session.getBasicRemote().sendText("Duke");
  } catch (IOException ex) {
    //. . .
  }
}
```

An inbound message from the endpoint can be received in any Java method decorated with @OnMessage:

```
@OnMessage
public void processMessage(String message, Session session) {
  //. . .
}
```

In this code:

- The `processMessage` method is invoked when a message is received from the endpoint.
- The `message` parameter is bound to the payload of the message.
- The `session` parameter provides more details about the other end of the connection.

The client can connect to the endpoint via `ContainerProvider`:

```
WebSocketContainer container = ContainerProvider.getWebSocketContainer();
String uri = "ws://localhost:8080/myApp/websocket";
container.connectToServer(MyClient.class, URI.create(uri));
```

In this code:

- `ContainerProvider` uses the ServiceLoader mechanism to load an implementation of `ContainerProvider` and provide a new instance of `WebSocketContainer`.
- `WebSocketContainer` allows us to initiate a WebSocket handshake with the endpoint.
- The server endpoint is published at the `ws://localhost:8080/myApp/websocket` URI. The client connects to the endpoint by invoking the `connectToServer` method and providing the decorated client class and the URI of the endpoint. This method blocks until the connection is established, or throws an error if either the connection could not be made or there was a problem with the supplied endpoint class.

You can use an optional `configurator` attribute to specify a custom configuration class for configuring new instances of this endpoint:

```
public class MyConfigurator extends ClientEndpointConfig.Configurator {
  @Override
  public void beforeRequest(Map<String, List<String>> headers) {
    //. . .
  }
  //. . .
}

@ClientEndpoint(configurator = MyConfigurator.class)
public class MyClientEndpoint {
  //. . .
}
```

In this code:

- The `MyConfigurator` class provides an implementation of `ClientEndpointConfig.Configurator`. This abstract class provides two methods to configure the client endpoint: `beforeRequest` and `afterResponse`. The `beforeRequest` method is called after the handshake request that will be used to initiate the connection to the

server is formulated, but before any part of the request is sent. The `afterRes`
`ponse` method is called after a handshake response is received from the server as a
result of a handshake interaction it initiated.

- The `headers` parameter is a mutable map of handshake request headers the implementation is about to send to start the handshake interaction.

- The `configurator` attribute is used to specify the custom configurator class as part
of `@ClientEndpoint`.

As for annotation-based server endpoints, the WebSocket annotation behaviors are not
passed down the Java class inheritance hierarchy. They apply only to the Java class on
which they are marked. For example, a Java class that inherits from a Java class annotated
with a class-level `@ClientEndpoint` annotation does not itself become an annotated
endpoint, unless it itself is annotated with a class-level `@ClientEndpoint` annotation.

Subclasses of an annotated endpoint may not use method-level WebSocket annotations
unless they themselves use a class-level WebSocket annotation. Subclasses that override
methods annotated with WebSocket method annotations do not obtain WebSocket
callbacks unless those subclass methods themselves are marked with a method-level
WebSocket annotation.

Programmatic Client Endpoint

You can also create a WebSocket client endpoint by extending the `Endpoint` class. Such
an endpoint is also called a *programmatic endpoint*:

```
public class MyClientEndpoint extends Endpoint {
  @Override
  public void onOpen(final Session session, EndpointConfig ec) {
    //. . .
  }
}
```

In this code, the `onOpen` method is called when a new connection is initiated. `Endpoint`
`Config` identifies the configuration object used to configure this endpoint.

This endpoint is configured via multiple `MessageHandlers`, as for the interface-based
server endpoint. Similarly, you can initiate a synchronous or an asynchronous communication with the other end of the communication using `session.getBasicRe`
`mote` and `session.getAsyncRemote`, respectively. You can receive the whole message
by registering the `Messagehandler.Whole<T>` handler, where `T` is a `String` for text messages, and `ByteBuffer` or `byte[]` is for binary messages. You receive a multipart message
by overriding `MessageHandler.Partial<T>`.

The programmatic client endpoint can connect to the endpoint via `ContainerProvider`:

```
WebSocketContainer container = ContainerProvider.getWebSocketContainer();
String uri = "ws://localhost:8080/myApp/websocket";
container.connectToServer(MyClientEndpoint.class, null, URI.create(uri));
```

In this code:

- `ContainerProvider` uses the ServiceLoader mechanism to load an implementation of `ContainerProvider` and provide a new instance of `WebSocketContainer`.

- `WebSocketContainer` allows us to initiate a WebSocket handshake with the endpoint.

- The server endpoint is published at the `ws://localhost:8080/myApp/websocket` URI. The client connects to the endpoint by invoking the `connectToServer` method and providing the programmatic client endpoint and the URI of the endpoint as parameters. This method blocks until the connection is established, or throws an error if either the connection could not be made or there was a problem with the supplied endpoint class. You use the default configuration of the client endpoint by passing `null` as the second parameter.

You can configure a programmatic client endpoint by providing an instance of `ClientEndpointConfig.Configurator`:

```
public class MyConfigurator extends ClientEndpointConfig.Configurator {

    @Override
    public void beforeRequest(Map<String, List<String>> headers) {
        //. . .
    }

    @Override
    public void afterResponse(HandshakeResponse response) {
        //. . .
    }
}
```

In this code, the `MyConfigurator` class provides an implementation of `ClientEndpointConfig.Configurator`. This abstract class provides two methods to configure the client endpoint: `beforeRequest` and `afterResponse`. The `beforeRequest` method is called after the handshake request that will be used to initiate the connection to the server is formulated, but before any part of the request is sent. The `afterResponse` method is called after a handshake response is received from the server as a result of a handshake interaction it initiated.

This configuration element can be specified in `connectToServer`:

```
container.connectToServer(MyClientEndpoint.class,
  ClientEndpointConfig
    .Builder
```

```
        .create()
        .configurator(new MyConfigurator()).build(), URI.create(uri));
```

For endpoints deployed in the Java EE platform, full dependency injection support as described in the CDI specification is available. Field, method, and constructor injection is available in all WebSocket endpoint classes. Interceptors may be enabled for these classes via the standard mechanism:

```
public class MyClientEndpoint extends Endpoint {
  @Inject MyBean bean;
  //. . .
}
```

In this code, the `MyBean` bean is injected using the standard injection mechanism.

JavaScript WebSocket Client

You can invoke a WebSocket endpoint using the W3C-defined JavaScript API (*http://www.w3.org/TR/websockets/*). The API allows us to connect to a WebSocket endpoint by specifying the URL and an optional list of subprotocols:

```
var websocket = new WebSocket("ws://localhost:8080/myapp/chat");
```

In this code:

- We invoke the `WebSocket` constructor by specifying the URI where the endpoint is published.
- The `ws://` protocol scheme defines the URL to be a WebSocket endpoint. The `wss://` scheme may be used to initiate a secure connection.
- WebSocket endpoint is hosted at `localhost` host and port `8080`.
- Application is deployed at the `myapp` context root.
- The endpoint is published at the `/chat` URI.
- You can specify an optional array of subprotocols in the constructor; the default value is an empty array.
- An established WebSocket connection is available in the JavaScript `websocket` variable.

The API defines event handlers that are invoked for different life-cycle methods:

- The `onopen` event handler is called when a new connection is initiated.
- The `onerror` event handler is called when an error is received during the communication.
- The `onclose` event handler is called when the connection is terminated:

```
websocket.onopen = function() {
  //. . .
}
websocket.onerror = function(evt) {
  //. . .
}
websocket.onclose = function() {
  //. . .
}
```

Text or binary data can be sent via any of the `send` methods:

```
websocket.send(myField.value);
```

This code reads the value entered in a text field, `myField`, and sends it as a text message:

```
websocket.binaryType = "arraybuffer";
var buffer = new ArrayBuffer(myField.value);
var bytes = new Uint8Array(buffer);
for (var i=0; i<bytes.length; i++) {
  bytes[i] = i;
}
websocket.send(buffer);
```

This code reads the value entered in a text field called `myField`, creates a binary array `buffer` of the length specified in that field, and sends it as a binary message to the WebSocket endpoint. The `binaryType` attribute can be set to `blob` or `arraybuffer` to send different types of binary data.

A message can be received via the `onmessage` event handler:

```
websocket.onmessage = function(evt) {
  console.log("message received: " + evt.data);
}
```

WebSocket defines a low-level message protocol. Any message exchange patterns, such as request-response, need to be explicitly built at the application level.

Encoders and Decoders

Applications can receive and send a payload in raw text and binary format. You can convert the text payload to an application-specific class by implementing `Decod er.Text<T>` and `Encoder.Text<T>`. You can convert the binary payload to an application-specific class by implementing the `Decoder.Binary<T>` and `Encoder.Bina ry<T>` interfaces.

JSON is a typical format for a text payload. Instead of receiving the payload as text and then converting it to a `JsonObject` (for example, using the APIs defined in the `jav ax.json` package), you can define an application-specific class to capture `JsonObject`:

```
public class MyMessage {

  private JsonObject jsonObject;

  //. . .
}
```

MyMessage is an application-specific class that contains JsonObject to capture the payload of the message.

The Decoder.Text<T> interface can be implemented to decode the incoming string payload to the application-specific class:

```
public class MyMessageDecoder implements Decoder.Text<MyMessage> {

  @Override
  public MyMessage decode(String string) throws DecodeException {
    MyMessage myMessage = new MyMessage(
            Json.createReader(
              new StringReader(string))
                .readObject()
            );
    return myMessage;
  }

  @Override
  public boolean willDecode(String string) {
    return true;
  }

  //. . .
}
```

This code shows how a String payload is decoded to MyMessage type. The decode method decodes the String parameter into an object of type MyMessage, and the will Decode method returns true if the string can be decoded into the object of type MyMessage. Standard javax.json.* APIs are used to generate the JSON representation from a string:

```
public class MyMessageEncoder implements Encoder.Text<MyMessage> {
  @Override
  public String encode(MyMessage myMessage) throws EncodeException {
    return myMessage.getJsonObject().toString();
  }

  //. . .
}
```

This code defines how a MyMessage type is encoded to a String, and the encode method encodes the message parameter into a String.

You can specify the encoders and decoders on an annotated endpoint using the `encoders` and `decoders` attributes of `@ServerEndpoint`:

```
@ServerEndpoint(value = "/encoder",
      encoders = {MyMessageEncoder.class},
      decoders = {MyMessageDecoder.class})
public class MyEndpoint {
  //. . .
}
```

Multiple encoders and decoders can be specified:

```
@ServerEndpoint(value = "/encoder",
      encoders = {MyMessageEncoder.class, MyMessageEncoder2.class},
      decoders = {MyMessageDecoder.class, MyMessageDecoder2.class})
public class MyEndpoint {
  //. . .
}
```

The first encoder that matches the given type is used. The first decoder where the `willDecode` method returns `true` is used.

The encoders and decoders can be specified on a programmatic server endpoint during endpoint configuration in `ServerEndpointConfig.Builder`:

```
public class MyEndpointConfiguration implements ServerApplicationConfig {

    List<Class<? extends Encoder>> encoders = new ArrayList<>();
    List<Class<? extends Decoder>> decoders = new ArrayList<>();

    public MyEndpointConfiguration() {
      encoders.add(MyMessageEncoder.class);
      decoders.add(MyMessageDecoder.class);
    }

    @Override
    public Set<ServerEndpointConfig> getEndpointConfigs(
                              Set<Class<? extends Endpoint>> set) {
      return new HashSet<ServerEndpointConfig>() {
          {
            add(ServerEndpointConfig
                  .Builder
                  .create(MyEndpoint.class, "/chat")
                  .encoders(encoders)
                  .decoders(decoders)
                  .build());
          }
      };
    }

    //. . .
}
```

In this code, the `Encoder` and `Decoder` list is initialized in the constructor and sets the encoder and decoder implementation using the `encoders` and `decoders` methods.

You can specify the encoders and decoders on a client endpoint using the `encoders` and `decoders` attributes of `@ClientEndpoint`:

```
@ClientEndpoint(
  encoders = {MyMessageEncoder.class},
  decoders = {MyMessageDecoder.class}
)
public class MyClientEndpoint {
  @OnOpen
  public void onOpen(Session session) {
    MyMessage message = new MyMessage("{ \"foo\" : \"bar\"}");
    session.getBasicRemote().sendObject(message);
  }
}
```

In this code:

- `MyMessageEncoder` is specified via the `encoders` attribute.
- `MyMessageDecoder` is specified via the `decoders` attribute.
- `MyMessage` object is initialized with a JSON payload.
- The client endpoint sends a message using `sendObject` instead of `sendString`.

You can specify the encoders and decoders on the programmatic client endpoint during endpoint configuration using `ClientEndpointConfig.Builder`:

```
List<Class<? extends Encoder>> encoders = new ArrayList<>();
List<Class<? extends Decoder>> decoders = new ArrayList<>();

encoders.add(MyMessageEncoder.class);
decoders.add(MyMessageDecoder.class);

WebSocketContainer container = ContainerProvider.getWebSocketContainer();
String uri = "ws://localhost:8080" + request.getContextPath() + "/websocket";
container.connectToServer(MyClient.class,
            ClientEndpointConfig
            .Builder
            .create()
            .encoders(encoders)
            .decoders(decoders)
            .build(),
          URI.create(uri));
```

In this code, the `Encoder` and `Decoder` list is initialized with the encoder and decoder implementations. The `encoders` and `decoders` methods on `ClientEndpointCon fig.Builder` can be used to set the encoders and decoders.

Integration with Java EE Security

A WebSocket mapped to a given `ws://` URI is protected in the deployment descriptor with a listing to an `http://` URI with same hostname, port, and path since this is the URL of its opening handshake. The authentication and authorization of the WebSocket endpoint builds on the servlet-defined security mechanism.

A WebSocket that requires authentication must rely on the opening handshake request that seeks to initiate a connection to be previously authenticated. Typically, this will be performed by an HTTP authentication (perhaps basic or form-based) in the web application containing the WebSocket prior to the opening handshake to the WebSocket.

Accordingly, WebSocket developers may assign an authentication scheme, user-role-based access, and a transport guarantee to their WebSocket endpoints.

You can set up basic authentication by using the *web.xml* deployment descriptor:

```
<web-app xmlns="http://xmlns.jcp.org/xml/ns/javaee"
         xmlns:xsi="http://www.w3.org/2001/XMLSchema-instance"
         xsi:schemaLocation="http://xmlns.jcp.org/xml/ns/javaee
                             http://xmlns.jcp.org/xml/ns/javaee/web-app_3_1.xsd"
         version="3.1">
  <security-constraint>
    <web-resource-collection>
      <web-resource-name>WebSocket Endpoint</web-resource-name>
        <url-pattern>/*</url-pattern>
        <http-method>GET</http-method>
    </web-resource-collection>
    <auth-constraint>
      <role-name>g1</role-name>
    </auth-constraint>
  </security-constraint>

  <login-config>
    <auth-method>BASIC</auth-method>
    <realm-name>file</realm-name>
  </login-config>

  <security-role>
    <role-name>g1</role-name>
  </security-role>
</web-app>
```

In this code:

- All HTTP `GET` requests require basic authentication defined by `BASIC` in `<auth-method>`. Invoking any page in the application will prompt the user to enter a username and password. The entered credentials must match one of the users in the group `g1`.

- Any subsequent requests, including the WebSocket opening handshake, will occur in the authenticated request.

If a client sends an unauthenticated opening handshake request for a WebSocket that is protected by the security mechanism, a 401 (Unauthorized) response to the opening handshake request is returned and the WebSocket connection is not initialized.

A transport guarantee of NONE allows unencrypted `ws://` connections to the WebSocket. A transport guarantee of CONFIDENTIAL only allows access to the WebSocket over an encrypted (`wss://`) connection.

CHAPTER 8

Enterprise JavaBeans

Enterprise JavaBeans (EJB) is defined as JSR 345, and the complete specification can be downloaded (*http://jcp.org/aboutJava/communityprocess/final/jsr345/index.html*).

Enterprise JavaBeans are used for the development and deployment of component-based distributed applications that are scalable, transactional, and secure. An EJB typically contains the business logic that operates on the enterprise's data. The service information, such as transaction and security attributes, may be specified in the form of metadata annotations, or separately in an XML deployment descriptor.

A bean instance is managed at runtime by a container. The bean is accessed on the client and is mediated by the container in which it is deployed. The client can also be on the server in the form of a managed bean, a CDI bean, or a servlet of some sort. In any case, the EJB container provides all the plumbing required for an enterprise application. This allows the application developer to focus on the business logic and not worry about low-level transaction and state management details, remoting, concurrency, multithreading, connection pooling, or other complex low-level APIs.

There are two types of enterprise beans:

- Session beans
- Message-driven beans

Entity beans were marked for pruning in the EJB 3.1 version of the specification and are made optional in EJB 3.2. It is strongly recommended to use the Java Persistence API for all the persistence and object/relational mapping functionality.

Stateful Session Beans

A stateful session bean contains conversational state for a specific client. The state is stored in the session bean instance's field values, its associated interceptors and their instance field values, and all the objects and their instances' field values, reachable by following Java object references.

You can define a simple stateful session bean by using @Stateful:

```
package org.sample;

@Stateful
public class Cart {
    List<String> items;

    public ShoppingCart() {
        items = new ArrayList<>();
    }

    public void addItem(String item) {
        items.add(item);
    }

    public void removeItem(String item) {
        items.remove(item);
    }

    public void purchase() {
      //. . .
    }

    @Remove
    public void remove() {
        items = null;
    }
}
```

This is a POJO marked with the @Stateful annotation. That's all it takes to convert a POJO to a stateful session bean. All public methods of the bean may be invoked by a client. The method remove is marked with the @Remove annotation. A client may remove a stateful session bean by invoking the remove method. Calling this method will result in the container calling the method marked with the @PreDestroy annotation. Removing a stateful session bean means that the instance state specific to that client is gone.

This style of bean declaration is called as a *no-interface view*. Such a bean is only locally accessible to clients packaged in the same archive. If the bean needs to be remotely accessible, it must define a separate business interface annotated with @Remote:

```
@Remote
public interface Cart {
  public void addItem(String item);
  public void removeItem(String item);
  public void purchase();
}

@Stateful
```

```
public class CartBean implements Cart {
  public float addItem(String item) {
    //. . .
  }

  public void removeItem(String item) {
    //. . .
  }

  //. . .
}
```

Now the bean is injected via the interface:

```
@Inject Cart cart;
```

A client of this stateful session bean can access this bean:

```
@Inject Cart cart;

cart.addItem("Apple");
cart.addItem("Mango");
cart.addItem("Kiwi");
cart.purchase();
```

EJB 3.2 relaxed the default rules for designating implementing interfaces as local or remote. The bean class must implement the interface or the interface must be designated as a local or remote business interface of the bean by means of the Local or Remote annotation or in the deployment descriptor.

If the bean is implementing two interfaces:

```
@Stateless
public class CartBean implements Cart, Payment {
  //. . .
}
```

In this code, if Cart and Payment have no annotations of their own, then they are exposed as local views of the bean. The beans may be explicitly marked @Local:

```
@Local
@Stateless
public class CartBean implements Cart, Payment {
  //. . .
}
```

The two code fragments are semantically equivalent. If the bean is marked @Remote as:

```
@Remote
@Stateless
public class CartBean implements Cart, Payment {
  //. . .
}
```

then `Cart` and `Payment` are remote views. If one of the interfaces is marked `@Local` or `@Remote`, then each interface that needs to be exposed must be marked explicitly; otherwise, it is ignored:

```
@Remote
public interface Cart {
  //. . .
}

@Stateless
public class Bean implements Payment, Cart {
  //. . .
}
```

In this code, the bean `Bean` only exposes one remote interface, `Cart`.

The `PostConstruct` and `PreDestroy` lifecycle callback methods are available for stateful session beans.

An EJB container may decide to *passivate* a stateful session bean to some form of secondary storage and then *activate* it again. The container takes care of saving and restoring the state of the bean. However, if there are nonserializable objects such as open sockets or JDBC connections, they need to be explicitly closed and restored as part of that process.

EJB 3.2 adds the capability to opt out of passivation. For example, a stateful session bean may contain nonserializable attributes, which would lead to runtime exceptions during passivation, or passivation and acivation of such instances may cause degradation of an application performance:

```
@Stateful(passivationCapable=false)
public class Cart {
  List<String> items;
  //. . .
}
```

In this code, the stateful EJB will not be passivated.

The `@PrePassivate` life-cycle callback method is invoked to clean up resources before the bean is passivated, and the `PostActivate` callback method is invoked to restore the resources.

Stateless Session Beans

A stateless session bean does not contain any conversational state for a specific client. All instances of a stateless bean are equivalent, so the container can choose to delegate a client-invoked method to any available instance. Since stateless session beans do not contain any state, they don't need to be passivated.

You can define a simple stateless session bean by using `@Stateless`:

```
package org.sample;

@Stateless
public class AccountSessionBean {
    public float withdraw() {
        //. . .
    }

    public void deposit(float amount) {
        //. . .
    }
}
```

This is a POJO marked with the @Stateless annotation. That's all it takes to convert a POJO to a stateless session bean. All public methods of the bean may be invoked by a client.

You can access this stateless session bean by using @EJB:

```
@EJB AcountSessionBean account;
account.withdraw();
```

This style of bean declaration is called as a *no-interface view*. Such a bean is only locally accessible to clients packaged in the same archive. If the bean needs to be remotely accessible, it must define a separate business interface annotated with @Remote:

```
@Remote
public interface Account {
    public float withdraw();
    public void deposit(float amount);
}

@Stateless
public class AccountSessionBean implements Account {
    float balance;

    public float withdraw() {
        //. . .
    }

    public void deposit(float amount) {
        //. . .
    }
}
```

Now the bean is injected via the interface:

```
@EJB Account account;
```

The PostConstruct and PreDestroy life-cycle callbacks are supported for stateless session beans.

The PostConstruct callback method is invoked after the no-args constructor is invoked and all the dependencies have been injected, and before the first business method is invoked on the bean. This method is typically where all the resources required for the bean are initialized.

The PreDestroy life-cycle callback is called before the instance is removed by the container. This method is where all the resources acquired during PostConstruct are released.

As stateless beans do not store any state, the container can pool the instances, and all of them are treated equally from a client's perspective. Any instance of the bean can be used to service the client's request.

Singleton Session Beans

A singleton session bean is a session bean component that is instantiated once per application and provides easy access to shared state. If the container is distributed over multiple virtual machines, each application will have one instance of the singleton for each JVM. A singleton session bean is explicitly designed to be shared and supports concurrency.

You can define a simple singleton session bean by using @Singleton:

```
@Singleton
public class MySingleton {
    //. . .
}
```

The container is responsible for when to initialize a singleton bean instance. However, you can optionally mark the bean for eager initialization by annotating it with @Startup:

```
@Startup
@Singleton
public class MySingleton {
    //. . .
}
```

The container now initializes all such startup-time singletons, executing the code marked in @PostConstruct, before the application becomes available and any client request is serviced.

You can specify an explicit initialization of singleton session beans using @DependsOn:

```
@Singleton
public class Foo {
    //. . .
}

@DependsOn("Foo")
@Singleton
```

```
public class Bar {
    //. . .
}
```

The container ensures that Foo bean is initialized before Bar bean.

A singleton bean supports PostConstruct and PreDestroy life-cycle callback methods.

A singleton bean always supports concurrent access. By default, a singleton bean is marked for container-managed concurrency, but alternatively may be marked for bean-managed concurrency.

Container-managed concurrency is based on method-level locking metadata where each method is associated with either a Read (shared) or Write (exclusive) lock. A Read lock allows concurrent invocations of the method. A Write lock waits for the processing of one invocation to complete before allowing the next invocation to proceed.

By default, a Write lock is associated with each method of the bean. The @Lock(Lock Type.READ) and @Lock(LockType.WRITE) annotations are used to specify concurrency locking attributes. These annotations may be specified on the class, a business method of the class, or both. A value specified on a method overrides a value specified on the bean.

Bean-managed concurrency requires the developer to manage concurrency using Java language–level synchronization primitives such as synchronized and volatile.

Life-Cycle Event Callbacks

Life-cycle callback interceptor methods may be defined for session beans and message-driven beans.

The @AroundConstruct, @PostConstruct, @PreDestroy, @PostActivate, and @PrePas sivate annotations are used to define interceptor methods for life-cycle callback events. An AroundConstruct life-cycle callback interceptor method may be defined on an interceptor class only. All other interceptor methods can be defined on an interceptor class and/or directly on the bean class.

@AroundConstruct

The AroundConstruct callback annotation designates an interceptor method that receives a callback when the target class constructor is invoked. This callback interceptor method may be defined only on interceptor classes and/or superclasses of interceptor classes and cannot be defined on the target class.

An interceptor can be defined as:

```
@Inherited
@InterceptorBinding
@Retention(RUNTIME)
@Target({CONSTRUCTOR, METHOD, TYPE})
```

```
public @interface MyAroundConstruct {
}
```

Interceptor binding can be defined as:

```
@MyAroundConstruct
@Interceptor
public class MyAroundConstructInterceptor {

  @AroundConstruct
  public void validateConstructor(InvocationContext context) {
    //. . .
  }
}
```

And finally the interceptor can be specified on the bean like so:

```
@MyAroundConstruct
@Stateful
public class MyBean {
  //. . .
}
```

The `validateConstructor` method is called every time MyBean's constructor is called.

@PostConstruct

The `PostConstruct` annotation is used on a method that needs to be executed after dependency injection is done to perform any initialization and before the first business method invocation on the bean instance. The method annotated with `PostConstruct` is invoked even if the class does not request any resources to be injected. Only one method can be annotated with @PostConstruct:

```
@Stateless
public class MyBean {
  @Inject AnotherBean bean;

  @PostConstruct
  private void setupResources() {
    //. . .
  }

  //. . .
}
```

In this code, the bean's default constructor is called first, then `AnotherBean` is injected, and finally the `setupResources` method is called before any of the business methods can be called.

This life-cycle callback interceptor method for different types of session beans occurs in the following transaction contexts:

- For a stateless session bean, it executes in an unspecified transaction context.

- For a stateful session bean, it executes in a transaction context determined by the life-cycle callback method's transaction attribute.

- For a singleton session bean, it executes in a transaction context determined by the bean's transaction management type and any applicable transaction attribute.

@PreDestroy

The `PreDestroy` annotation is used on methods as a callback notification to signal that the instance is in the process of being removed by the container. The method annotated with `PreDestroy` is typically used to release resources that it has been holding:

```
@Stateless
public class MyBean {
  @Inject AnotherBean bean;

  @PreDestroy
  private void cleanupResources() {
    //. . .
  }

  //. . .
}
```

In this code, the `cleanupResources` method is called before the instance is removed by the container.

This life-cycle callback interceptor method for different types of session beans occurs in the following transaction contexts:

- For a stateless session bean, it executes in an unspecified transaction context.

- For a stateful session bean, it executes in a transaction context determined by the life-cycle callback method's transaction attribute.

- For a singleton session bean, it executes in a transaction context determined by the bean's transaction management type and any applicable transaction attribute.

@PrePassivate

The `PrePassivate` annotation can only be used on a stateful session bean. This annotation designates a method to receive a callback before a stateful session bean is passivated:

```
@Stateful
public class MyStatefulBean {
  @PrePassivate
  private void beforePassivation(InvocationContext context) {
    //. . .
  }
```

```
    //. . .
  }
```

These methods are ignored for stateless or singleton session beans.

This life-cycle callback interceptor method executes in a transaction context determined by the life-cycle callback method's transaction attribute.

@PostActivate

The `PostActivate` annotation can only be used on a stateful session bean. This annotation designates a method to receive a callback after a stateful session bean is activated:

```
@Stateful
public class MyStatefulBean {
  @PostActivate
  private void afterActivation(InvocationContext context) {
    //. . .
  }

  //. . .
}
```

These methods are ignored for stateless or singleton session beans.

This life-cycle callback interceptor method executes in a transaction context determined by the life-cycle callback method's transaction attribute.

Life-cycle callback interceptor methods may throw system runtime exceptions, but not application exceptions.

Message-Driven Beans

A message-driven bean (MDB) is a container-managed bean that is used to process messages asynchronously. An MDB can implement any messaging type, but is most commonly used to process Java Message Service (JMS) messages. These beans are stateless and are invoked by the container when a JMS message arrives at the destination. A session bean can receive a JMS message synchronously, but a message-driven bean can receive a message asynchronously.

You can convert a POJO to a message-driven bean by using `@MessageDriven`:

```
@MessageDriven(mappedName = "myDestination")
public class MyMessageBean implements MessageListener {

    @Override
    public void onMessage(Message message) {
        try {
            // process the message
        } catch (JMSException ex) {
```

```
            //. . .
        }
    }
}
```

In this code, @MessageDriven defines the bean to be a message-driven bean. The map
pedName attribute specifies the JNDI name of the JMS destination from which the bean
will consume the message. The bean must implement the MessageListener interface,
which provides only one method, onMessage. This method is called by the container
whenever a message is received by the message-driven bean and contains the
application-specific business logic.

This code shows how a text message is received by the onMessage method and how the
message body can be retrieved and displayed:

```
public void onMessage(Message message) {
    try {
        TextMessage tm = (TextMessage)message;
        System.out.println(tm.getText());
    } catch (JMSException ex) {
        //. . .
    }
}
```

Even though a message-driven bean cannot be invoked directly by a session bean, it can
still invoke other session beans. A message-driven bean can also send JMS messages.

@MessageDriven can take additional attributes to configure the bean. For example, the
activationConfig property can take an array of ActivationConfigProperty that provides information to the deployer about the configuration of the bean in its operational
environment.

Table 8-1 defines the standard set of configuration properties that are supported.

Table 8-1. Message-driven bean ActivationConfig properties

Property name	Description
acknowledgeMode	Specifies JMS acknowledgment mode for the message delivery when bean-managed transaction demarcation is used. Supported values are Auto_acknowledge (default) or Dups_ok_acknowledge.
messageSelector	Specifies the JMS message selector to be used in determining which messages an MDB receives.
destinationType	Specifies whether the MDB is to be used with a Queue or Topic. Supported values are javax.jms.Queue or javax.jms.Topic.
subscriptionDurability	If MDB is used with a Topic, specifies whether a durable or nondurable subscription is used. Supported values are Durable or NonDurable.

A single message-driven bean can process messages from multiple clients concurrently.
Just like stateless session beans, the container can pool the instances and allocate enough

bean instances to handle the number of messages at a given time. All instances of the bean are treated equally.

A message is delivered to a message-driven bean within a transaction context, so all operations within the onMessage method are part of a single transaction. The transaction context is propagated to the other methods invoked from within onMessage.

MessageDrivenContext may be injected in a message-driven bean. This provides access to the runtime message-driven context that is associated with the instance for its lifetime:

```
@Resource
MessageDrivenContext mdc;

public void onMessage(Message message) {
    try {
        TextMessage tm = (TextMessage)message;
        System.out.println(tm.getText());
    } catch (JMSException ex) {
        mdc.setRollbackOnly();
    }
}
```

EJB 3.2 allows a message-driven bean to implement a listener interface with no methods. A bean that implements a no-method interface exposes as message listener methods all public methods of the bean class and of any superclasses except the java.lang.Ob ject. This feature cannot be used today but provides an extension point that allows the MDBs to provide additional functionality in the future.

Portable Global JNDI Names

A session bean can be packaged in an *ejb-jar* file or within a web application module (*.war*). An optional EJB deployment descriptor, *ejb-jar.xml*, providing additional information about the deployment may be packaged in an *ejb-jar* or *.war* file. The *ejb-jar.xml* file can be packaged as either *WEB-INF/ejb-jar.xml* or *META-INF/ejb-jar.xml* within one of the *WEB-INF/lib* JAR files, but not both.

A local or no-interface bean packaged in the *.war* file is accessible only to other components within the same *.war* file, but a bean marked with @Remote is remotely accessible independent of its packaging. The *ejb-jar* file may be deployed by itself or packaged within an *.ear* file. The beans packaged in this *ejb-jar* can be accessed remotely.

You can access this EJB using a portable global JNDI name with the following syntax:

```
java:global[/<app-name>]
            /<module-name>
            /<bean-name>
            [!<fully-qualified-interface-name>]
```

<app-name> applies only if the session bean is packaged with an *.ear* file.

`<module-name>` is the name of the module in which the session bean is packaged.

`<bean-name>` is the *ejb-name* of the enterprise bean.

If the bean exposes only one client interface (or alternatively has only a no-interface view), the bean is also exposed with an additional JNDI name using the following syntax:

```
java:global[/<app-name>]/<module-name>/<bean-name>
```

The stateless session bean is also available through the `java:app` and `java:module` namespaces.

If the `AccountSessionBean` is packaged in *bank.war*, then the following JNDI entries are exposed:

```
java:global/bank/AccountSessionBean
java:global/bank/AccountSessionBean!org.sample.AccountSessionBean
java:app/AccountSessionBean
java:app/AccountSessionBean!org.sample.AccountSessionBean
java:module/AccountSessionBean
java:module/AccountSessionBean!org.sample.AccountSessionBean
```

Transactions

A bean may use programmatic transaction in the bean code, which is called a *bean-managed transaction*. Alternatively, a declarative transaction may be used in which the transactions are managed automatically by the container; this is called a *container-managed transaction*.

By default, transactions in a bean are container-managed. The `@TransactionManage ment` annotation is used to declare whether the session bean or message-driven bean uses a bean-managed or container-managed transaction. The value of this annotation is either `CONTAINER` (the default) or `BEAN`.

A bean-managed transaction requires you to specify `@TransactionManagement(BEAN)` on the class and use the `javax.transaction.UserTransaction` interface. Within the business method, a transaction is started with `UserTransaction.begin` and committed with `UserTransaction.commit`:

```
@Stateless
@TransactionManagement(BEAN)
public class AccountSessionBean {
  @Resource javax.transaction.UserTransaction tx;

  public float deposit() {
    //. . .
    tx.begin();
    //. . .
    tx.commit();
    //. . .
```

```
    }
  }
```

Container-managed transaction is the default and does not require you to specify any additional annotations on the class. The EJB container implements all the low-level transaction protocols, such as the two-phase commit protocol between a transaction manager and a database system or messaging provider, to honor the transactional semantics. The changes to the underlying resources are all committed or rolled back.

A stateless session bean using a container-managed transaction can use `@Transactio nAttribute` to specify transaction attributes on the bean class or the method. Specifying the `TransactionAttribute` on a bean class means that it applies to all applicable methods of the bean. The absence of `TransactionAttribute` on the bean class is equivalent to the specification of `TransactionAttribute(REQUIRED)` on the bean.

A bean class using a container-managed transaction looks like:

```
@Stateless
public class AccountSessionBean {

  public float deposit() {
    //. . .
  }
}
```

There are no additional annotations specified on the bean class or the method.

The `@TransactionAttribute` values and meaning are defined in Table 8-2.

Table 8-2. @TransactionAttribute values

Value	Description
MANDATORY	Always called in client's transaction context. If the client calls with a transaction context, then it behaves as REQUIRED. If the client calls without a transaction context, then the container throws the `jav ax.ejb.EJBTransactionRequiredException`.
REQUIRED	If the client calls with a transaction context, then it is propagated to the bean. Otherwise, the container starts a new transaction before delegating a call to the business method and attempts to commit the transaction when the business process has completed.
REQUIRES_NEW	The container always starts a new transaction context before delegating a call to the business method and attempts to commit the transaction when the business process has completed. If the client calls with a transaction context, then the suspended transaction is resumed after the new transaction has committed.
SUPPORTS	If the client calls with a transaction context, then it behaves as REQUIRED. If the client calls without a transaction context, then it behaves as NOT_SUPPORTED.
NOT_SUPPORTED	If the client calls with a transaction context, then the container suspends and resumes the association of the transaction context before and after the business method is invoked. If the client calls without a transaction context, then no new transaction context is created.

Value	Description
NEVER	The client is required to call without a transaction context. If the client calls with a transaction context, then the container throws `javax.ejb.EJBException`. If the client calls without a transaction context, then it behaves as `NOT_SUPPORTED`.

The `container-transaction` element in the deployment descriptor may be used instead of annotations to specify the transaction attributes. The values specified in the deployment descriptor override or supplement the transaction attributes specified in the annotation.

Only the `NOT_SUPPORTED` and `REQUIRED` transaction attributes may be used for message-driven beans. A JMS message is delivered to its final destination after the transaction is committed, so the client will not receive the reply within the same transaction.

By default, the methods designated with `@PostConstruct`, `@PreDestroy`, `@PrePassivate`, and `@PostActivate` are executed in an unspecified transactional context. EJB 3.2 specifies that for a stateful session bean with container-managed transaction demarcation, these methods can have `REQUIRES_NEW` and `NOT_SUPPORTED` attributes.

Asynchronous Invocation

Each method of a session bean is invoked synchronously (i.e., the client is blocked until the server-side processing is complete and the result returned). A session bean may tag a method for asynchronous invocation, and a client can then invoke that method asynchronously.

This returns control to the client before the container dispatches the instance to a bean. The asynchronous operations must have a return type of `void` or `Future<V>`. The methods with a `void` return type are used for a *fire-and-forget* pattern. The other version allows the client to retrieve a result value, check for exceptions, or attempt to cancel any in-progress invocations.

The `@Asynchronous` annotation is used to mark a specific method (method level) or all methods (class level) of the bean as asynchronous. Here is an example of a stateless session bean that is tagged as asynchronous at the class level:

```
@Stateless
@Asynchronous
public class MyAsyncBean {
  public Future<Integer> addNumbers(int n1, int n2) {
    Integer result;
    result = n1 + n2;
    // simulate a long running query
    //. . .
    return new AsyncResult(result);
    }
}
```

The method signature returns `Future<Integer>` and the return type is `AsyncResult(Integer)`. `AsyncResult` is a new class introduced in EJB 3.1 that wraps the result of an asynchronous method as a `Future` object. Behind the scenes, the value is retrieved and sent to the client. Adding any new methods to this class will automatically make them asynchronous as well.

This session bean can be injected and invoked in any Java EE component:

```
@EJB MyAsyncBean asyncBean;

Future<Integer> future = asyncBean.addNumbers(10, 20);
```

The methods on the `Future` API are used to query the availability of a result with `isDone` or cancel the execution with `cancel(boolean mayInterruptIfRunning)`.

The client transaction context does not propagate to the asynchronous business method. This means that the semantics of the `REQUIRED` transaction attribute on an asynchronous method are exactly the same as `REQUIRES_NEW`.

The client security principal propagates to the asynchronous business method. This means the security context propagation behaves the same way for synchronous and asynchronous method execution.

Timers

The EJB Timer Service is a container-managed service that allows callbacks to be scheduled for time-based events. These events are scheduled according to a calendar-based schedule at a specific time, after a specific elapsed duration, or at specific recurring intervals.

Time-based events can be scheduled in multiple ways:

- Automatic timers based upon the metadata specified with `@Schedule`
- Programmatically using `TimerService`
- Methods marked with `@Timeout`
- Deployment descriptors

The first way to execute time-based methods is by marking any method of the bean with `@Schedule`:

```
@Stateless
public class MyTimer {

    @Schedule(hour="*", minute="*", second="*/10")
    public void printTime() {
        //. . .
```

```
        }
    }
```

In this code, the `printTime` method is called every 10th second of every minute of every hour. `@Schedule` also takes `year` and `month` fields, with a default value of `*` indicating to execute this method each month of all years.

The EJB container reads the `@Schedule` annotations and automatically creates timers.

Table 8-3 shows some samples that can be specified via `@Schedule` and their meanings.

Table 8-3. @Schedule expressions and meanings

@Schedule	Meaning
`hour="1,2,20"`	1 am, 2 am, and 10 pm on all days of the year
`dayOfWeek="Mon-Fri"`	Monday, Tuesday, Wednesday, Thursday, and Friday, at midnight (based upon the default values of `hour`, `minute`, and `second`)
`minute="30"`, `hour="4"`, `time zone="America/Los_Angeles"`	Every morning at 4:30 US Pacific Time
`dayOfMonth="-1,Last"`	One day before the last day and the last day of the month at midnight

`@Schedules` may be used to specify multiple timers.

Note that there is no need for an `@Startup` annotation here, as life-cycle callback methods are not required. Each redeploy of the application will automatically delete and recreate all the schedule-based timers.

You can easily create interval timers by using the `ScheduleExpression.start` and `end` methods. You can easily create the single-action timer by specifying fixed values for each field:

```
@Schedule(year="A",
          month="B",
          dayOfMonth="C",
          hour="D",
          minute="E",
          second="F")
```

Timers are not for real time, as the container interleaves the calls to a timeout callback method with the calls to the business methods and the life-cycle callback methods of the bean. So the timed-out method may not be invoked at exactly the time specified at timer creation.

The Timer Service allows for programmatic creation and cancellation of timers. You can create programmatic timers using the create*XXX* methods on `TimerService`. The method to be invoked at the scheduled time may be the `ejbTimeout` method from `TimedObject`:

```
@Singleton
@Startup
public class MyTimer implements TimedObject {
  @Resource TimerService timerService;

  @PostConstruct
  public void initTimer() {
    if (timerService.getTimers() != null) {
      for (Timer timer : timerService.getTimers()) {
        timer.cancel();
      }
    }
    timerService.createCalendarTimer(
      new ScheduleExpression().
        hour("*").
        minute("*").
        second("*/10"),
        new TimerConfig("myTimer", true)
    );

    @Override
    public void ejbTimeout(Timer timer) {
      //. . .

    }
  }
}
```

The initTimer method is a life-cycle callback method that cleans up any previously created timers and then creates a new timer that triggers every 10th second. The ejbTimeout method, implemented from the TimedObject interface, is invoked every time the timeout occurs. The timer parameter in this method can be used to cancel the timer, get information on when the next timeout will occur, get information about the timer itself, and gather other relevant data.

Note that the timers are created in the life-cycle callback methods, thus ensuring that they are ready before any business method on the bean is invoked.

EJB 3.2 adds the Timer.getAllTimers API, which returns all active timers associated with the beans in the same module in which the caller bean is packaged. These include both the programmatically created timers and the automatically created timers.

The third way to create timers is for a method to have the following signatures:

```
void <METHOD>() {
    //. . .
}
void <METHOD>(Timer timer) {
    //. . .
}
```

The method needs to be marked with @Timeout:

```
public class MyTimer {

  //. . .

  @Timeout
  public void timeout(Timer timer) {
    //. . .
  }
}
```

The fourth way to create timers is by tagging a method for execution on a timer expiration using *ejb-jar.xml*. Let's say the method looks like:

```
public class MyTimer {
  public void timeout(Timer timer) {
    //. . .
  }
}
```

You can convert the method `timeout` into a timer method by adding the following fragment to *ejb-jar.xml*:

```
<enterprise-beans>
  <session>
    <ejb-name>MyTimer</ejb-name>
    <ejb-class>org.sample.MyTimer</ejb-class>
    <session-type>Stateless</session-type>
    <timer>
      <schedule>
        <second>*/10</second>
        <minute>*</minute>
        <hour>*</hour>
        <month>*</month>
        <year>*</year>
      </schedule>
      <timeout-method>
        <method-name>timeout</method-name>
        <method-params>
          <method-param>javax.ejb.Timer</method-param>
        </method-params>
      </timeout-method>
    </timer>
  </session>
</enterprise-beans>
```

Timers can be created in stateless session beans, singleton session beans, and message-driven beans, but not stateful session beans. This functionality may be added to a future version of the specification.

Timers are persistent by default and can be made nonpersistent programmatically:

```
timerService.createCalendarTimer(
  new ScheduleExpression().
```

```
    hour("*").
    minute("*").
    second("*/10"),
    new TimerConfig("myTimer", true)
);
```

Alternatively, `timerConfig.setPersistent(false);` can be used to make the timer nonpersistent.

Timers defined via annotations can be made nonpersistent:

```
@Schedule(hour="*", minute="*", second="*/10", persistent="false")
public void printTime() {
    //. . .
}
```

Persistent timers are not allowed in Web Profile.

The timer-based events can only be scheduled in stateless session beans and singleton session beans.

Embeddable API

The Embeddable EJB API allows client code and its corresponding enterprise beans to run within the same JVM and class loader. The client uses the bootstrapping API from the `javax.ejb` package to start the container and identify the set of enterprise bean components for execution. This provides better support for testing, offline processing, and executing EJB components within a Java SE environment.

The following sample code shows how to write a test case that starts the embeddable EJB container, looks up the loaded EJB using the Portable Global JNDI Name, and invokes a method on it:

```
public void testEJB() throws NamingException {
    EJBContainer ejbC = EJBContainer.createEJBContainer();
    Context ctx = ejbC.getContext();
    MyBean bean = (MyBean) ctx.lookup ("java:global/classes/org/sample/MyBean");
    assertNotNull(bean);
    //. . .
    ejbC.close();
}
```

With EJB 3.2, if Java SE 7 is used to run the embeddable container, then the client may close the container implicitly by using the `try-with-resources` statement when acquiring the `EJBContainer` instance:

```
public void testEJB() throws NamingException {
    try (EJBContainer ejbC = EJBContainer.createEJBContainer()) {
        //. . .
        // no need to call ejbC.close();
```

```
    }
}
```

The embeddable EJB container uses the JVM classpath to scan for the EJB modules to be loaded. The client can override this behavior during setup by specifying an alternative set of target modules:

```
Properties props = new Properties();
props.setProperty(EJBContainer.EMBEDDABLE_MODULES_PROPERTY, "bar");
EJBContainer ejbC = EJBContainer.createEJBContainer(props);
```

This code will load only the `bar` EJB module in the embeddable container.

Table 8-4 explains the properties that may be used to configure the EJB container.

Table 8-4. Embeddable EJB container initialization properties

Name	Type	Purpose
`javax.ejb.embeddable.initial` or `EJBContainer.EMBEDDABLE_INI TIAL_PROPERTY`	`String`	Fully qualified name of the embeddable container provider class to be used for this application.
`javax.ejb.embeddable.modules` or `EJBContainer.EMBEDDABLE_MOD ULES_PROPERTY`	`String` or `String[]` `java.io.File` or `java.io.File[]`	Modules to be initialized. If included in the classpath, specified as `String` or `String[]`. If not in the classpath, specified as `File` or `File[]` where each object refers to an *ejb-jar* or exploded *ejb-jar* directory.
`javax.ejb.embeddable.appName` or `EJBContainer.EMBEDDA BLE_APP_NAME_PROPERTY`	`String`	Application name for an EJB module. It corresponds to the`<app-name>` portion of the Portable Global JNDI Name syntax.

The embeddable container implementation may support additional properties.

EJB Lite

The full set of EJB functionality may not be required for all enterprise applications. As explained earlier, the Web Profile offers a reasonably complete stack composed of standard APIs, and is capable out-of-the-box of addressing a wide variety of web applications. The applications targeted toward web profiles will want to use transactions, security, and other functionality defined in the EJB specification. EJB Lite was created to meet that need.

EJB Lite is a minimum set of the complete EJB functionality. No new functionality is defined as part of EJB Lite; it is merely a proper subset of the full functionality. This allows the EJB API to be used in applications that may have much smaller installation and runtime footprints than a typical full Java EE implementation.

Table 8-5 highlights the difference between EJB 3.2 Lite and EJB 3.2 Full API.

Table 8-5. Difference between EJB 3.2 Lite and EJB 3.2 Full API

	EJB 3.2 Lite	EJB 3.2 Full API
Session beans	✓	✓
Message-driven beans	✗	✓
Java Persistence 2.0	✓	✓
Local business interface/No-interface	✓	✓
3.x Remote	✗	✓
2.x Remote/Home component	✗	✓
2.x Local/Home component	✗	✓
JAX-WS web service endpoint	✗	✓
Nonpersistent EJB Timer Service	✓	✓
Persistent EJB Timer Service	✗	✓
Local asynchronous session bean invocations	✓	✓
Remote asynchronous session bean invocations	✗	✓
Interceptors	✓	✓
RMI-IIOP interoperability	✗	✓
Container-managed/bean-managed transactions	✓	✓
Declarative and programmatic security	✓	✓
Embeddable API	✓	✓

Local asynchronous session bean invocations and the nonpersistent EJB Timer Service are new additions in EJB 3.2 Lite. Everything else was categorized in EJB 3.1.

Functionality defined by EJB Lite is available in a Java EE Web Profile–compliant application server. A full Java EE–compliant application server is required to implement the complete set of functionality.

CHAPTER 9

Contexts and Dependency Injection

Contexts and Dependency Injection (CDI) is defined as JSR 346, and the complete specification can be downloaded (*http://jcp.org/aboutJava/communityprocess/final/jsr346/index.html*).

CDI defines a type-safe dependency injection mechanism in the Java EE platform. A bean specifies only the type and semantics of other beans it depends upon, without a string name and using the type information available in the Java object model. This allows compile-time validation in addition to deployment. It also provides for easy refactoring.

The injection request need not be aware of the actual life cycle, concrete implementation, threading model, or other clients of the bean. This "strong typing, loose coupling" combination makes your code easier to maintain. The bean so injected has a well-defined life cycle and is bound to *life-cycle contexts*. The injected bean is also called a *contextual instance* because it is always injected in a context.

Almost any POJO can be injected as a CDI bean. This includes EJBs, JNDI resources, entity classes, and persistence units and contexts. Even the objects that were earlier created by a factory method can now be easily injected. Specifically, CDI allows EJB components to be used as JSF managed beans, thus bridging the gap between the transactional and the web tier. It is also integrated with Unified Expression Language (UEL), allowing any contextual object to be used directly within a JSF or JSP page.

Discovery of Beans

Bean classes are deployed in *bean archives*. A bean archive has the bean discovery modes listed in Table 9-1.

Table 9-1. Bean discovery mode values

Value	Meaning
all	All types in the archive are considered for injection.
annotated	Only types with bean-defining annotations will be considered for injection.
none	Disable CDI.

A bean archive that does not contain *beans.xml* but contains one or more bean classes with a bean-defining annotation, or one or more session beans, is considered an *implicit bean archive*. A bean with a declared scope type is said to have a *bean-defining annotation*.

An *explicit bean archive* is an archive that contains a *beans.xml* file with any of the following conditions:

- A version number of 1.1 (or later), with the `bean-discovery-mode` of `all`:

```
<beans
  xmlns="http://xmlns.jcp.org/xml/ns/javaee"
  xmlns:xsi="http://www.w3.org/2001/XMLSchema-instance"
  xsi:schemaLocation="http://xmlns.jcp.org/xml/ns/javaee
                     http://xmlns.jcp.org/xml/ns/javaee/beans_1_1.xsd"
  bean-discovery-mode="all">
</beans>
```

A sample *beans.xml* file contains the starting and ending `beans` tag, with namespaces and attributes.

- No version number:

```
<beans xmlns="http://xmlns.jcp.org/xml/ns/javaee">
</beans>
```

- An empty file.

An explicit bean archive has a bean discovery mode of `all`.

A bean archive that contains a *beans.xml* file with version `1.1` (or later) must specify the `bean-discovey-mode` attribute. The default value for the attribute is `annotated`.

If it exists in the archive, then it must be present in the following locations:

- The *WEB-INF* or *WEB-INF/classes/META-INF* directory for web applications.
- The *META-INF* directory for EJB modules or JAR files.

beans.xml can define *exclude filters* to exclude beans and package names from discovery. You define these by using `<exclude>` elements as children of the `<scan>` element:

```
<beans ...>
  <scan>
```

```
      <exclude name="...">
      . . .
      </exclude>
    </scan>
  </beans>
```

Package names can be excluded if a particular class is found:

```
<exclude name="org.sample.beans.*">
  <if-class-available name="org.sample.beans.SimpleGreeting"/>
</exclude>
```

In this code, all beans in the `org.sample.beans.*` package are excluded if the `org.sample.beans.SimpleGreeting` class is found.

Package names can be excluded if a particular class is not found:

```
<exclude name="org.sample.beans.*">
  <if-class-not-available name="org.sample.beans.FancyGreeting"/>
</exclude>
```

In this code, all beans in the `org.sample.beans.*` package are excluded if the `org.sample.beans.FancyGreeting` class is not found.

Package names can be excluded if a system property is not defined for a particular name or a system property is not defined with a particular value:

```
<exclude name="org.sample.beans.*">
  <if-system-property name="myProperty" value="myValue"/>
</exclude>
```

In this code, all beans in the `org.sample.beans.*` package are excluded if a system property with the name `myProperty` is not defined with the value `myValue`.

The package name and all subpackages can be excluded if the filter name ends with `.**`:

```
<exclude name="org.sample.beans.**">
  <if-system-property name="exclude-beans"/>
</exclude>
```

In this code, all beans in the `org.sample.beans.*` package and subpackages are excluded if a system property with the name `exclude-beans` is set.

CDI 1.1 introduces a new annotation, `@Vetoed`. You can prevent a bean from injection by adding this annotation:

```
@Vetoed
public class SimpleGreeting implements Greeting {
  ...
}
```

In this code, the `SimpleGreeting` bean is not considered for injection.

All beans in a package may be prevented from injection:

```
@Vetoed
package org.sample.beans;

import javax.enterprise.inject.Vetoed;
```

This code in `package-info.java` in the `org.sample.beans` package will prevent all beans from this package from injection.

Java EE components, such as stateless EJBs or JAX-RS resource endpoints, can be marked with `@Vetoed` to prevent them from being considered beans.

Injection Points

You can inject a bean at a field, method, or constructor using `@Inject`.

The following code shows a `Greeting` interface, a POJO `SimpleGreeting` as its implementation, and the injection of the interface as a field in `GreetingService`:

```
public interface Greeting {
    public String greet(String name);
}

public class SimpleGreeting implements Greeting {
    public String greet(String name) {
        return "Hello" + name;
    }
}

@Stateless
public class GreetingService {
    @Inject Greeting greeting;

    public String greet(String name) {
        return greeting.greet(name);
    }
}
```

`@Inject` specifies the injection point, `Greeting` specifies what needs to be injected, and `greeting` is the variable that gets the injection.

A bean may define one or more methods as targets of injection as well:

```
Greeting greeting;

@Inject
public setGreeting(Greeting greeting) {
  this.greeting = greeting;
}
```

Finally, a bean can have at most one constructor marked with `@Inject`:

```
Greeting greeting;
```

```
@Inject
public SimpleGreeting(Greeting greeting) {
  this.greeting = greeting;
}
```

All method parameters are then automatically injected. This constructor may have any number of parameters, and all of them are injection points. A constructor marked with @Inject need not have public access. This allows a bean with constructor injection to be immutable.

Here is the bean initialization sequence:

1. Default constructor or the one annotated with @Inject

2. All fields of the bean annotated with @Inject

3. All methods of the bean annotated with @Inject (the call order is not portable, though)

4. The @PostConstruct method, if any

Qualifier and Alternative

Qualifier allows you to uniquely specify a bean to be injected among its multiple implementations. For example, this code declares a new qualifier, @Fancy:

```
@Qualifier
@Retention(RUNTIME)
@Target({METHOD, FIELD, PARAMETER, TYPE})
public @interface Fancy {
}
```

This defines a new implementation of the Greeting interface:

```
@Fancy
public class FancyGreeting implements Greeting {
    public String greet(String name) {
        return "Nice to meet you, hello" + name;
    }
}
```

and injects it in the GreetingService by specifying @Fancy as the qualifer:

```
@Stateless
public class GreetingService {
    @Inject @Fancy Greeting greeting;

    public String sayHello(String name) {
        return greeting.greet(name);
    }
}
```

This removes any direct dependency to any particular implementation of the interface. Qualifiers may take parameters for further discrimination. Multiple qualifiers may be specified at an injection point.

Table 9-2 lists the built-in qualifiers and their meanings.

Table 9-2. Built-in CDI qualifiers

Qualifier	Description
@Named	String-based qualifier, required for usage in Expression Language
@Default	Default qualifier on all beans without an explicit qualifier, except @Named
@Any	Default qualifier on all beans except @New
@New	Allows the application to obtain a new instance independent of the declared scope; deprecated in CDI 1.1, and injecting @Dependent scoped beans is encouraged instead

Using the `SimpleGreeting` and `FancyGreeting` implementations defined earlier, the injection points are explained as follows:

```
@Inject Greeting greeting;
@Inject @Default Greeting greeting;
@Inject @Any @Default Greeting greeting;
```

The three injection points are equivalent, as each bean has **@Default** and **@Any** (except for **@New**) qualifiers and specifying them does not provide any additional information. The `SimpleGreeting` bean is injected in each statement. Thus:

```
@Inject @Any @Fancy Greeting greeting;
```

will inject the `FancyGreeting` implementation. This is because specifying **@Fancy** on `FancyGreeting` means it does not have the **@Default** qualifier. This statement:

```
@Inject @Any Greeting greeting;
```

will result in *ambiguous dependency* and require us to further qualify the bean by specifying **@Default** or **@Fancy**.

The use of **@Named** as an injection point qualifier is not recommended, except in the case of integration with legacy code that uses string-based names to identify beans.

The beans marked with **@Alternative** are unavailable for injection, lookup, or EL resolution. We need to explicitly enable them in *beans.xml* using `<alternatives>`:

```
@Alternative
public class SimpleGreeting implements Greeting {
    //. . .
}

@Fancy @Alternative
public class FancyGreeting implements Greeting {
    //. . .
}
```

Now the following injection will give an error about *unresolved dependency*:

```
@Inject Greeting greeting;
```

because both the beans are disabled for injection. We can resolve this error by explicitly enabling one of the beans in *beans.xml*:

```
<beans
    xmlns="http://xmlns.jcp.org/xml/ns/javaee"
    xmlns:xsi="http://www.w3.org/2001/XMLSchema-instance"
    xsi:schemaLocation="
        http://xmlns.jcp.org/xml/ns/javaee
        http://xmlns.jcp.org/xml/ns/javaee/beans_1_1.xsd"
    bean-discovery-mode="annotated">
    <alternatives>
        <class>org.sample.FancyGreeting</class>
    </alternatives>
</beans>
```

`@Alternative` allows us to package multiple implementations of a bean with the same qualifiers in the *.war* file and selectively enable them by changing the deployment descriptor based upon the environment. For example, this can allow you to target separate beans for injection in development, testing, and production environments by enabling the classes in *beans.xml*. This provides deployment-type polymorphism.

Producer and Disposer

`@Inject` and `@Qualifier` provide static injection of a bean (i.e., the concrete type of the bean to be injected is known). However, this may not always be possible. The *producer methods* provide runtime polymorphism where the concrete type of the bean to be injected may vary at runtime, the injected object may not even be a bean, and objects may require custom initialization. This is similar to the well-known *factory pattern*.

Here is an example that shows how `List<String>` can be made available as a target for injection:

```
@Produces
public List<String> getGreetings() {
    List<String> response = new ArrayList<String>();
    //. . .
    return response;
}
```

In this code, the `getGreetings` method can populate `List<String>` from a `Data Source` or by invoking some other external operation.

And now it can be injected as:

```
@Inject List<String> list;
```

By default, a bean is injected in `@Dependent` scope, but we can change it by explicitly specifying the required scope. Let's say `Connection` is a bean that encapsulates a connection to a resource—for example, a database accessible via JDBC—and `User` provides credentials to the resource. The following code shows how a `Connection` bean is available for injection in request scope:

```
@Produces @RequestScoped
Connection connect(User user) {
    return createConnection(user.getId(), user.getPassword());
}
```

Here is another example of how `PersistenceContext` may be exposed as a type-safe bean. This is typical of how an `EntityManager` is injected:

```
@PersistenceContext(unitName="...")
EntityManager em;
```

All such references can be unified in a single file as:

```
@Produces
@PersistenceContext(unitName="...")
@CustomerDatabase
EntityManager em;
```

where `CustomerDatabase` is a qualifier. The `EntityManager` can now be injected as:

```
@Inject @CustomerDatabase
EntityManager em;
```

Similarly, JMS factories and destinations can be injected in a type-safe way.

Some objects that are made available for injection via `@Produces` may require explicit destruction. For example, the JMS factories and destinations need to be closed. Here is a code example that shows how the `Connection` produced earlier may be closed:

```
void close(@Disposes Connection connection) {
    connection.close();
}
```

Interceptors

Interceptors are used to implement cross-cutting concerns, such as logging, auditing, and security, from the business logic.

The specification is not entirely new, as the concept already existed in the EJB 3.0 specification. However, it is now abstracted at a higher level so that it can be more generically applied to a broader set of specifications in the platform. Interceptors do what their name implies—they intercept invocations and life-cycle events on an associated target class. Basically, an interceptor is a class whose methods are invoked when business methods on a target class are invoked, life-cycle events such as methods that create/

destroy the bean occur, or an EJB timeout method occurs. The CDI specification defines a type-safe mechanism for associating interceptors to beans using interceptor bindings.

We need to define an *interceptor binding type* in order to intercept a business method. We can do this by specifying the @InterceptorBinding meta-annotation:

```
@InterceptorBinding
@Retention(RUNTIME)
@Target({METHOD,TYPE})
public @interface Logging {
}
```

@Target defines the program element to which this interceptor can be applied. In this case, the annotation @Logging can be applied to a method or a type (class, interface, or enum).

The interceptor is implemented as follows:

```
@Interceptor
@Logging
public class LoggingInterceptor {
  @AroundInvoke
  public Object log(InvocationContext context) throws Exception {
    String name = context.getMethod().getName();
    String params = context.getParameters().toString();
    //. . .
    return context.proceed();
  }
}
```

Adding the @Interceptor annotation marks this class as an interceptor, and @Logging specifies that this is an implementation of the earlier defined interceptor binding type. @AroundInvoke indicates that this interceptor method interposes on business methods. Only one method of an interceptor may be marked with this annotation. InvocationContext provides context information about the intercepted invocation and operations and can be used to control the behavior of the invocation chain. Name of the business method invoked and the parameters passed to it can be retrieved from the context.

This interceptor may be attached to any managed bean:

```
@Logging
public class SimpleGreeting {
  //. . .
}
```

Alternatively, we can log individual methods by attaching the interceptor:

```
public class SimpleGreeting {
  @Logging
  public String greet(String name) {
    //. . .
```

```
    }
}
```

You can define multiple interceptors using the same interceptor binding.

By default, all interceptors are disabled. They need to be explicitly enabled and ordered via the @Priority annotation, along with a priority value on the interceptor class:

```
@Priority(Interceptor.Priority.APPLICATION+10)
@Interceptor
@Logging
public class LoggingInterceptor {
  //. . .
}
```

The priority values are defined in the javax.interceptor.Interceptor.Priority class, as specified in Table 9-3.

Table 9-3. Interceptor priority values

Priority value	Constant field value
Interceptor.Priority.PLATFORM_BEFORE	0
Interceptor.Priority.LIBRARY_BEFORE	1000
Interceptor.Priority.APPLICATION	2000
Interceptor.Priority.LIBRARY_AFTER	3000
Interceptor.Priority.PLATFORM_AFTER	4000

Interceptors with the smaller priority values are called first. If more than one interceptor has the same priority, the relative order of these interceptor is undefined.

The values in Table 9-4 define the following interceptor ranges to order interceptors for a specific interposed method or event in the interceptor chain.

Table 9-4. Interceptor priority value ranges

Range	Invocation sequence
> PLATFORM_BEFORE and < LIBRARY_BEFORE	Interceptors defined by the Java EE Platform specifications that are to be executed at the beginning of the interceptor chain
> LIBRARY_BEFORE and < APPLICATION	Interceptors defined by extension libraries that are intended to be executed earlier in the interceptor chain
> APPLICATION and < LIBRARY_AFTER	Interceptors defined by applications
> LIBRARY_AFTER and < PLATFORM_AFTER	Interceptors defined by extension libraries that are intended to be executed later in the interceptor chain
> PLATFORM_AFTER	Interceptors defined by the Java EE Platform specifications that are to be executed at the end of the interceptor chain

The LoggingInterceptor defined earlier is executed after all application-specific interceptors are called but before interceptors defined by extension libraries.

You can also explicitly enable interceptors by specifying them in *beans.xml*:

```
<beans xmlns="http://xmlns.jcp.org/xml/ns/javaee"
    xmlns:xsi="http://www.w3.org/2001/XMLSchema-instance"
    xsi:schemaLocation="
        http://xmlns.jcp.org/xml/ns/javaee
        http://xmlns.jcp.org/xml/ns/javaee/beans_1_1.xsd"
    bean-discovery-mode="annotated">
    <interceptors>
        <class>org.sample.LoggingInterceptor</class>
    </interceptors>
</beans>
```

Note that the actual interceptor implementation class is mentioned here.

Defining interceptor bindings provides one level of indirection but removes the dependency from the actual interceptor implementation class. It also allows you to vary the actual interceptor implementation based upon the deployment environment as well, and to provide a central ordering of interceptors for that archive. The interceptors are invoked in the order in which they are specified inside the <interceptors> element.

Interceptors also support dependency injection. An interceptor that adds basic transactional behavior to a managed bean may be defined thusly:

```
@Interceptor
@MyTransactional
public class MyTransactionInterceptor {
    @Resource UserTransaction tx;

    @AroundInvoke
    public Object manageTransaction(InvocationContext context) {
        tx.begin();
        //. . .
        Object response = context.proceed();
        //. . .
        tx.commit();
        return response;
    }
}
```

UserTransaction is injected in the interceptor and is then used to start and commit the transaction in the interceptor method. @MyTransactional can now be specified on any managed bean or a method thereof to indicate the transactional behavior.

The Java Transaction API introduces a new @javax.transaction.Transactional annotation that enables an application to declaratively control transaction boundaries on CDI-managed beans, as well as classes defined as managed beans, such as servlets, JAX-RS resource classes, and JAX-WS service endpoints.

A life-cycle callback interceptor can be implemented as follows:

```
public class LifecycleInterceptor {
    @PostConstruct
    public void init(InvocationContext context) {
        //. . .
    }
}
```

An EJB timeout interceptor can be implemented like so:

```
public class TimeoutInterceptor {
    @AroundTimeout
    public Object timeout(InvocationContext context) {
        //. . .
    }
}
```

Decorators

Decorators are used to implement business concerns. Interceptors are unaware of the business semantics of the invoked bean and thus are more widely applicable; decorators complement interceptors, as they are business-semantics-aware and applicable to beans of a particular type. A decorator is a bean that implements the bean it decorates and is annotated with the @Decorator stereotype (see "Stereotypes" on page 181 for more details):

```
@Decorator
class MyDecorator implements Greeting {
    public String greet(String name) {
        //. . .
    }
}
```

The decorator class may be abstract, as it may not be implementing all methods of the bean.

A decorator class has a *delegate injection point* that is an injection point for the same type as the bean it decorates. The delegate injection point follows the normal rules for injection and therefore must be an injected field, initializer method parameter, or bean constructor method parameter:

```
@Inject @Delegate @Any Greeting greeting;
```

This delegate injection point specifies that the decorator is bound to all beans that implement Greeting.

A delegate injection point may specify qualifiers, and the decorator is then bound to beans with the same qualifiers.

By default, all decorators are disabled and need to be explicitly enabled and ordered via the @Priority annotation, along with a priority value on the decorator class:

```
@Decorator
@Priority(Interceptor.Priority.APPLICATION+10)
class MyDecorator implements Greeting {
    public String greet(String name) {
        //. . .
    }
}
```

The priority values are defined in the `javax.interceptor.Interceptor.Priority` class, as explained earlier in Table 9-3. Decorators with the smaller priority values are called first. The order of more than one decorator with the same priority is undefined.

A decorator enabled via the `@Priority` annotation is enabled for the entire application. Just like interceptors, this allows you to specify a central ordering of decorators for that archive and vary the set of decorators based upon the deployment environment.

The priority value ranges for decorators were defined previously in Table 9-4.

You can enable a decorator by specifying it in *beans.xml*:

```
<beans xmlns="http://xmlns.jcp.org/xml/ns/javaee"
    xmlns:xsi="http://www.w3.org/2001/XMLSchema-instance"
    xsi:schemaLocation="
      http://xmlns.jcp.org/xml/ns/javaee
      http://xmlns.jcp.org/xml/ns/javaee/beans_1_1.xsd"
    bean-discovery-mode="annotated">
    <decorators>
        <class>org.sample.MyDecorator</class>
    </decorators>
</beans>
```

In this case, the decorator is enabled for the bean archive that contains *beans.xml*.

The order of the decorator declarations using `<class>` determines the decorator ordering. Decorators that occur earlier in the list are called first.

Decorators enabled via `@Priority` are called before decorators enabled via *beans.xml*.

In order of execution, the interceptors for a method are called before the decorators that apply to the method.

Scopes and Contexts

A bean is said to be in a *scope* and is associated with a *context*. The associated context manages the life cycle and visibility of all beans in that scope. A bean is created once per scope and then reused. When a bean is requested in a particular scope, a new instance is created if it does not exist already. If it does exist, that instance is returned instead. The runtime makes sure the bean in the right scope is created, if required; the client does not have to be scope-aware. This provides loose coupling between the client and the bean to be injected.

There are four predefined scopes and one default scope, as shown in Table 9-5.

Table 9-5. Predefined scopes in CDI

Scope	Description
@RequestScoped	A bean is scoped to a request. The bean is available during a single request and destroyed when the request is complete.
@SessionScoped	A bean is scoped to a session. The bean is shared between all requests that occur in the same HTTP session, holds state throughout the session, and is destroyed when the HTTP session times out or is invalidated.
@ApplicationScoped	A bean is scoped to an application. The bean is created when the application is started, holds state throughout the application, and is destroyed when the application is shut down.
@ConversationScoped	A bean is scoped to a conversation and is of two types: *transient* or *long-running*. By default, a bean in this scope is transient, is created with a JSF request, and is destroyed at the end of the request. A transient conversation can be converted to a long-running one via `Conversation.begin`. This long-running conversation can be ended via `Conversation.end`. All long-running conversations are scoped to a particular HTTP servlet session and may be propagated to other JSF requests. Multiple parallel conversations can run within a session, each uniquely identified by a string-valued identifier that is either set by the application or generated by the container. This allows multiple tabs in a browser to hold state corresponding to a conversation, unike session cookies, which are shared across tabs.
@Dependent	A bean belongs to the dependent pseudoscope. This is the default scope of the bean that does not explicitly declare a scope.

A contextual reference to the bean is not a direct reference to the bean (unless it is in @Dependent scope). Instead, it is a *client proxy object*. This client proxy is responsible for ensuring that the bean instance that receives a method invocation is the instance that is associated with the current context. This allows you to invoke the bean in the current context instead of using a stale reference.

If the bean is in @Dependent scope, then the client holds a direct reference to its instance. A new instance of the bean is bound to the life cycle of the newly created object. A bean in @Dependent scope is never shared between multiple injection points. If an @Dependent-scoped bean is used in an EL expression, then an instance of the bean is created for each EL expression. So a wider life-cycle context, such as @RequestScoped or @SessionScoped, needs to be used if the values evaluated by the EL expression need to be accessible in other beans.

You can define a new scope using the extensible context model (@Contextual, @CreationalContext, and @Context interfaces), but that is generally not required by an application developer.

Stereotypes

A stereotype encapsulates *architectural patterns* or *common metadata* for beans that produce recurring roles in a central place. It encapsulates scope, interceptor bindings, qualifiers, and other properties of the role.

A stereotype is a meta-annotation annotated with `@Stereotype`:

```
@Stereotype
@Retention(RUNTIME)
@Target(TYPE)
//. . .
public @interface MyStereotype { }
```

A stereotype that adds transactional behavior can be defined as:

```
@Stereotype
@Retention(RUNTIME)
@Target(TYPE)
@Transactional
public @interface MyStereotype { }
```

In this code, an interceptor binding defined earlier, `@Transactional`, is used to define the stereotype. A single interceptor binding defines this stereotype instead of the interceptor binding. However, it allows you to update the stereotype definition later with other scopes, qualifiers, and properties, and those values are then automatically applied on the bean.

A stereotype can be specified on a target bean like any other annotation:

```
@MyStereotype
public class MyBean {
    //. . .
}
```

The metadata defined by the stereotype is now applicable on the bean.

A stereotype may declare the default scope of a bean:

```
@Stereotype
@RequestScoped
@Retention(RUNTIME)
@Target(TYPE)
public @interface MyStereotype { }
```

Specifying this stereotype on a bean marks it to have `@RequestScoped` unless the bean explicitly specifies the scope. A stereotype may declare at most one scope.

A stereotype may declare zero, one, or multiple interceptor bindings:

```
@Stereotype
@Transactional
@Logging
@Retention(RUNTIME)
```

```
@Target(TYPE)
public @interface MyStereotype { }
```

Adding @Alternative to the stereotype definition marks all the target beans to be alternatives.

Stereotypes can be *stacked* together to create new stereotypes as well.

@Interceptor, @Decorator, and @Model are predefined stereotypes. The @Model stereotype is predefined:

```
@Named
@RequestScoped
@Stereotype
@Target({TYPE, METHOD})
@Retention(RUNTIME)
public @interface Model {}
```

This stereotype provides a default name for the bean and marks it @RequestScoped. Adding this stereotype on a bean will enable it to pass values from a JSF view to a controller, say, an EJB.

Events

Events provide an annotation-based event model based upon the *observer* pattern. Event *producers* raise events that are consumed by *observers*. The event object, typically a POJO, carries state from producer to consumer. The producer and the observer are completely decoupled from each other and only communicate using the state.

A producer bean will fire an event using the Event interface:

```
@Inject @Any Event<Customer> event;
//. . .
event.fire(customer);
```

An observer bean with the following method signature will receive the event:

```
void onCustomer(@Observes Customer event) {
    //. . .
}
```

In this code, Customer is carrying the state of the event.

The producer bean can specify a set of qualifiers when injecting the event:

```
@Inject @Any @Added Event<Customer> event;
```

The observer bean's method signature has to match the exact set of qualifiers in order to receive the events fired by this bean:

```
void onCustomer(@Observes @Added Customer event) {
    //. . .
}
```

Qualifiers with parameters and multiple qualifiers may be specified to further narrow the scope of an observer bean.

By default, an existing instance of the bean or a new instance of the bean is created in the current context to deliver the event. This behavior can be altered so that the event is delivered only if the bean already exists in the current scope:

```
void onCustomer(
        @Observes(
          notifyObserver= Reception.IF_EXISTS)
          @Added Customer event){
    //. . .
}
```

Transactional observer methods receive their event notifications during the *before completion* or *after completion* phases of the transaction in which the event was fired. `Trans actionPhase` identifies the kind of transactional observer methods, as defined in Table 9-6.

Table 9-6. Transactional observers

Transactional observers	Description
IN_PROGRESS	Default behavior; observers are called immediately
BEFORE_COMPLETION	Observers are called during the *before completion* phase of the transaction
AFTER_COMPLETION	Observers are called during the *after completion* phase of the transaction
AFTER_FAILURE	Observers are called during the *after completion* phase of the transaction, only when the transaction fails
AFTER_SUCCESS	Observers are called during the *after completion* phase of the transaction, only when the transaction succeeds

For example, the following observer method will be called after the transaction has successfully completed:

```
void onCustomer(
        @Observes(
    during= TransactionPhase.AFTER_SUCCESS)
    @Added Customer event) {
    //. . .
}
```

An event is not fired for any bean annotated with @Vetoed, or in a package annotated with @Vetoed.

Portable Extensions

CDI exposes an Service Provider Interface (SPI) allowing portable extensions to extend the functionality of the container easily. A portable extension may integrate with the container by:

- Providing its own beans, interceptors, and decorators to the container
- Injecting dependencies into its own objects using the dependency injection service
- Providing a contextual implementation for a custom scope
- Augmenting or overriding the annotation-based metadata with metadata from some other source

Here is a simple extension:

```
public class MyExtension implements Extension {

    <T> void processAnnotatedType(
                @Observes ProcessAnnotatedType<T> pat) {
        Logger.global.log(Level.INFO,
            "processing annotation: {0}",
            pat.
                getAnnotatedType().
                getJavaClass().
                getName());
    }
}
```

This extension prints the list of annotations on a bean packaged in a web application.

The extension needs to implement the Extension marker interface. You then need to register this extension using the *service provider* mechanism by creating a file named *META-INF/services/javax.enterprise.inject.spi.Extension*. This file contains the fully qualified name of the class implementing the extension:

```
org.sample.MyExtension
```

The bean can listen to a variety of container life-cycle events, as listed in Table 9-7.

Table 9-7. CDI container life-cycle events

Event	When fired?
BeforeBeanDiscovery	Before the bean discovery process begins
AfterBeanDiscovery	After the bean discovery process is complete
AfterDeploymentValidation	After no deployment problems are found and before contexts are created and requests processed
BeforeShutdown	After all requests are finished processing and all contexts destroyed
ProcessAnnotatedType	For each Java class or interface discovered in the application, before the annotations are read
ProcessInjectionTarget	For every Java EE component class supporting injection
ProcessProducer	For each producer method or field of each enabled bean

Each of these events allows a portable extension to integrate with the container initialization. For example, BeforeBeanDiscovery can be used to add new interceptors, qualifiers, scope, and stereotypes on an existing bean.

BeanManager provides operations for obtaining contextual references for beans, along with many other operations of use to portable extensions. It can be injected into the observer methods as follows:

```
<T> void processAnnotatedType(
        @Observes ProcessAnnotatedType<T> pat,
        BeanManager bm) {
    //. . .
}
```

BeanManager is also available for field injection and can be looked up by the name java:comp/BeanManager.

Built-in Beans

A Java EE or embeddable EJB container must provide the following built-in beans, all of which have the qualifer @Default:

- A bean with bean type javax.transaction.UserTransaction, allowing injection of a reference to the JTA UserTransaction:

```
@Stateless
@TransactionManagement(TransactionManagementType.BEAN)
public class SimpleGreeting {
  @Inject UserTransaction ut;
  //. . .

  public String greet(String name) {
    ut.start();
    //. . .
    ut.commit();
  }
}
```

In this code, a UserTransaction instance is injected in a *bean-managed transaction* EJB. The injected instance can be used to start and commit/roll back the transaction.

- A bean with bean type javax.security.Principal, allowing injection of a Principal representing the current caller identity:

```
@Stateless
public class SimpleGreeting {
  @Inject Principal principal;
  public String greet(String name) {
    if (principal.getName().equals("manager")) {
      //. . .
```

```
        } else {
          //. . .
        }
      }
    }
```

In this code, a `Principal` instance is injected in an EJB. The injected instance can be used to check the security principal name.

A servlet container must provide the following built-in beans, all of which have the qualifer `@Default`:

- A bean with bean type `javax.servlet.http.HttpServletRequest`, allowing injection of a reference to the `HttpServletRequest`:

  ```
  @Inject HttpServletRequest request;
  ```

- A bean with bean type `javax.servlet.http.HttpSession`, allowing injection of a reference to the `HttpSession`:

  ```
  @Inject HttpSession session;
  ```

- A bean with bean type `javax.servlet.ServletContext`, allowing injection of a reference to the `ServletContext`:

  ```
  @Inject ServletContext context;
  ```

Life-Cycle Callbacks

The standard annotations `javax.annotation.PostConstruct` and `javax.annotation.PreDestroy` from JSR 250 can be applied to any methods in a bean to perform resource initialization or cleanup:

```
public class MyBean {
  @PostConstruct
  public void setupResources() {
    //. . .
  }

  @PreDestroy
  public void cleanupResources() {
    //. . .
  }

  public String sayHello() {
    return "Hello " + name;
  }
}
```

The setupResources method is where any resources required during business method execution can be acquired, and the cleanupResources method is where those resources are closed or released. The life-cycle callback methods are invoked after the no-args constructor.

CHAPTER 10

Concurrency Utilities

Concurrency Utilities for Java EE are defined as JSR 236, and the complete specification can be downloaded (*http://jcp.org/aboutJava/communityprocess/final/jsr236/index.html*).

Concurrency Utilities for Java EE provides a simple, standardized API for using concurrency from application components without compromising container integrity while still preserving the Java EE platform's fundamental benefits.

Java EE containers such as the EJB or web container do not allow using common Java SE concurrency APIs such as `java.util.concurrent.ThreadPoolExecutor`, `java.lang.Thread`, or `java.util.Timer` directly. This is because all application code is run on a thread managed by the container, and each container typically expects all access to container-supplied objects to occur on the same thread. This allows the container to manage the resources and provide centralized administration. Further, using resources in a nonmanaged way is discouraged, because it can potentially undermine the enterprise features that the platform is designed to provide, such as availability, security, reliability, and scalability.

This API extends the Concurrency Utilities API developed under JSR-166y and found in Java 2 Platform, Standard Edition 7 (*http://bit.ly/15rkVhX*) (Java SE 7) in the `java.util.concurrent` package. Application developers familiar with this API can leverage existing libraries and usage patterns with little modification. This will allow you to add concurrency design principles to existing Java EE applications using existing design patterns.

Asynchronous Tasks

`javax.enterprise.concurrent.ManagedExecutorService` is a managed version of `java.util.concurrent.ExecutorService` and provides methods for submitting asynchronous tasks in a Java EE environment.

You can obtain an instance of `ManagedExecutorService` with a JNDI lookup using resource environment references. A default `ManagedExecutorService` is available under the JNDI name `java:comp/DefaultManagedExecutorService`.

You can obtain `ManagedExecutorService` as follows:

```
InitialContext ctx = new InitialContext();
ManagedExecutorService executor =
   (ManagedExecutorService)ctx.lookup("java:comp/DefaultManagedExecutorService");
```

You can also inject `ManagedExecutorService` into the application using `@Resource`:

```
@Resource(lookup="java:comp/DefaultManagedExecutorService")
ManagedExecutorService executor;
```

You can obtain an application-specific `ManagedExecutorService` by adding the following fragment to *web.xml*:

```
<resource-env-ref>
  <resource-env-ref-name>
    concurrent/myExecutor
  </resource-env-ref-name>
  <resource-env-ref-type>
    javax.enterprise.concurrent.ManagedExecutorService
  </resource-env-ref-type>
</resource-env-ref>
```

In this code:

- `<resource-env-ref-name>` defines the JNDI name of the resource relative to `java:comp/env`. It is recommended that you have resource environment references in the `java:comp/env/concurrent` subcontext.

- `<resource-env-ref-type>` defines the type of resource environment reference.

- `ManagedScheduledExecutor` can then be obtained with the usual JNDI reference or `@Resource`, but with the lookup name of `concurrent/myExecutor`.

The unit of work that needs to be executed concurrently is called a *task*. A task is a concrete implementation of the `java.lang.Runnable` interface:

```
public class MyTask1 implements Runnable {
  @Override
  public void run() {
    //. . .
  }
}
```

A task may be defined as a concrete implementation of the `java.util.concurrent.Callable` interface:

```
public class MyTask2 implements Callable<Product> {
  private int id;
```

```
  public MyTask2(int id) {
    this.id = id;
  }

  @Override
  public Product call() {
    Product product = new Product(id);
    //. . .
    return product;
  }
}
```

In this code:

- `Product` is an application-specific class.
- `id` provides an identifier of the task and is used to initialize the `Product`.
- The `call` method is called to compute the result of the task, and throws an exception if unable to do so.

There are two differences between a task implementing `Callable` and `Runnable`:

- A `Callable` task can return a result, whereas a `Runnable` task does not.
- A `Callable` task can throw checked exceptions, whereas a `Runnable` task cannot.

Each task runs within the application component context that submitted the task.

CDI beans may be submitted as tasks, but it is recommended that they not be in `@Re questScoped`, `@SessionScoped`, or `@ConversationScoped`. CDI beans with the `@Appli cation` or `@Dependent` scope can be used as tasks. It is possible that the task could be running beyond the life cycle of the submitting component, such as when the component is destroyed.

You submit task instances to a `ManagedExecutorService` using any of the `submit`, `execute`, `invokeAll`, or `invokeAny` methods.

- The `submit` method submits a `Runnable` or `Callable` task and returns a `Future` representing that task:

  ```
  Future future = executor.submit(new MyTask1());
  ```

- The `execute` method executes a `Runnable` task at some time in the future:

  ```
  executor.execute(new MyTask1());
  ```

- The `invokeAll` method executes all the submitted `Collection<? extends Calla ble<T>>` tasks and returns a `List<Future<T>>` holding their status and results, when completed:

```
Collection<Callable<Product>> tasks = new ArrayList<>();
tasks.add(new MyTask2(1));
tasks.add(new MyTask2(2));
//. . .
List<Future<Product>> results = executor.invokeAll(tasks);
Product result = results.get(0).get();
```

In this code, a Collection of Callable<Product> is created and submitted via invokeAll. The result is returned as List<Future<Product>> and the first result is accessed.

The invokeAll method has another variation where the timeout can be specified.

- The invokeAny method executes any of the submitted Collection<? extends Callable<T>> tasks, and returns the result of one that has completed successfully (i.e., without throwing any exception), if any do:

```
Collection<Callable<Product>> tasks = new ArrayList<>();
tasks.add(new MyTask2(1));
tasks.add(new MyTask2(2));
//. . .
Product result = executor.invokeAny(tasks);
```

In this code, a Collection of Callable<Product> is created and submitted via invokeAny. The result of one task that has completed successfully is returned.

The invokeAny method has another variation where the timeout can be specified.

ManagedExecutorService supports at most one quality of service. This ensures that a task will execute at most one time.

The security context of the calling thread is propagated to the called thread. The transaction context is not propagated. However, transactions can be explicitly started and committed or rolled back via javax.transaction.UserTransaction:

```
public class MyTask implements Runnable {
  @Override
  public void run() {
    InitialContext context = new InitialContext();
    UserTransaction tx = (UserTransaction)context
                .lookup("java:comp/UserTransaction");
    tx.start();
    //. . .
    tx.commit();
  }
}
```

Each task can implement the ManagedTask interface to provide identity information about the task, get notification of life-cycle events of the task, or provide additional execution properties.

A task can also implement the `ManagedTaskListener` interface to receive life-cycle event notifications. This interface provides the methods listed in Table 10-1.

Table 10-1. ManagedTaskListener methods

Method	Description
taskSubmitted	Called after the task is submitted to the `Executor`
taskStarting	Called before the task is about to start
taskDone	Called when a submitted task has completed running, successful or otherwise
taskAborted	Called when a task's `Future` has been cancelled any time during the life of a task

A task implementing these methods looks like:

```
public class MyTask implements Runnable, ManagedTask, ManagedTaskListener {

  @Override
  public void run() {
    //. . .
  }

  @Override
  public void taskSubmitted(Future<?> f,
                            ManagedExecutorService m,
                            Object o) {
    //. . .
  }

  @Override
  public void taskStarting(Future<?> f,
                           ManagedExecutorService m,
                           Object o) {
    //. . .
  }

  @Override
  public void taskAborted(Future<?> f,
                          ManagedExecutorService m,
                          Object o,
                          Throwable t) {
    //. . .
  }

  @Override
  public void taskDone(Future<?> f,
                       ManagedExecutorService m,
                       Object o,
                       Throwable t) {
    //. . .
  }

  @Override
```

```
public ManagedTaskListener getManagedTaskListener() {
  return this;
}

@Override
public Map<String, String> getExecutionProperties() {
  //. . .
}

}
```

In this code, the getManagedTaskListener and getExecutionProperties methods are implemented from the ManagedTask interface. The execution properties provide additional information to ManagedExecutorService when executing this task. Some standard property keys are defined in this class, such as the ManagedTask.IDENTITY_NAME property, which can be used to uniquely identify a task. The run method is implemented from the Runnable interface, and all other methods are implemented from the Managed TaskListener interface.

Each listener method will run with an unspecified context. All listeners run without an explicit transaction (they do not enlist in the application component's transaction). UserTransaction instance can be used if transactions are required.

ManagedExecutorService can be configured with Application Server–specific attributes. The specification does not define any standard configuration attributes.

Schedule Tasks

javax.enterprise.concurrent.ManagedScheduledExecutorService provides a managed version of ScheduledExecutorService and can be used to schedule tasks at specified and periodic times.

You can obtain an instance of ManagedScheduledExecutorService with a JNDI lookup using resource environment references. A default ManagedScheduledExecutorSer vice is available under the JNDI name java:comp/DefaultManagedScheduledExecu torService.

You can then obtain ManagedScheduledExecutorService like so:

```
InitialContext ctx = new InitialContext();
ManagedScheduledExecutorService executor =
    (ManagedScheduledExecutorService)ctx
      .lookup("java:comp/DefaultManagedScheduledExecutorService");
```

You can also inject ManagedScheduledExecutorService into the application using @Resource:

```
@Resource(lookup="java:comp/DefaultManagedScheduledExecutorService")
ManagedScheduledExecutorService executor;
```

You can obtain an application-specific `ManagedScheduledExecutorService` by adding the following fragment to *web.xml*:

```
<resource-env-ref>
  <resource-env-ref-name>
    concurrent/myScheduledExecutor
  </resource-env-ref-name>
  <resource-env-ref-type>
    javax.enterprise.concurrent.ManagedScheduledExecutorService
  </resource-env-ref-type>
</resource-env-ref>
```

In this code:

- `<resource-env-ref-name>` defines the JNDI name of the resource relative to `java:comp/env`. It is recommended that you have resource environment references in the `java:comp/env/concurrent` subcontext.

- `<resource-env-ref-type>` defines the type of resource environment reference.

- `ManagedScheduledExecutorService` can then be obtained with the usual JNDI reference and `@Resource`, but with the lookup name of `concurrent/mySchedule dExecutor`.

As in `ManagedExectorService`, a task is a concrete implementation of `java.lang.Runn able` or `java.util.concurrent.Callable` interface.

You submit task instances to a `ManagedScheduledExecutorService` using any of the `submit`, `execute`, `invokeAll`, `invokeAny`, `schedule`, `scheduleAtFixedRate`, or `schedu leWithFixedDelay` methods.

The `submit`, `execute`, `invokeAll`, and `invokeAny` methods behave as in `ManagedExecu torService`. The other methods are explained next.

- `<V> ScheduledFuture<V> schedule(Callable<V> callable, Trigger trig ger)` creates and executes a task based on a `Trigger`.

- `ScheduledFuture<?> schedule(Runnable command, Trigger trigger)` creates and executes a task based on a `Trigger`.

- `<V> ScheduledFuture<V> schedule(Callable<V> callable, long delay, TimeUnit unit)` creates and executes a one-shot `ScheduledFuture` that becomes enabled after the given delay.

  A task using `Callable` can be defined as:

  ```
  public class MyTask implements Callable<Product> {
    @Override
    public Product call() {
      Product product = ...;
      //. . .
      return product;
  ```

```
    }
  }
```

`Product` is an application-specific class. This task can be scheduled as:

```
ScheduledFuture<Product> future =
  executor.schedule(new MyTask(), 5, TimeUnit.SECONDS);
```

This code will schedule the task after five seconds of initial delay. The returned `ScheduledFuture` can be used to check the status of the task, cancel the execution, and retrieve the result.

• `ScheduledFuture<V> schedule(Runnable command, long delay, TimeUnit unit)` creates and executes a one-shot action that becomes enabled after the given delay.

A task using `Runnable` can be defined as:

```
public class MyTask implements Runnable {
  @Override
  public void run() {
    //. . .
  }
}
```

This task can be scheduled as:

```
ScheduledFuture<?> f = executor.schedule(new MyTask(),
                                         5,
                                         TimeUnit.SECONDS);
```

This code will schedule the task after five seconds of initial delay. The returned `ScheduledFuture` can be used to check the status of the task, cancel the execution, and retrieve the result.

• `ScheduledFuture<?> scheduleAtFixedRate(Runnable command, long initialDelay, long period, TimeUnit unit)` creates and executes a periodic action that becomes enabled first after the given initial delay, and subsequently with the given period; that is, executions will commence after `initialDelay`, then `initialDelay` `+period`, then `initialDelay + 2 * period`, and so on:

```
ScheduledFuture<?> f = executor
                .scheduleAtFixedRate(new MyRunnableTask(5),
                                     2,
                                     3,
                                     TimeUnit.SECONDS);
```

This code will schedule the task after an initial delay of two seconds and then every three seconds after that. If any execution of the task encounters an exception, subsequent executions are suppressed. If any execution of this task takes longer than its period, then subsequent executions may start late, but will not concurrently execute. Otherwise, the task will only terminate via cancellation or termination of the executor.

The returned `ScheduledFuture` can be used to check the status of the task, cancel the execution, and retrieve the result.

- `ScheduledFuture <?> scheduleWithFixedDelay(Runnable command, long initialDelay, long delay, TimeUnit unit)` creates and executes a periodic action that becomes enabled first after the given initial delay, and subsequently with the given delay between the termination of one execution and the commencement of the next:

```
ScheduledFuture<?> f = executor
                .scheduleAtFixedRate(new MyRunnableTask(5),
                                     2,
                                     3,
                                     TimeUnit.SECONDS);
```

This code will schedule the task after an initial delay of two seconds and then every three seconds after that. A new task is started only after the previous task has terminated successfully. If any execution of the task encounters an exception, subsequent executions are suppressed. Otherwise, the task will only terminate via cancellation or termination of the executor.

Each task can implement the `ManagedTask` and `ManagedTaskListener` interfaces to provide identity information about the task, get notification of life-cycle events of the task, or provide additional execution properties. This behaves in a similar manner to `ManagedExecutorService`.

Managed Threads

`javax.enterprise.concurrent.ManagedThreadFactory` can be used to create managed threads for execution in a Java EE environment.

You can obtain an instance of `ManagedThreadFactory` with a JNDI lookup using resource environment references. A default `ManagedThreadFactory` is available under the JNDI name `java:comp/DefaultManagedThreadFactory`.

You can then obtain `ManagedThreadFactory` like so:

```
InitialContext ctx = new InitialContext();
ManagedThreadFactory factory =
  (ManagedThreadFactory)ctx.lookup("java:comp/DefaultManagedThreadFactory");
```

You can also inject `ManagedThreadFactory` into the application using `@Resource`:

```
@Resource(lookup="java:comp/DefaultManagedThreadFactory")
ManagedThreadFactory factory;
```

You can obtain an application-specific `ManagedThreadFactory` by adding the following fragment to *web.xml*:

```
<resource-env-ref>
  <resource-env-ref-name>
    concurrent/myFactory
  </resource-env-ref-name>
  <resource-env-ref-type>
    javax.enterprise.concurrent.ManagedThreadFactory
  </resource-env-ref-type>
</resource-env-ref>
```

In this code:

- `<resource-env-ref-name>` defines the JNDI name of the resource relative to `java:comp/env`. It is recommended that you have resource environment references in the `java:comp/env/concurrent` subcontext.

- `<resource-env-ref-type>` defines the type of resource environment reference.

- `ManagedThreadFactory` can then be obtained with the usual JNDI reference and `@Resource`, but with the lookup name of `concurrent/myFactory`.

You can create new threads from this factory using `newThread(Runnable r)`. For a task definition:

```
public class MyTask implements Runnable {
  @Override
  public void run() {
    //. . .
  }
}
```

A new thread can be created and started:

```
Thread thread = factory.newThread(new MyTask());
thread.start();
```

The returned threads implement the `ManageableThread` interface.

The container context information is propagated to the thread's `Runnable`. Naming context, class loader, and security context information is propagated to the thread. Use a `UserTransaction` instance if a transaction is required.

Dynamic Contextual Objects

Application component container contexts, such as classloading, namespace, and security, can be associated with an object instance via `ContextService`. Dynamic proxy capabilities found in the `java.lang.reflect` package are used for the context association. The object becomes a contextual object, and whenever a method on the contextual object is invoked, the method executes with the thread context of the associated application component instance.

The JNDI naming context, classloader, and security context is propagated to the proxied object. Proxy methods suspend any transactional context on the thread and allow components to manually control global transaction demarcation boundaries. The User Transaction instance can be used if a transaction is required within the proxy object.

This allows non–Java EE service callbacks, such as JMS MessageListeners, to run in the context of the container instead of the implementation provider's undefined thread context. This also allows customized Java SE platform ExecutorService to be used.

You can obtain an instance of ContextService with the JNDI lookup using resource environment references. A default ContextService is available under the JNDI name java:comp/DefaultContextService.

You can then obtain ContextService like so:

```
InitialContext ctx = new InitialContext();
ContextService cs =
  (ContextService)ctx.lookup("java:comp/DefaultContextService");
```

You can also inject ContextService into the application using @Resource:

```
@Resource(lookup="java:comp/DefaultContextService")
ContextService cs;
```

You can obtain an application-specific ContextService by adding the following fragment to *web.xml*:

```
<resource-env-ref>
  <resource-env-ref-name>
    concurrent/myContextService
  </resource-env-ref-name>
  <resource-env-ref-type>
    javax.enterprise.concurrent.ContextService
  </resource-env-ref-type>
</resource-env-ref>
```

In this code:

- <resource-env-ref-name> defines the JNDI name of the resource relative to java:comp/env. It is recommended that you have resource environment references in the java:comp/env/concurrent subcontext.

- <resource-env-ref-type> defines the type of resource environment reference.

- ContextExecutor can then be obtained with the usual JNDI reference or @Resource, but with the lookup name of concurrent/myContextService.

You create contextual object proxy instances with a ContextService instance using the createContextualProxy method. Contextual object proxies will run as an extension of the application component instance that created the proxy and may interact with Java EE container resources.

A contextual instance of a `Runnable` executed with Java SE `ExecutorService` can be created as:

```java
public class MyRunnable implements Runnable {
  @Override
  public void run() {
    //. . .
  }
}

@Resource(lookup="DefaultContextService")
ContextService cs;

@Resource(lookup="DefaultManagedThreadFactory")
ThreadFactory factory;

MyRunnable r = new MyRunnable();

Runnable proxy = cs.createContextualProxy(r, Runnable.class);

ExecutorService es = Executors.newFixedThreadPool(10, factory);

Future f = es.submit(proxy);
```

In this code:

- `MyRunnable` is the object to be proxied.
- A default `ContextService` and `ManagedThreadFactory` are obtained via `@Resource`.
- You create the contextual proxy of a `Runnable` task by calling the `createContextualProxy` method.
- The Java SE–style `ExecutorService` is obtained with `ManagedThreads` and submits the contextual proxy.

If the object instance supports multiple interfaces, then you can specify the interfaces for which the contextual proxy needs to be created as follows:

```java
public class MyRunnableWork implements Runnable, MyWork {
  @Override
  public void run() {
    //. . .
  }

  @Override
  public void myWork() {
    //. . .
  }
}

//. . .
```

```
MyRunnableWork r = new MyRunnableWork();

Object proxy = cs.createContextualProxy(r, Runnable.class, MyWork.class);
((MyWork)proxy).myWork();

ExecutorService es = Executors.newThreadPool(10, factory);

Future f = es.submit((Runnable)proxy);
```

In this code:

- MyRunnableWork is the object to be proxied and implements the Runnable and MyWork interfaces.
- You create the contextual proxy by passing both the interfaces, and the return type is Object.
- You can invoke methods on a non-Runnable interface by casting to the MyWork interface.
- You can submit a proxied instance to the ExecutorService by casting to the Runnable interface.

CHAPTER 11

Bean Validation

Bean Validation is defined as JSR 349, and the complete specification can be downloaded (*http://jcp.org/aboutJava/communityprocess/final/jsr349/index.html*).

Bean Validation provides a class-level constraint declaration and validation facility for Java applications.

The constraints can be declared in the form of annotations placed on a field, property, method parameter, or class. Constraints can be defined on interfaces or superclasses. Specifying a constraint on an interface ensures the constraint is enforced on classes implementing the interface. Similarly, all classes inheriting from a superclass inherit the validation behavior as well. Constraints declared on an interface or superclass are validated along with any constraints defined on the implementing or overriding class.

Validation constraints and configuration information can also be defined through XML validation descriptors in *META-INF/validation.xml*. The descriptors override and extend the metadata defined via annotations. This chapter will cover annotation-based constraint validations only.

The specification also includes a constraint metadata repository and the capability to query it. This is primarily targeted toward tool development as well as integration with other frameworks and libraries.

Built-in Constraints

Bean Validation offers a built-in set of constraint definitions that can be used on beans. Multiple constraints can be specified on a bean to ensure different validation requirements are met. These constraints can also be used for composing other constraints.

All built-in constraints are defined in the `javax.validation.constraints` package and are explained as follows:

@Null

Annotated element must be `null` and can be applied to any type:

```
@Null
String httpErrorCode;
```

The `httpErrorCode` field captures the HTTP status code from a RESTful endpoint.

@NotNull

Annotated element must not be `null` and can be applied to any type:

```
@NotNull
String name;
```

`name` captures the name of, say, a customer. Specifying `@NotNull` will trigger a validation error if the instance variable is assigned a `null` value.

@AssertTrue

The annotated element must be `true` and can be applied to `boolean` or `Boolean` types only:

```
@AssertTrue
boolean isConnected;
```

`isConnected` can be a field in a class managing resource connections.

@AssertFalse

The annotated element must be `false` and can be applied to `boolean` or `Boolean` types only:

```
@AssertFalse
Boolean isWorking;
```

`isWorking` can be a field in an `Employee` class.

@Min, @DecimalMin

The annotated element must be a number whose value is higher or equal to the specified minimum. `byte`, `short`, `int`, `long`, `Byte`, `Short`, `Integer`, `Long`, `BigDecimal`, and `BigInteger` are supported types:

```
@Min(10)
int quantity;
```

`quantity` can be a field in a class storing the quantity of stock.

@Max, @DecimalMax

The annotated element must be a number whose value is lower or equal to the specified maximum. `byte`, `short`, `int`, `long`, `Byte`, `Short`, `Integer`, `Long`, `BigDecimal`, and `BigInteger` are supported types:

```
@Max(20)
int quantity;
```

quantity can be a field in a class storing the quantity of stock.

Multiple constraints may be specified on the same field:

```
@Min(10)
@Max(20)
int quantity;
```

@Size

The annotated element size must be between the specified boundaries. String, Collection, Map, and Array are supported types:

```
@Size(min=5, max9)
String zip;
```

zip can be a field capturing the zip code of a city. The length of the string is used for validation critieria. min and max define the length of the targeted field, specified values included. By default, min is 0 and max is 2147483647.

Another example is:

```
@Size(min=1)
@List<Item> items;
```

The List.size method is used for validation in this case.

@Digits

The annotated element must be a number within the accepted range. byte, short, int, long, Byte, Short, Integer, Long, BigDecimal, BigInteger, and String are supported types:

```
@Digits(integer=3,fraction=0)
int age;
```

integer defines the maximum number of integral digits and fraction defines the number of fractional digits for this number. So 1, 28, 262, and 987 are valid values. Specifying multiple constraints may make this field more meaningful:

```
@Min(18)
@Max(25)
@Digits(integer=3,fraction=0)
int age;
```

@Past

The annotated element must be a date in the past. The present time is defined as the current time according to the virtual machine. Date and Calendar are supported:

```
@Past
Date dob;
```

dob captures the date of birth.

`@Future`

The annotated element must be a date in the future. The present time is defined as the current time according to the virtual machine. `Date` and `Calendar` are supported:

```
@Future
Date retirementDate;
```

`retirementDate` stores the retirement date of an employee.

`@Pattern`

The annotated string must match the specified regular expression:

```
@Pattern(regexp="[0-9]*")
String zip;
```

`zip` stores the zip code of a city. The regular expression says that only digits from 0 to 9 are permitted. You can make this field more meaningful by adding the `@Size` constraint:

```
@Pattern(regexp="[0-9]*")
@Size(min=5, max=5)
String zip;
```

Each constraint declaration can also override the `message`, `group`, and `payload` fields.

`message` is used to override the default error message when the constraint is violated. `group` is used to override the default validation group, explained later. `payload` is used to associate metadata with the constraint.

Java EE 7 adds a new attribute, `validationAppliesTo`, to constraint declaration that defines the constraint target (i.e., the annotated element, the method return value, or the method parameters). The attribute can have the following values:

`ConstraintTarget.IMPLICIT`

This is the default value and discovers the target when no ambiguity is present. It implies the annotated element if it is not specified on a method or a constructor. If specified on a method or constructor with no parameter, it implies RETURN_VALUE. If specified on a method with no return value, then it implies PARAMETERS. If there is ambiguity, then either RETURN_VALUE or PARAMETERS is required.

`ConstraintTarget.RETURN_VALUE`

Applies to the return value of a method or constructor.

`ConstraintTarget.PARAMETERS`

Applies to the parameters of a method or constructor.

Defining a Custom Constraint

Custom constraints designed to meet specific validation criteria can be defined by the combination of a constraint annotation and a list of custom validation implementations.

This code shows a custom constraint annotation to validate a zip code:

```
@Documented
@Target({ ElementType.ANNOTATION_TYPE,
          ElementType.METHOD,
          ElementType.FIELD,
          ElementType.CONSTRUCTOR,
          ElementType.PARAMETER })
@Retention(RetentionPolicy.RUNTIME)
@Constraint(validatedBy=ZipCodeValidator.class)
@Size(min=5, message="{org.sample.zipcode.min_size}")
@Pattern(regexp="[0-9]*")
@NotNull(message="{org.sample.zipcode.cannot_be_null}")
public @interface ZipCode {
    String message() default
        "{org.sample.zipcode.invalid_zipcode}";

    Class<?>[] groups() default {};

    Class<? extends Payload>[] payload() default {};

    Country country() default Country.US;
    public enum Country {
        US,
        CANADA,
        MEXICO,
        BRASIL
    }
}
```

In this code:

- **@Target** indicates that this constraint can be declared on types, methods, fields, constructors, and method parameters.

- **@Constraint** marks the annotation as a constraint definition. It also creates a link with its constraint validation implementation, defined by the attribute **validated By**. **ZipCodeValidator.class** provides the validation implementation in this case. Multiple validator implementations may be specified as an array of classes.

- **@Size**, **@Pattern**, and **@NotNull** are primitive constraints used to create this composite custom constraint. Annotating an element with **@ZipCode** (the *composed annotation*) is equivalent to annotating it with **@Size**, **@Pattern**, and **@NotNull** (the *composing annotations*) and **@ZipCode**.

By default, each violation of a composing annotation raises an individual error report. All the error reports are collected together, and each violation is reported. However, @ReportAsSingleViolation on a constraint annotation can be used to suppress the error reports generated by the composing annotations. In this case, the error report from the composed annotation is generated instead.

- message's value is used to create the error message. In this case, the message value is a resource bundle key that enables internationalization.

- group specifies a validation group, which is used to perform partial validation of the bean or control the order in which constraints are evaluated. By default, the value is an empty array and belongs to the Default group.

- payload is used to associate metadata information with a constraint.

- country is defined as an additional element to parameterize the constraint. The possible set of values for this parameter is defined as an enum with the constraint definition. A default value of the parameter, Country.US, is also specified.

A simple zip code constraint validator implementation looks like:

```
public class ZipCodeValidator
    implements ConstraintValidator<ZipCode, String> {

    List<String> zipcodes;

    @Override
    public void initialize(ZipCode constraintAnnotation) {
        zipcodes = new ArrayList<>();
        switch (constraintAnnotation.country()) {
            case US:
                zipcodes.add("95054");
                zipcodes.add("95051");
                zipcodes.add("94043");
                break;
            case CANADA:
                //
                break;
            case MEXICO:
                //
                break;
            case BRASIL:
                //
                break;
        }
    }

    @Override
    public boolean isValid(
            String value,
            ConstraintValidatorContext context) {
        return zipcodes.contains(value);
```

```
        }
    }
```

In this code:

- The constraint validator implementation class implements the `ConstraintValida
tor` interface. A given constraint can apply to multiple Java types. This requires
defining multiple constraint validator implementations, one each for a specific type.
This validator can only be applied to string types:

  ```
  @ZipCode
  String zip;
  ```

- The `initialize` method initializes any resources or data structures used for validation. This code initializes the array of valid zip codes for a specific country. The
values of the `country` attribute and other attributes are available from the `con
straintAnnotation` parameter. This method is guaranteed to be called before any
use of this instance for validation.

- The `isValid` method implements the validation logic. The method returns `true` if
the constraint is valid, and `false` otherwise. The `value` parameter is the object to
validate, and `ConstraintValidatorContext` provides the context in which the
constraint is executed. This method's implementation must be thread-safe. This
code returns `true` if the zip code exists in the array of valid zip codes.

If a bean X contains a field of type Y, by default, the validation of type X does not trigger
the validation of type Y. However, annotating the field of type Y with `@Valid` will be
cascaded along with the validation of X.

`@Valid` also provides polymorphic validation. If field Y is an interface or an abstract
class, then the validation constraints applied at runtime are from the actual implementing class or subtype.

Any `Iterable` fields and properties may also be decorated with `@Valid` to ensure all
elements of the iterator are validated. `@Valid` is applied recursively, so each element of
the iterator is validated as well:

```
public class Order {
    @Pattern(...)
    String orderId;

    @Valid
    private List<OrderItem> items;
}
```

In this code, the list of order items is recursively validated along with the `orderId` field,
because `@Valid` has been specified on `items`. If `@Valid` is not specified, only the `order
Id` field is validated when the bean is validated.

The `validationAppliesTo` attribute can be used to specify the target of the constraint:

```
@ZipCode(validationAppliesTo=ConstraintTarget.PARAMETERS)
public void addPerson(Person person, String zip) {
  //. . .
}
```

In this code, the ZipCode constraint is applied to method parameters only (i.e., zip parameter in this case).

Validation Groups

By default, all constraints are defined in the Default validation group. Also by default, all validation constraints are executed and in no particular order. A constraint may be defined in an explicitly created validation group in order to perform partial validation of the bean or control the order in which constraints are evaluated.

A validation group is defined as an interface:

```
public interface ZipCodeGroup {
}
```

This validation group can now be assigned to a constraint definition:

```
@ZipCode(groups=ZipCodeGroup.class)
String zip;
```

In this code, zip will be validated only when the ZipCodeGroup validation group is targeted for validation.

By default, the Default validation group is not included if an explicit set of groups is specified:

```
@ZipCode(groups={Default.class,ZipCodeGroup.class})
String zip;
```

Groups can inherit other groups through interface inheritance. You can define a new group that consists of Default and ZipCodeGroup:

```
public interface DefaultZipCodeGroup
    extends Default, ZipCodeGroup {
}
```

This new validation group can now be specified as part of the constraint, and is semantically equivalent to specifying two groups separately:

```
@ZipCode(groups=DefaultZipCodeGroup.class)
String zip;
```

Partial validation of a bean may be required when validation of certain fields is optional or resource intensive. For example, entering data in a multipage HTML form requires only the field values entered in each page to be validated. Validating previously validated fields will be redundant, and validating fields that do not yet have a value assigned will throw a validation error. You can achieve partial validation by creating a validation group for each page:

```
public interface Page1Group {
}

public interface Page2Group {
}

public interface Page3Group {
}
```

Assign the group to the corresponding fields:

```
@Size(min=4, groups=Page1Group.class)
private String name;

@Digits(integer=3,fraction=0, groups=Page2Group.class)
int age;

@ZipCode(groups={Page3Group.class})
private String zipcode;
```

And finally, pass the validation group in the JSF page using f:validateBean:

```
<h:form>
    Name: <h:inputText value="#{person.name}" id="name">
            <f:validateBean validationGroups="org.sample.Page1Group"/>
        </h:inputText>
        <h:commandButton action="index2" value="Next >"/>
</h:form>
```

The fully qualified class name of the validation group needs to be specified in the validationGroups attribute of f:validateBean. Other pages will specify the corresponding validation group.

You can specify multiple validation groups using a comma-separated list:

```
<h:form>
    Name:
    <h:inputText value="#{person.name}" id="name">
            <f:validateBean
    validationGroups="org.sample.Page1Group,
                    org.sample.OtherGroup"/>
        </h:inputText>
        <h:commandButton action="index2" value="Next >"/>
</h:form>
```

@GroupSequence is used to define a sequence of groups in which the groups must be validated. This can be useful where simple validation constraints such as @NotNull or @Size can be validated before more complex constraints are enforced:

```
@GroupSequence({Simple.class, Complex.class})
```

In this code, `Simple` and `Complex` are validation groups that are specified on simple and complex validators of a bean. The definitions of simple and complex will depend upon the business domain, of course.

If one of the groups from the sequence generates a constraint violation, the subsequent groups are not processed.

Specifying `@GroupSequence` on a class changes the default validation group for that class.

Method and Constructor Constraint

Bean Validaton 1.1 allows us to specify constraints on arbitrary methods and constructors, and/or the parameters of a POJO by directly adding constraint annotations. In the former case, all the parameters or the return value is constrained. In the latter, individual parameters are constrained.

This allows us to describe and validate the contract by ensuring that the preconditions must be met by the caller before the method or constructor may be invoked. This also ensures that the postconditions are guaranteed to the caller after a method or constructor invocation returns. This enables a programming style known as *Programming by Contract* (PbC). This approach has two advantages:

- Checks are expressed declaratively and don't have to be performed manually, which results in less code to write, read, and maintain.

- The pre- and postconditions applying for a method or constructor don't have to be expressed again in the documentation, since any of its annotations will automatically be included in the generated JavaDoc. This reduces redundancies, thus avoiding efforts and inconsistencies between implementation and documentation.

You can specify the constraints using either actual Java annotations or an XML constraint mapping file:

```
public class AddressBook {
  public void addNames(@NotNull @PriorityCode String priority,
                       @NotNull @Size(min=1, max=10) List<Name> names) {
    //. . .
  }

  @NotNull
  public String getName(@NotNull @Past Date dob) {
    //. . .
  }
}
```

In this code:

- `AddressBook` is a POJO with two methods, `addNames` and `getName`.

- The `addNames` method takes two parameters. The first parameter, `priority`, cannot be `null` and is also validated by a custom constraint, `@PriorityCode`. The second parameter, `names`, cannot be `null` and the list must have a minimum of 1 element and a maximum of 10 elements.

- Method `getNames` takes a parameter, `dob`, that cannot be `null` and must be in the past. The return value also cannot be `null`.

Annotating the methods or constructors with parameter or return value constraints does not automatically enforce these constraints. The declared constraints need to be explicitly triggered via a method interceptor or a similar mechanism. In Java EE, typically you achieve this by using CDI interceptors or dynamic proxies. Meeting all the constraints ensures that the method or constructor is called if the caller has satisified the preconditions and returns to the caller if the postconditions are guaranteed. If the specified constraints are not met, then a `ConstraintViolationException` is thrown.

Cross-parameter constraints can be declared on a method and allow you to express constraints based on the value of several method parameters:

```
@ValidateDates
public List<Name> getNames(@NotNull Date startDob,
                           @NotNull Date endDob) {
    //. . .
}
```

This method retrieves the list of names born between `startDob` and `endDob`. `@ValidateDates` is a cross-parameter constraint that checks that the `startDob` is before `endDob`. It is often useful to combine constraints directly placed on individual parameters and cross-parameter constraints.

Some constraints can target the return value as well as its array of parameters. They are known to be both generic and cross-parameter constraints. `validationAppliesTo` can be used to resolve ambiguity in this case. Even without ambiguity, it is recommended that you explicitly set `validationAppliesTo` to `ConstraintTarget.PARAMETERS`, as it improves readability.

The `ParameterNameProvider` interface can be used to identify the parameter that resulted in `ConstraintViolation`.

By default, only constructors and nongetter methods are validated. You can change this default behavior by specifying `@ValidateExecutable` on the class or the method to be validated (see Table 11-1).

Table 11-1. @ValidateExecutable values

Value	What is validated?
NONE	No constructors or methods
CONSTRUCTORS	Only constructors
NON_GETTER_METHODS	All methods except the ones following the JavaBeans getter pattern
GETTER_METHODS	All methods following the JavaBeans getter pattern
ALL	All constructors and methods (this is the default value)

```
@ValidateExecutable
public class AddressBook {
  public class AddressBook() {
  }

  @Size(min=5)
  List<Name> getNames() {
    //. . .
  }

  public void addName(@Valid Name name) {
    //. . .
  }
}
```

In this code, all constructors and methods are validated. If `@ValidateExecutable` is not specified on the class, then only the constructor and the `addName` method are validated.

Static methods are ignored by validation. Putting constraints on a static method is not portable.

CHAPTER 12

Java Transaction

The Java Transaction API (JTA) is defined as JSR 907, and the complete specification can be downloaded (*http://jcp.org/aboutJava/communityprocess/maintenance/jsr907/index5.html*).

The JTA specifies local interfaces between a transaction manager and the parties involved in a distributed transaction system: the application, the resource manager, and the application server.

The API defines a high-level interface, annotation, and scope to demarcate transaction boundaries in a transactional application.

User-Managed Transactions

The UserTransaction interface enables the application to control transaction boundaries programmatically. This interface is typically used in EJBs with bean-managed transactions (BMT).

You can obtain UserTransaction using injection:

```
@Inject UserTransaction ut;
```

or through a JNDI lookup using the name java:comp/UserTransaction:

```
Context context = new InitialContext();
UserTransaction ut = (UserTransaction)context.lookup("java:comp/UserTransaction");
```

The begin method starts a global transaction and associates the transaction with the calling thread. The commit method completes the transaction associated with the current thread. All statements within begin and commit execute in the transaction scope:

```
ut.begin();
//. . .
ut.commit();
```

When the `commit` method completes, the thread is no longer associated with a transaction.

A transaction can be rolled back via the `rollback` method:

```
ut.begin();
//. . .
ut.rollback();
```

When the `rollback` method completes, the thread is no longer associated with a transaction.

You can change the timeout value associated with the transaction started by the current thread with the `begin` method:

```
ut.setTransactionTimeout(3);
```

In this code, the transaction timeout is set to three seconds. If the value is zero, the transaction service restores the default value.

Support for nested transactions is not required.

Container-Managed Transactions

JTA 1.2 introduces the `@javax.transaction.Transactional` annotation. It enables an application to declaratively control transaction boundaries on CDI-managed beans, as well as classes defined as managed beans, such as servlets, JAX-RS resource classes, and JAX-WS service endpoints. The annotation can be specified at both the class and method level, where method-level annotations override those at the class level:

```
@Transactional
public class MyBean {
  //. . .
}
```

In this code, all methods of the bean are executed in a transaction:

```
public class MyBean {
  public void myMethod1() {
    //. . .
  }

  @Transactional
  public void myMethod2() {
    //. . .
  }
}
```

In this code, only the `myMethod2` method is executed in a transaction context.

This support is provided via an implementation of CDI interceptors that conduct the necessary suspending, resuming, etc. The `Transactional` interceptor interposes on business method invocations and life-cycle events. Life-cycle methods are invoked in an unspecified transaction context unless the method is annotated explicitly with @Transactional.

The Transactional interceptors must have a priority of Interceptor.Priority.PLAT FORM_BEFORE+200.

The TxType element of the annotation provides the semantic equivalent of the transaction attributes in EJB (see Table 12-1).

Table 12-1. Transactional.TxType

TxType	Outside a transaction context	Inside a transaction context
REQUIRED (default)	The interceptor must begin a new JTA transaction, the managed bean method execution must then continue inside this transaction context, and the transaction must be completed by the interceptor.	The managed bean method execution must then continue inside this transaction context.
REQUIRES_NEW	The interceptor must begin a new JTA transaction, the managed bean method execution must then continue inside this transaction context, and the transaction must be completed by the interceptor.	The current transaction context must be suspended, a new JTA transaction will begin, the managed bean method execution must then continue inside this transaction context, the transaction must be completed, and the previously suspended transaction must be resumed.
MANDATORY	A TransactionalException with a nested TransactionRequiredExcep tion must be thrown.	The managed bean method execution will then continue under that context.
SUPPORTS	The managed bean method execution must then continue outside a transaction context.	The managed bean method execution must then continue inside this transaction context.
NOT_SUPPORTED	The managed bean method execution must then continue outside a transaction context.	The current transaction context must be suspended, the managed bean method execution must then continue outside a transaction context, and the previously suspended transaction must be resumed by the interceptor that suspended it after the method execution has completed.
NEVER	The managed bean method execution must then continue outside a transaction context.	A TransactionalException with a nested In validTransactionException must be thrown.

You can change the transaction type semantics by specifying the value of TxType:

```
@Transactional(TxType.REQUIRES_NEW)
public class MyBean {
  //. . .
}
```

By default, checked exceptions do not result in the transactional interceptor marking the transaction for rollback, and instances of RuntimeException and its subclasses do.

The `rollbackOn` element can be set to indicate exceptions that must cause the interceptor to mark the transaction for rollback:

```
@Transactional(rollbackOn={Exception.class})
```

This code will override behavior for checked exceptions, causing the transaction to be marked for rollback for all checked exceptions.

The `dontRollbackOn` element can be set to indicate exceptions that must not cause the interceptor to mark the transaction for rollback:

```
@Transactional(dontRollbackOn={IllegalStateException.class})
```

This code will prevent transactions from being marked for rollback by the interceptor when an `IllegalStateException` or any of its subclasses are thrown. When a class is specified for either of these elements, the designated behavior applies to subclasses of that class as well.

If both elements are specified, `dontRollbackOn` takes precedence.

@TransactionScoped

JTA 1.2 defines a new CDI scope: `javax.transaction.TransactionScoped`. It defines a bean instance whose life cycle is scoped to the currently active JTA transaction. If multiple instances of such a bean are injected within a transaction, the underlying CDI proxy refers to the same instance, ensuring that only one instance of the bean is injected.

The transaction scope is active when the return from a call to `UserTransaction.get Status` or `TransactionManager.getStatus` is one of the following states:

- `Status.STATUS_ACTIVE`
- `Status.STATUS_MARKED_ROLLBACK`
- `Status.STATUS_PREPARED`
- `Status.STATUS_UNKNOWN`
- `Status.STATUS_PREPARING`
- `Status.STATUS_COMMITTING`
- `Status.STATUS_ROLLING_BACK`

The object with this annotation will be associated with the current active JTA transaction when the object is used. The way in which the JTA transaction is begun and completed (for example, via `UserTransaction`, `Transactional interceptor`, etc.) is of no consequence.

CHAPTER 13

Java Persistence

The Java Persistence API (JPA) is defined as JSR 338, and the complete specification can be downloaded (*http://jcp.org/aboutJava/communityprocess/final/jsr338/index.html*).

JPA defines an API for the management of persistence and object/relational mapping using a Java domain model.

A database table, typically with multiple columns, stores the persistent state of an application. Multiple rows are stored in the database table to capture different states. A single column or combination of columns may define the uniqueness of each row using primary key constraint. Typically, an application accesses and stores data to multiple tables. These tables generally have relationships defined among them using foreign key constraint.

JPA defines a standard mapping between a database table and a POJO. It defines syntax to capture primary and foreign key constraints and how these rows can be created, read, updated, and deleted using these POJOs. Transactions, caching, validation, and other similar capabilities required by an application accessing a database are also defined by JPA.

This chapter will discuss the key concepts of JPA.

Entities

A POJO with a no-arg public constructor is used to define the mapping with one or more relational database tables. Each such class is annotated with @Entity, and the instance variables that follow JavaBeans-style properties represent the persistent state of the entity. The mapping between the table column and the field name is derived following reasonable defaults and can be overridden by annotations. For example, the table name is the same as the class name, and the column names are the same as the persistent field names.

Here is a simple entity definition describing a student:

```
@Entity
public class Student implements Serializable {
  @Id
  private int id;
  private String name;
  private String grade;
  @Embedded
  private Address address;

  @ElementCollection
  @CollectionTable("StudentCourse")
  List<Course> courses;

  //. . .
}
```

A few things to observe in this code:

- This class has a no-arg constructor by default, as no other constructors are defined.
- The entity's persistent state is defined by four fields; the identity is defined by the field `id` and is annotated with `@Id`. A composite primary key may also be defined where the primary key corresponds to one or more fields of the entity class.
- The class implements a `Serializable` interface, and that allows it to be passed by value through a remote interface.
- `Address` is a POJO class that does not have a persistent identity of its own and exclusively belongs to the `Student` class. This class is called as an *embeddable class*, is identified by `@Embedded` on the field in the entity class, and is annotated with `@Embeddable` in the class definition:

```
@Embeddable
public class Address {
  private String street;
  private String city;
  private String zip;
  //. . .
}
```

  This allows the database structure to be more naturally mapped in Java.

- The `@ElementCollection` annotation signifies that a student's courses are listed in a different table. By default, you derive the table name by combining the name of the owning class, the string "_," and the field name. `@CollectionTable` can be used to override the default name of the table, and `@AttributeOverrides` can be used to override the default column names. `@ElementCollection` can also be applied to an embeddable class.

The persistent fields or properties of an entity may be of the following types:

- Java primitive type
- `java.lang.String`
- `java.math.BigInteger` and `java.math.BigDecimal`
- `java.util.Date` and `java.util.Calendar`; the `@Temporal` annotation may be specified on fields of type `java.util.Date` and `java.util.Calendar` to indicate the temporal type of the field
- `java.sql.Date`, `java.sql.Time`, and `java.sql.Timestamp`
- `byte[]`, `Byte[]`, `char[]`, `Character[]`, enums, and other Java serializable types
- Entity types, collections of entity types, embeddable classes, and collections of basic and embeddable classes

An entity may inherit from a superclass that provides persistent entity state and mapping information, but which itself may or may not be an entity. An entity superclass is abstract and cannot be directly instantiated but can be used to create polymorphic queries.

The `@Inheritance` and `@Discriminator` annotations are used to specify the inheritance from an entity superclass. The `@MappedSuperclass` annotation is used to designate a nonentity superclass and captures state and mapping information that is common to multiple entity classes. Such a class has no separate table defined for it, so the mappings will only apply to its subclasses. An entity may inherit from a superclass that provides inheritance of behavior only. Such a class does not contain any persistent state.

You define the relationships between different entities using the `@OneToOne`, `@OneToMany`, `@ManyToOne`, and `@ManyToMany` annotations on the corresponding field of the referencing entity. A unidirectional relationship requires the owning side to specify the annotation. A bidirectional relationship also requires the nonowning side to refer to its owning side by use of the `mappedBy` element of the `OneToOne`, `OneToMany`, or `ManyToMany` annotation.

The `FetchType.EAGER` annotation may be specified on an entity to eagerly load the data from the database. The `FetchType.LAZY` annotation may be specified as a hint that the data should be fetched lazily when it is first accessed.

The entities may display a collection of elements and entity relationships as `java.util.Map` collections. The map key may be the primary key or a persistent field or property of the entity. `@MapKey` is used to specify the key for the association. For example, all the `Courses` by a `Student` can be modeled as:

```
public class Student {
  @MapKey
  private Map<Integer, Course> courses;
  //. . .
}
```

In this code, specifying `@MapKey` on the `Map` indicates that the map key is the primary key as well.

The map key can be a basic type, an embeddable class, or an entity. If a persistent field or property other than the primary key is used as a map key, then it is expected to have a uniqueness constraint associated with it. In this case, `@MapKeyColumn` is used to specify the mapping for the key column of the map:

```
public class Student {
  @MapKeyColumn(name="year")
  private Map<Integer, Course> courses;
  //. . .
}
```

In this code, `Map` represents all the `Courses` taken by a `Student` in a year. If the `name` element is not specified, it defaults to the concatenation of the following: the name of the referencing relationship field or property, "_," and "KEY." In this case, the default name will be `COURSES_KEY`.

`@MapKeyClass` can be used to specify the map key for the association. If the value is an entity, then `@OneToMany` and `@ManyToMany` may be used to specify the mapping:

```
public class Student {
  @OneToMany
  @MapKeyClass(PhoneType.class)
  private Map<PhoneType, Phone> phones;
  //. . .
}
```

`@MapKeyClass` and `@MapKey` are mutually exclusive.

If the value is a basic type or embeddable class, then `@ElementCollection` is used to specify the mapping.

Persistence Unit, Persistence Context, and Entity Manager

An entity is managed within a *persistence context*. Each entity has a unique instance for any persistent entity identity within the context. Within the persistence context, the entity instances and their life cycles are managed by the *entity manager*. The entity manager may be *container-managed* or *application-managed*.

A container-managed entity manager is obtained by the application directly through dependency injection:

```
@PersistenceContext
EntityManager em;
```

The entity manager can also be obtained via JNDI:

```
@PersistenceContext(name="persistence/myJNDI")
. . .
```

```
Context context = new InitialContext();
EntityManager em = context.lookup("java:comp/env/persistence/myJNDI");
```

In this code, we assign a JNDI name to the entity manager and then look it up using `InitialContext`.

The persistence context is propagated across multiple transactions for a container-managed entity manager, and the container is responsible for managing the life cycle of the entity manager.

An application-managed entity manager is obtained by the application from an entity manager factory:

```
@PersistenceUnit
EntityManagerFactory emf;
//. . .
EntityManager em = emf.createEntityManager();
```

A new isolated persistence context is created when a new entity manager is requested, and the application is responsible for managing the life cycle of the entity manager.

A container-managed entity manager is typically used in a Java EE environment. The application-managed entity manager is typically used in a Java SE environment and will not be discussed here.

An entity manager and persistence context are not required to be threadsafe. This requires an entity manager to be obtained from an entity manager factory in Java EE components that are not required to be threadsafe, such as servlets.

The entity managers, together with their configuration information, the set of entities managed by the entity managers, and metadata that specifies mapping of the classes to the database, are packaged together as a *persistence unit*. A persistence unit is defined by a *persistence.xml* file and is contained within an *ejb-jar*, *.war*, *.ear*, or application-client *JAR*. Multiple persistence units may be defined within a *persistence.xml* file.

A sample *persistence.xml* for the entity can be defined like so:

```
<?xml version="1.0" encoding="UTF-8"?>
<persistence version="2.1"
    xmlns="http://xmlns.jcp.org/xml/ns/persistence"
    xmlns:xsi="http://www.w3.org/2001/XMLSchema-instance"
    xsi:schemaLocation=
        "http://xmlns.jcp.org/xml/ns/persistence
http://xmlns.jcp.org/xml/ns/persistence/persistence_2_1.xsd">
  <persistence-unit name="MyPU" transaction-type="JTA">
    <jta-data-source>jdbc/sample</jta-data-source>
    <exclude-unlisted-classes>
        false
    </exclude-unlisted-classes>
    <properties/>
```

```
    </persistence-unit>
</persistence>
```

In this code:

- The persistence unit's name is `MyPU`.

- The `transaction-type` attribute's value of `JTA` signifies that a JTA data source is provided.

- The `jta-data-source` element defines the global JNDI name of the JTA data source defined in the container. In a Java EE environment, this ensures that all the database configuration information, such as host, port, username, and password, are specified in the container, and just the JTA data source name is used in the application.

- You can specify an explicit list of entity classes to be managed using multiple `class` elements, or include all the entities (as above) by specifying the `exclude-unlisted-classes` element.

- The `<properties>` element is used to specify both standard and vendor-specific properties. The following standard properties may be specified:

  — `javax.persistence.jdbc.driver`

  — `javax.persistence.jdbc.url`

  — `javax.persistence.jdbc.user`

  — `javax.persistence.jdbc.password`

  JPA 2.1 introduces new `javax.persistence.schema-generation.*` property names that allow generation of database artifacts. These are explained in the next section.

The Java EE 7 platform defines a new default `DataSource` that must be provided by a Java EE 7–compliant runtime. This preconfigured data source can be used by the application for accessing the associated database. It is accessible to the application under the JNDI name:

```
java:comp/DefaultDataSource
```

The *persistence.xml* file can then be defined:

```
<?xml version="1.0" encoding="UTF-8"?>
<persistence version="2.1"
    xmlns="http://xmlns.jcp.org/xml/ns/persistence"
    xmlns:xsi="http://www.w3.org/2001/XMLSchema-instance"
    xsi:schemaLocation=
        "http://xmlns.jcp.org/xml/ns/persistence
http://xmlns.jcp.org/xml/ns/persistence/persistence_2_1.xsd">
  <persistence-unit name="MyPU" transaction-type="JTA">
    <jta-data-source>java:comp/DefaultDataSource</jta-data-source>
  </persistence-unit>
</persistence>
```

The JPA 2.1 specification says that if neither the `jta-data-source` nor the `non-jta-data-source` element is specified, the deployer must specify a JTA data source at deployment or the default JTA data source must be provided by the container, and a JTA `EntityManagerFactory` will be created to correspond to it.

This *persistence.xml* file defined earlier is then semantically equivalent to:

```
<?xml version="1.0" encoding="UTF-8"?>
<persistence version="2.1"
    xmlns="http://xmlns.jcp.org/xml/ns/persistence"
    xmlns:xsi="http://www.w3.org/2001/XMLSchema-instance"
    xsi:schemaLocation=
        "http://xmlns.jcp.org/xml/ns/persistence
http://xmlns.jcp.org/xml/ns/persistence/persistence_2_1.xsd">
  <persistence-unit name="MyPU" transaction-type="JTA">
  </persistence-unit>
</persistence>
```

In both cases, the default data source will be provisioned and available to the application.

By default, a container-managed persistence context is scoped to a single transaction, and entities are detached at the end of a transaction. For stateful session beans, the persistence context may be marked to span multiple transactions and is called an *extended persistence context*. The entities stay managed across multiple transactions in this case. An extended persistence context can be created:

```
@PersistenceContext(type=PersistenceContextType.EXTENDED)
EntityManager em;
```

In JPA 2, the persistence context is of the type `SynchronizationType.SYNCHRONIZED`. Such a context is automatically joined to the current JTA transaction, and updates made to the persistence context are propagated to the resource manager (i.e., stored in the database). JPA 2.1 introduces `SynchronizedType.UNSYNCHRONIZED`. Such a persistence context is not enlisted in any JTA transaction unless explicitly joined to that transaction by the application:

```
@PersistenceContext(synchronization=SynchronizationType.UNSYNCHRONIZED)
EntityManager em;
```

Such an `EntityManager` can be enlisted in a JTA transaction and registered for subsequent transaction notifications by the invocation of `EntityManager.joinTransac tion`. The persistence context remains joined to the transaction until the transaction commits or rolls back. The persistence context remains unsynchronized after that and explicitly needs to join a transaction in the new scope.

The application can invoke the `persist`, `merge`, `remove`, and `refresh` entity life-cycle operations on an unsynchronized persistence context. After joining the transaction, any changes in persistence context may be flushed to the database either explicitly by application via `flush` or by the provider. If not explicitly flushed, then the persistence provider may defer flushing until commit time depending on the operations invoked and the flush mode setting in effect.

Schema Generation

JPA 2.1 in the Java EE 7 platform introduces a new set of properties that allows generation of database artifacts like tables, indexes, and constraints in a database schema. It may or may not involve generation of a proper database schema depending upon the credentials and authorization of the user. This helps in prototyping of your application where the required artifacts are generated either prior to application deployment or as part of `EntityManagerFactory` creation. This is also useful in environments that require provisioning a database on demand (e.g., in a cloud).

This feature will allow your JPA domain object model to be directly generated in a database. The generated schema may need to be tuned for the actual production environment. This use case is supported by allowing the schema generation to occur into DDL scripts, which can then be further tuned by a DBA.

Table 13-1 lists the set of properties in *persistence.xml* or specified during `EntityMana gerFactory` creation that control the behavior of schema generation.

Table 13-1. JPA 2.1 schema generation properties

Property name	Purpose	Values
`javax.persistence.schema-generation.database.action`	Specifies the action to be taken by the persistence provider. If this property is not specified, no schema generation actions must be taken on the database.	`none`, `create`, `drop-and-create`, `drop`
`javax.persistence.schema-generation.scripts.action`	Specifies which scripts are to be generated by the persistence provider. A script will only be generated if the script target is specified. If this property is not specified, no scripts will be generated.	`none`, `create`, `drop-and-create`, `drop`
`javax.persistence.schema-generation.create-source`, `javax.persistence.schema-generation.drop-source`	Specifies whether the creation or deletion of database artifacts is to occur on the basis of the object/relational mapping metadata, DDL script, or a combination of the two.	`metadata`, `script`, `metadata-then-script`, `script-then-metadata`
`javax.persistence.schema-generation.create-database-schemas`	Specifies whether the persistence provider needs to create schema in addition to creating database objects such as tables, sequences, constraints, etc.	`true`, `false`
`javax.persistence.schema-generation.scripts.create-target`, `javax.persistence.schema-generation.scripts.drop-target`	Controls target locations for writing of scripts. Writers are preconfigured for the persistence provider. Need to be specified only if scripts are to be generated.	`java.io.Writer` (e.g., `MyWriter.class`) or URL strings

Property name	Purpose	Values
`javax.persistence.schema-generation.create-script-source`, `javax.persistence.schema-generation.drop-script-source`	Specifies locations from which DDL scripts are to be read. Readers are preconfigured for the persistence provider.	`java.io.Reader` (e.g., `MyReader.class`) or URL strings
`javax.persistence.database-product-name`, `javax.persistence.database-major-version`, `javax.persistence.database-minor-version`	Needed if scripts are to be generated and no connection to the target database is supplied. Values are those obtained from JDBC `DatabaseMetaData`.	
`javax.persistence.schema-generation-connection`	JDBC connection to be used for schema generation.	
`javax.persistence.sql-load-script-source`	Specifies location of SQL bulk load script.	`java.io.Reader` (e.g., `MyReader.class`) or URL string

An application that requires database tables to be dropped and created via the scripts bundled in the *META-INF* directory of the application can have the following *persistence.xml*:

```
<persistence version="2.1"
  xmlns="http://xmlns.jcp.org/xml/ns/persistence"
  xmlns:xsi="http://www.w3.org/2001/XMLSchema-instance"
  xsi:schemaLocation="http://xmlns.jcp.org/xml/ns/persistence
    http://xmlns.jcp.org/xml/ns/persistence/persistence_2_1.xsd">
  <persistence-unit name="myPU" transaction-type="JTA">
    <properties>
      <property name="javax.persistence.schema-generation.database.action"
              value="drop-and-create"/>
      <property name="javax.persistence.schema-generation.create-source"
              value="script"/>
      <property name="javax.persistence.schema-generation.drop-source"
              value="script"/>
      <property name="javax.persistence.schema-generation.create-script-source"
              value="META-INF/create.sql"/>
      <property name="javax.persistence.schema-generation.drop-script-source"
              value="META-INF/drop.sql"/>
      <property name="javax.persistence.sql-load-script-source"
              value="META-INF/load.sql"/>
    </properties>
  </persistence-unit>
</persistence>
```

The usual annotations—such as `@Table`, `@Column`, `@CollectionTable`, `@JoinTable`, and `@JoinColumn`—are used to define the generated schema. Several layers of defaulting may be involved. For example, the table name is defaulted from the entity name and the entity name (which can be specified explicitly as well) is defaulted from the class name. However, annotations may be used to override or customize the values:

```
@Entity public class Employee {
    @Id
    private int id;

    private String name;
    . . .
    @ManyToOne
    private Department dept;
}
```

This entity is generated in the database with the following attributes:

- Maps to the EMPLOYEE table in the default schema.
- The id field is mapped to the ID column as the primary key.
- The name is mapped to the NAME column with a default VARCHAR(255). The length of this field can be easily tuned via @Column.
- @ManyToOne is mapped to the DEPT_ID foreign key column and can be customized via JOIN_COLUMN.

In addition to these properties, a couple of new annotations are added to JPA 2.1.

@Index

An index for the primary key is generated by default in a database. This new annotation will allow you to define additional indexes, over a single or multiple columns, for better performance. This is specified as part of @Table, @SecondaryTable, @CollectionTable, @JoinTable, and @TableGenerator:

```
@Table(indexes = {
        @Index(columnList="NAME"),
         @Index(columnList="DEPT_ID DESC")
      })
@Entity public class Employee {
    //. . .
}
```

In this case, the generated table will have a default index on the primary key. In addition, two new indexes are defined on the NAME column (default ascending) and the foreign key that maps to the department in descending order.

@ForeignKey

This is used to define a foreign key constraint or to otherwise override or disable the persistence provider's default foreign key definition. It can be specified as part of JoinColumn(s), MapKeyJoinColumn(s), and PrimaryKeyJoinColumn(s):

```
@Entity public class Employee {
  @Id private int id;
```

```
    private String name;
    @ManyToOne
    @JoinColumn(foreignKey=@ForeignKey(
        foreignKeyDefinition="FOREIGN KEY (MANAGER_ID) REFERENCES MANAGER"))
    private Manager manager;
    //. . .
}
```

In this entity, the employee's manager is mapped by the MANAGER_ID column in the
MANAGER table. The value of foreignKeyDefinition would be a database-specific
string.

Create, Read, Update, and Delete Entities

An entity goes through create, read, update, and delete (CRUD) operations during its
life cycle. A create operation means a new entity is created and persisted in the database.
A read operation means querying for an entity from the database based upon selection
criteria. An update operation means updating the state of an existing entity in the database. And a delete operation means removing an entity from the database. Typically,
an entity is created once, read and updated a few times, and deleted once.

The JPA specification outlines the following ways to perform CRUD operations:

Java Persistence Query Language (JPQL)

> The Java Persistence Query Language is a string-based typed query language used
> to define queries over entities and their persistent state. The query language uses a
> SQL-like syntax and uses the abstract persistence schema of entities as its data
> model. This portable query language syntax is translated into SQL queries that are
> executed over the database schema where the entities are mapped. The EntityMan
> ager.createNamed*XXX* methods are used to create the JPQL statements. The query
> statements can be used to select, update, or delete rows from the database.

Criteria API

> The Criteria API is an object-based, type-safe API and operates on a metamodel of
> the entities. Criteria queries are very useful for constructing dynamic queries. Typ-
> ically, the static metamodel classes are generated by way of an annotation processor,
> and model the persistent state and relationships of the entities. The javax.persis
> tence.criteria and javax.persistence.metamodel APIs are used to create the
> strongly typed queries. In JPA 2, the Criteria API allowed only querying the entities.
> JPA 2.1 allows you to update and delete entities using the Criteria API as well.

Native SQL statement

> Create a native SQL query specific to a database. @SQLResultSetMapping is used to
> specify the mapping of the result of a native SQL query. The EntityManager.cre
> ateNative*XXX* methods are used to create native queries.

A new entity can be persisted in the database with an entity manager:

```
Student student = new Student();
student.setId(1234);
//. . .
em.persist(student);
```

In this code, em is an entity manager obtained as explained earlier. The entity is persisted to the database at the transaction commit.

A simple JPQL statement to query all the Student entities and retrieve the results looks like:

```
em.createQuery("SELECT s FROM Student s").getResultList();
```

@NamedQuery and @NamedQueries are used to define a mapping between a static JPQL query statement and a symbolic name. This follows the "Don't Repeat Yourself" (DRY) design pattern and allows you to centralize the JPQL statements:

```
@NamedQuery(
  name="findStudent"
  value="SELECT s FROM Student s WHERE p.grade = :grade")
//. . .
Query query = em.createNamedQuery("findStudent");
List<Student> list = List<Student>query
                           .setParameter("grade", "4")
                           .getResultList();
```

This code will query the database for all the students in grade 4 and return the result as List<Student>.

The usual WHERE, GROUP BY, HAVING, and ORDER BY clauses may be specified in the JPQL statements to restrict the results returned by the query. Other SQL keywords such as JOIN and DISTINCT and functions like ABS, MIN, SIZE, SUM, and TRIM are also permitted. The KEY, VALUE, and ENTRY operators may be applied where map-valued associations or collections are returned.

The return type of the query result list may be specified:

```
TypedQuery<Student> query = em.createNamedQuery(
                                "findStudent",
                                Student.class);
List<Student> list = query.setParameter("grade", "4")
                           .getResultList();
```

Typically, a persistence provider will precompile the static named queries.

You can define a dynamic JPQL query by directly passing the query string to the corresponding createQuery methods:

```
TypedQuery<Student> query = em.createQuery(
                                "SELECT s FROM Student s",
                                Student.class);
```

The query string is dynamically constructed in this case.

Dynamic queries can also be constructed via the type-safe Criteria API. Here is a code sample that explains how to use the Criteria API to query the list of Students:

```
CriteriaBuilder builder = em.getCriteriaBuilder();
CriteriaQuery criteria = builder.createQuery(Student.class);

Root<Student> root = criteria.from(Student.class);
criteria.select(root);
TypedQuery<Student> query = em.createQuery(criteria);
List<Student> list = query.getResultList();
```

The Criteria API is very useful in building dynamic queries at runtime—for example, an elaborate search page in an application that searches for content based on input fields. Using the Critiera API, instead of JPQL, would eliminate the need for string concatenation operations to build the query.

The static @NamedQuery may be more appropriate for simple use cases. In a complex query where SELECT, FROM, WHERE, and other clauses are defined at runtime, the dynamic JPQL may be more error prone, typically because of string concatenation. The type-safe Criteria API offers a more robust way of dealing with such queries. All the clauses can be easily specified in a type-safe manner, providing the advantages of compile-time validation of queries.

The JPA2 metamodel classes capture the metamodel of the persistent state and relationships of the managed classes of a persistence unit. This abstract persistence schema is then used to author the type-safe queries via the Criteria API. The canonical metamodel classes can be generated statically by way of an annotation processor following the rules defined by the specification. The good thing is that no extra configuration is required to generate these metamodel classes.

To update an existing entity, you need to first find it, change the fields, and call the EntityManager.merge method:

```
Student student = em.find(Student.class, 1234);
//. . .
student.setGrade("5");
em.merge(student);
```

You can then update the entity using JPQL:

```
Query query = em.createQuery("UPDATE Student s"
+ "SET s.grade = :grade WHERE s.id = :id");
query.setParameter("grade", "5");
query.setParameter("id", "1234");
query.executeUpdate();
```

With JPA 2.1, you can update the entity using the Criteria API:

```
CriteriaBuilder builder = em.getCriteriaBuilder();
CriteriaUpdate updateCriteria = builder.createCriteriaUpdate(Student.class);
Root<Student> updateRoot = updateCriteria.from(Student.class);
```

```
updateCriteria.where(builder.equal(updateRoot.get(Student_.id), "1234"));
updateCriteria.set(updateRoot.get(Student_.grade), "5");
Query q = em.createQuery(updateCriteria);
q.executeUpdate();
```

To remove an existing entity, you need to find it and then call the `EntityManager.re move` method:

```
Student student = em.find(Student.class, 1234);
em.remove(student);
```

You may delete the entity using JPQL:

```
Query query = em.createQuery("DELETE FROM Student s"
+ "WHERE s.id = :id");
query.setParameter("id", "1234");
query.executeUpdate();
```

Removing an entity removes the corresponding record from the underlying data store as well.

With JPA 2.1, you can delete the entity using the Criteria API:

```
CriteriaBuilder builder = em.getCriteriaBuilder();
CriteriaDelete deleteCriteria = builder.createCriteriaDelete(Student.class);
Root<Student> updateRoot = deleteCriteria.from(Student.class);
deleteCriteria.where(builder.equal(updateRoot.get(Student_.id), "1234"));
Query q = em.createQuery(deleteCriteria);
q.executeUpdate();
```

Entity Listeners

An entity goes through multiple life-cycle events such as load, persist, update, and re-move. You can place the annotations listed in Table 13-2 on methods in the entity class or mapped superclass to receive notification of these life-cycle events.

Table 13-2. Entity listener annotations

Annotation	Description
@PostLoad	Executed after an entity has been loaded in the current persistence context or an entity has been refreshed.
@PerPersist	Executed before the entity manager persist operation is actually executed or cascaded. If entities are merged, then this is invoked after the entity state has been copied. This method is synchronous with the persist operation.
@PostPersist	Executed after the entity has been persisted or cascaded. Invoked after the database INSERT is executed. Generated key values are available in this method.
@PreUpdate	Executed before the database UPDATE operation.
@PostUpdate	Executed after the database UPDATE operation.
@PreRemove	Executed before the entity manager remove operation is actually executed or cascaded. This method is synchronous with the remove operation.

Annotation	Description
@PostRemove	Executed after the entity has been removed. Invoked after the database DELETE is executed.

```
@Entity
public class Student implements Serializable {
  //. . .

  @PostLoad
  public void studentLoaded() {
    //. . .
  }

  @PostPersist
  public void newStudentAlert() {
    //. . .
  }

  @PostUpdate
  public void studentUpdateAlert() {
    //. . .
  }

  @PreRemove
  public void studentDeleteAlert() {
    //. . .
  }
}
```

In this code:

- The method studentLoaded is called after the entity has been loaded into the current persistence context or after the refresh operation has been applied to it.

- The method newStudentAlert is called after the entity has been persisted to the data store.

- The method studentUpdateAlert is called after the entity has been updated.

- The method studentDeleteAlert is called before the entity is deleted.

The callback methods can have public, private, protected, or package-level access, but must not be static or final.

JPA 2.1 supports dependency injection. For a Java EE 7 archive where CDI is enabled by default, additional life-cycle callback methods annotated with @PostConstruct and @PreDestroy may be used.

The callback methods may be defined on a separate class and associated with this entity via @EntityListeners. The method signature in that case will be different:

```
@Entity
@EntityListeners(StudentListener.class)
```

```
public class Student implements Serializable {
  //. . .
}
public class StudentListener
  @PostLoad
  public void studentLoaded(Student student) {
    //. . .
  }

  @PostPersist
  public void newStudentAlert(Student student) {
    //. . .
  }

  @PostUpdate
  public void studentUpdateAlert(Student student) {
    //. . .
  }

  @PreRemove
  public void studentDeleteAlert(Student student) {
    //. . .
  }
}
```

The argument is the entity instance for which the callback method is invoked.

Multiple entity listeners may be defined for an entity class or mapped superclass. Each listener is invoked in the same order as it is specified in the `EntityListeners` annotation.

You can define the callback listeners using the XML descriptors bundled in *META-INF/orm.xml*:

```
<entity-mappings xmlns="http://xmlns.jcp.org/xml/ns/persistence/orm"
        xsi:schemaLocation="http://xmlns.jcp.org/xml/ns/persistence/orm
        http://xmlns.jcp.org/xml/ns/persistence/orm/orm_2_1.xsd"
        version="2.1">
  <persistence-unit-metadata>
    <entity class="org.sample.Student">
      <entity-listeners>
        <entity-listener class="org.sample.StudentListener">
          <post-load method-name="studentLoaded"/>
        </entity-listener>
      </entity-listeners>
    </entity>
  </persistence-unit-metadata>
</entity-mappings>
```

Default entity listeners can be specified by way of the XML descriptor. The callback methods from such a listener class will apply to all entities in the persistence unit:

```
<entity-mappings xmlns="http://xmlns.jcp.org/xml/ns/persistence/orm"
        xsi:schemaLocation="http://xmlns.jcp.org/xml/ns/persistence/orm
        http://xmlns.jcp.org/xml/ns/persistence/orm/orm_2_1.xsd"
        version="2.1">
  <persistence-unit-metadata>
    <persistence-unit-defaults>
      <entity-listeners>
        <entity-listener class="MyListener"/>
      </entity-listeners>
    </persistence-unit-defaults>
  </persistence-unit-metadata>
</entity-mappings>
```

In this code, `MyListener` is defined as the default entity listener that will be applied to all entities in the persistence unit.

The order specified in the XML descriptor overrides the order specified via metadata annotations, either in the entity class or through `@EntityListeners`.

Stored Procedures

JPA 2.1 adds the capability to execute queries that invoke stored procedures defined in the database. You can specify stored procedures either using `@NamedStoredProcedure` `Query` or dynamically.

Similar to `@NamedQuery`, there is `@NamedStoredProcedureQuery`, which specifies and names a stored procedure, its parameters, corresponding parameter modes (`IN`, `OUT`, `INOUT`, `REF_CURSOR`) and its result type, if any. Unlike `@NamedQuery`, `@NamedStoredProcedureQuery` names a stored procedure that exists in the database rather than providing a stored procedure definition. This annotation can be specified on an entity or mapped superclass:

```
@Entity
@NamedStoredProcedureQuery(name="topGiftsStoredProcedure",
    procedureName="Top10Gifts")
public class Product {
  // . . .
}
```

In this code, `name` uniquely defines this stored procedure query element within a persistence unit, and `procedureName` identifies the name of the stored procedure in the database.

There are different variants of the `EntityManager.createXXXStoredProcedureQuery` methods that return a `StoredProcedureQuery` for executing a stored procedure. The name specified in the annotation is used in `EntityManager.createNamedStoredProce` `dureQuery`. You specify different parameters of the stored procedure using the `setPara` `meter` method. The parameters must be specified in the order in which they occur in the parameter list of the stored procedure. Either the parameter name or position can be used to bind the parameter with the value or to extract the value (if the parameter is OUT or INOUT):

```
StoredProcedureQuery query = EntityManager.createNamedStoredProcedureQuery
    ("topGiftsStoredProcedure");
query.setParameter(1, "top10");
query.setParameter(2, 100);
query.execute();
String response = query.getOutputParameterValue(1);
```

In this code:

- The stored procedure name from @NamedStoredProcedureQuery is used to create StoredProcedureQuery.

- Positional parameters are used to bind the value of the two parameters. There are different setParameter methods for defining the temporal type of a parameter.

- After the query is executed, the results are extracted via getOutputParameterValue with positional parameters as well.

  If the execute method returns true, then the first result is a result set; it returns false if it is an update count or there are no other results other than through the INOUT and OUT parameters, if any. If a single result set plus any other results are passed back via the INOUT and OUT parameters, then you can obtain the results using the getResultList and getSingleResult methods. The getUpdateCount method may be called to obtain the results if it is an update count. The results from getResultList, getSingleResult, and getUpdateCount must be processed before the INOUT or OUT parameter values are extracted.

If you do not define the stored procedure using parameters, resultClasses, and resultSetMappings in @NamedStoredProcedureQuery, you must provide the parameter and result information dynamically:

```
StoredProcedureQuery query =
  EntityManager
    .createNamedStoredProcedureQuery("topGiftsStoredProcedure");
query.registerStoredProcedureParameter(1, String.class, ParameterMode.INOUT);
query.setParameter(1, "top10");
query.registerStoredProcedureParameter(2, Integer.class, ParameterMode.IN);
query.setParameter(2, 100);
query.execute();
String response = query.getOutputParameterValue(1);
```

In this code, the two parameters are registered via the registerStoredProcedureParameter method. The parameter mode is specified during the registration.

You can provide result mapping information using the EntityManager.createStoredProcedureQuery method.

Validating the Entities

Bean Validation allows you to specify validation metadata on JavaBeans. For JPA, all managed classes (entities, managed superclasses, and embeddable classes) may be configured to include Bean Validation constraints. These constraints are then enforced when the entity is persisted, updated, or removed in the database. Bean Validation has some predefined constraints like @Min, @Max, @Pattern, and @Size. You can easily create a custom constraint by using the mechanisms defined in the Bean Validation specification and explained in this book.

The Student entity with validation constraints can be defined as:

```
@Entity
public class Student implements Serializable {
  @NotNull
  @Id private int id;

  @Size(max=30)
  private String name;  @Size(min=2, max=5)
  private String grade;

  //. . .
}
```

This ensures that the id field is never null, the size of the name field is at most 30 characters with a default minimum of 0, and the size of the grade field is a minimum of 2 characters and a maximum of 5. With these constraints, attempting to add the following Student to the database will throw a ConstraintViolationException, as the grade field must be at least 2 characters long:

```
Student student = new Student();
student.setId(1234);
student.setName("Joe Smith");
student.setGrade("1");
em.persist(student);
```

Embeddable attributes are validated only if the Valid annotation has been specified on them. So the updated Address class will look like:

```
@Embeddable
@Valid
public class Address {
  @Size(max=20)
  private String street;

  @Size(max=20)
  private String city;

  @Size(max=20)
  private String zip;
```

```
//. . .
}
```

By default, the validation of entity beans is automatically turned on. You can change the default validation behavior by specifying the `validation-mode` element in *persistence.xml*. Its values are defined in Table 13-3.

Table 13-3. Values for validation-mode in persistence.xml

validation-mode	Description
auto	Automatic validation of entities; this is the default behavior. No validation takes place if no Bean Validation provider is found.
callback	Life-cycle validation of entities. An error is reported if no Bean Validation provider is found.
none	No validation is performed.

You can specify this attribute in *persistence.xml*:

```
<persistence-unit name="MySamplePU" transaction-type="JTA">
    <validation-mode>CALLBACK</validation-mode>
</persistence-unit>
```

You can also specify these values using the `javax.persistence.validation.mode` property if you create the entity manager factory using `Persistence.createEntityManagerFactory`:

```
Map props = new HashMap();
props.put("javax.persistence.validation.mode", "callback");
EntityManagerFactory emf =
    Persistence.createEntityManagerFactory("MySamplePU", props);
```

By default, all entities in a web application are in the `Default` validation group. The `Default` group is targeted in pre-persist and pre-update events, and no groups are targeted in pre-remove events. So the constraints are validated when an entity is persisted or updated, but not when it is deleted.

You can override this default behavior by specifying the target groups using the following validation properties in *persistence.xml*:

- `javax.persistence.validation.group.pre-persist`
- `javax.persistence.validation.group.pre-update`
- `javax.persistence.validation.group.pre-remove`

You can define a new validation group by declaring a new interface:

```
public interface MyGroup { }
```

You can target a field in the `Student` entity to this validation group:

```
@Entity
public class Student implements Serializable {
```

```
@Id @NotNull int id;

@AssertTrue(groups=MyGroup.class)
private boolean canBeDeleted;

}
```

And *persistence.xml* needs to have the following property defined:

```
//. . .
<property
   name="javax.persistence.validation.group.pre-remove"
   value="org.sample.MyGroup"/>
```

These properties can also be passed to `Persistence.createEntityManagerFactory` in a `Map`.

You can also achieve validation in the application by calling the `Validator.validate` method upon an instance of a managed class. The life-cycle event validation only occurs when a Bean Validation provider exists in the runtime.

If a constraint is violated, the current transaction is marked for rollback.

Transactions and Locking

The `EntityManager.persist`, `.merge`, `.remove`, and `.refresh` methods must be invoked within a transaction context when an entity manager with a transaction-scoped persistence context is used. The transactions are controlled either through JTA or through the use of the resource-local `EntityTransaction` API. A container-managed entity manager must use JTA and is the typical way of having transactional behavior in a Java EE container. A resource-local entity manager is typically used in a Java SE environment.

A transaction for a JTA entity manager is started and committed external to the entity manager:

```
@Stateless
public class StudentSessionBean {
  @PersistenceContext
  EntityManager em;

  public void addStudent(Student student) {
    em.persist(student);
  }
}
```

In this Enterprise JavaBean, a JTA transaction is started before the `addStudent` method and committed after the method is completed. The transaction is automatically rolled back if an exception is thrown in the method.

The resource-local `EntityTransaction` API can be used:

```
EntityManagerFactory emf = Persistence.createEntityManagerFactory("student");
EntityManager em = emf.getEntityManager();
em.getTransaction().begin();
Student student = new Student();
//. . .
em.persist(student);
em.getTransaction().commit();
em.close();
emf.close();
```

The transaction may be rolled back via the `EntityTransaction.rollback` method.

In addition to transactions, an entity may be locked when the transaction is active.

By default, *optimistic concurrency control* is assumed. Optimistic locking allows anyone to read and update an entity; however, a version check is made upon commit and an exception is thrown if the version was updated in the database since the entity was read.

The `@Version` attribute can be specified on an entity's field of type `int`, `Integer`, `short`, `Short`, `long`, `Long`, or `java.sql.Timestamp`. An entity is automatically enabled for optimistic locking if it has a property or field mapped with a `Version` mapping.

The application must never update this field. Only the persistence provider is permitted to set or update the value of the version attribute. This field is used by the persistence provider to perform optimistic locking:

```
@Entity
public class Student implements Serializable {
  @Id
  @NotNull
  private int id;

  @Version
  private int version;

  //. . .
}
```

The version attribute is incremented with a successful commit. If another concurrent transaction tries to update the entity and the version attribute has been updated since the entity was read, then `javax.persistence.OptimisticLockException` is thrown.

No database locks are held in optimistic locking, which delivers better scalability. The disadvantages are that the user or application must refresh and retry failed updates.

Pessimistic locking gives an exclusive lock on the entity until the application is finished processing it. Pessimistic locking ensures that multiple transactions cannot update the same entity at the same time, which can simplify application code, but it limits concurrent access to the data.

You can obtain a pessimistic lock on an entity by passing a LockModeType enum value during the find method:

```
Student student = em.find(Student.class, 1234, LockModeType.PESSIMISTIC_WRITE);
```

Alternatively, you can obtain a lock on an entity afterward:

```
em.lock(student, LockModeType.PESSIMISTIC_WRITE);
```

This code can throw OptimisticLockException during flush or commit if the entity was updated after reading but before locking.

When an entity instance is locked via pessimistic locking, the persistence provider must lock the database row(s) that correspond to the non-collection-valued persistent state of that instance. Element collections and relationships owned by the entity that are contained in join tables will be locked if the javax.persistence.lock.scope property is specified with a value of PessimisticLockScope.EXTENDED.

This property may be specified on @NamedQuery:

```
@NamedQuery(
  name="findStudent"
  value="SELECT s FROM Student s WHERE p.grade = :grade",
  lockMode = PessimisticLockScope.EXTENDED)
```

Caching

JPA provides two levels of caching. The entities are cached by the entity manager at the first level in the persistence context. The entity manager guarantees that within a single persistence context, for any particular database row, there will only be one object instance. However, the same entity could be managed in another transaction, so appropriate locking should be used.

Second-level caching by the persistence provider can be enabled by the value of the shared-cache-mode element in *persistence.xml*. This element can have the values defined in Table 13-4.

Table 13-4. shared-cache-mode values in persistence.xml

Value	Description
ALL	All entities and entity-related state are cached.
NONE	No entities or entity-related state is cached.
ENABLE_SELECTIVE	Only cache entities marked with @Cacheable(true) are cached.
DISABLE_SELECTIVE	Only cache entities that are not marked @Cacheable(false) are cached.
UNSPECIFIED	Persistence-provider-specific defaults apply.

The exact value can be specified:

```
<shared-cache-element>ALL</shared-cache-element>
```

This allows entity state to be shared across multiple persistence contexts.

The Cache interface can be used to interface with the second-level cache as well. This interface can be obtained from EntityManagerFactory, and can be used to check whether a particular entity exists in the cache or to invalidate a particular entity, an entire class, or the entire cache:

```
@PersistenceUnit
EntityMangagerFactory emf;

public void myMethod() {
    //. . .
    Cache cache = emf.getCache();
    boolean inCache = cache.contains(Student.class, 1234);
    //. . .
}
```

A specific entity can be cleared:

```
cache.evict(Student.class, 1234);
```

All entities of a class can be invalidated:

```
cache.evict(Student.class);
```

And the complete cache can be invalidated as:

```
cache.evictAll();
```

A standard set of query hints are also available to allow refreshing or bypassing the cache. The query hints are specified as javax.persistence.cache.retrieveMode and javax.persistence.cache.storeMode properties on the Query object. The first property is used to specify the behavior when data is retrieved by the find methods and by queries. The second property is used to specify the behavior when data is read from the database and committed into the database:

```
Query query = em.createQuery("SELECT s FROM Student s");
query.setHint("javax.persistence.cache.storeMode",
            CacheStoreMode.BYPASS);
```

The property values are defined on CacheRetrieveMode and CacheStoreMode enums and explained in Table 13-5.

Table 13-5. CacheStoreMode and CacheRetrieveMode values

Cache query hint	Description
CacheStoreMode.BYPASS	Don't insert into cache.
CacheStoreMode.REFRESH	Insert/update entity data into cache when read from database and when committed into database.
CacheStoreMode.USE	Insert/update entity data into cache when read from database and when committed into database; this is the default behavior.
CacheRetrieveMode.BYPASS	Bypass the cache: get data directly from the database.
CacheRetrieveMode.USE	Read entity data from the cache; this is the default behavior.

CHAPTER 14

Java Message Service

The Java Message Service is defined as JSR 343, and the complete specification can be downloaded (*http://jcp.org/aboutJava/communityprocess/final/jsr343/index.html*).

Message-oriented middleware (MOM) allows sending and receiving messages between distributed systems. Java Message Service (JMS) is a MOM that provides a way for Java programs to create, send, receive, and read an enterprise messaging system's messages.

JMS defines the following concepts:

JMS provider
> An implementation of the JMS interfaces, included in a Java EE implementation.

JMS client
> A Java program that produces and/or receives messages. Any Java EE application component can act as a JMS client.

JMS message
> An object that contains the data transferred between JMS clients. A JMS producer/ publisher creates and sends messages. A JMS consumer/subscriber receives and consumes messages.

Administered objects
> Objects created and preconfigured by an administrator. They typically refer to `ConnectionFactory` and `Destination`, and are identified by a JNDI name. The `ConnectionFactory` is used to create a connection with the provider. The `Destina tion` is the object used by the client to specify the destination of messages it is sending and the source of messages it is receiving.

JMS supports two messaging models: *Point-to-Point* and *Publish-Subscribe.*

In the Point-to-Point model, a publisher sends a message to a specific destination, called a *queue*, targeted to a subscriber. Multiple publishers can send messages to the queue, but each message is delivered and consumed by one consumer only. Queues retain all messages sent to them until the messages are consumed or expire.

In the Publish-Subscribe model, a publisher publishes a message to a particular destination, called a *topic*, and a subscriber registers interest by subscribing to that topic. Multiple publishers can publish messages to the topic, and multiple subscribers can subscribe to the topic. By default, a subscriber will receive messages only when it is active. However, a subscriber may establish a *durable* connection, so that any messages published while the subscriber is not active are redistributed whenever it reconnects.

The publisher and subscriber are loosely coupled from each other; in fact, they have no knowledge of each other's existence. They only need to know the destination and the message format.

Different levels of quality of service, such as missed or duplicate messages or deliver-once, can be configured. The messsages may be received synchronously or asynchronously.

A JMS message is composed of three parts:

Header
> This is a required part of the message and is used to identify and route messages. All messages have the same set of header fields. Some fields are initialized by the JMS provider and others are initialized by the client on a per-message basis.

The standard header fields are defined in Table 14-1.

Table 14-1. JMS header fields

Message header field	Description
JMSDestination	Destination to which the message is sent.
JMSDeliveryMode	Delivery mode is PERSISTENT (for durable topics) or NON_PERSISTENT.
JMSMessageID	String value with the prefix "ID:" that uniquely identifies each message sent by a provider.
JMSTimestamp	Time the message was handed off to a provider to be sent. This value may be different from the time the message was actually transmitted.
JMSCorrelationID	Used to link one message to another (e.g., a response message with its request message).
JMSReplyTo	Destination supplied by a client where a reply message should be sent.
JMSRedelivered	Set by the provider if the message was delivered but not acknowledged in the past.
JMSType	Message type identifier; may refer to a message definition in the provider's respository.
JMSExpiration	Expiration time of the message.
JMSPriority	Priority of the message.

Properties
> These are optional header fields added by the client. Just like standard header fields, these are name/value pairs. The value can be boolean, byte, short, int, long, float,

double, and `String`. The producer/publisher can set these values and the consumer/subscriber can use these values as selection criteria to fine-tune the selection of messages to be processed.

Properties may be either application-specific (standard properties defined by JMS) or provider-specific. JMS-defined properties are prefixed `JMSX`, and provider-specific properties are prefixed with `JMS_<vendor_name>`.

Body

This is the actual payload of the message, which contains the application data.

Different types of body messages are shown in Table 14-2.

Table 14-2. JMS message types

Message type	Description
StreamMessage	Payload is a stream of Java primitive types, written and read sequentially.
MapMessage	Payload is a set of name/value pairs; order of the entries is undefined, and can be accessed randomly or sequentially.
TextMessage	Payload is a `String`.
ObjectMessage	Payload is a serializable Java object.
ByteMessage	Payload is a stream of uninterpreted bytes.

JMS refers to the API introduced in JMS 1.1 as the *classic API*. It provides a single set of interfaces that could be used for both point-to-point and pub/sub messaging. JMS 2.0 introduces a *simplified API* that offers all the features of classic API but requires fewer interfaces and is simpler to use. The following sections will explain the key JMS concepts using both the classic API and the simplified API.

Sending a Message

Using the JMS 2 simplified API, you can send a message from a stateless session bean:

```
@Stateless
@JMSDestinationDefinitions(
  {
    @JMSDestinationDefinition(name = "java:global/jms/myQueue",
      interfaceName = "javax.jms.Queue")
  }
)
public class MessageSender {

  @Inject
  JMSContext context;

  @Resource(mappedName="java:global/jms/myQueue")
  Destination myQueue;
```

```
    public void sendMessage(String message) {
      context.createProducer().send(myQueue, message);
    }
}
```

In this code:

- `@JMSDestinationDefinitions` is used to define one or more `JMSDestinationDe` `finition`.

- `@JMSDestinationDefinition` defines a JMS `Destination` required in the operational environment. This annotation provides information that can be used at the application's deployment to provision the required resource and allows an application to be deployed into a Java EE environment with less administrative configuration. (See Table 14-3.)

Table 14-3. @JMSDestinationDefinition attributes

Attribute	Meaning
`interfaceName`	Required fully qualified name of the JMS destination interface. Permitted values are `javax.jms.Queue` or `javax.jms.Topic`.
`name`	Required JNDI name of the destination resource being defined.
`className`	Optional fully qualified name of the JMS destination implementation class.
`description`	Optional description of this JMS destination.
`destinationName`	Optional name of the queue or topic.
`properties`	Optional properties of the JMS destination. Properties are specified in the format `property` `Name=propertyValue` with one property per array element.
`resourceAdapter`	Optional resource adapter name.

- `JMSContext` is the main interface in the simplified JMS API. This combines in a single object the functionality of two separate objects from the JMS 1.1 API: a `Connection` and a `Session`. It provides a physical link to the JMS server and a single-threaded context for sending and receiving messages.

A container-managed `JMSContext` is injected via the `@Inject` annotation. Such a context is created and closed by the container, not the application. The annotation `@JMSConnectionFactory` may be used to specify the JNDI lookup name of the connection factory used to create the `JMSContext`:

```
@Inject
@JMSConnectionFactory("jms/myConnectionFactory")
private JMSContext context;
```

A preconfigured and a default `JMSConnectionFactory` are accessible under the JNDI name `java:comp/DefaultJMSConnectionFactory`. If the `@JMSConnection` `Factory` annotation is omitted, then the platform default connection factory is used.

The @JMSPasswordCredential annotation can be used to specify the username and password that will be used when the JMSContext is created. Passwords may be specified as an alias, which allows the password to be defined in a secure manner separately from the application.

- Destination encapsulates a provider-specific address. A Queue or Topic may be injected here instead. You inject both of these objects by using @Resource and specifying the JNDI name of the resource.

- When an application needs to send messages, it uses the createProducer method to create a JMSProducer, which provides methods to configure and send messages. It provides various send methods to send a message to a specified destination.

Note that no explicit exception handling is required, as send methods throw only an instance of a runtime exception.

Various setter methods on JMSProducer all return the JMSProducer object. This allows method calls to be chained together, allowing a fluid programming style:

```
context
  .createProducer()
  .setProperty(...)
  .setTimeToLive(...)
  .setDeliveryMode(...)
  .setPriorty(...)
  .send(...);
```

By default, a message is sent synchronously. You can send messages asynchronously by calling setAsync(CompletionListener listener) on the JMSProducer. This is not permitted in the Java EE or EJB container because it registers a callback method that is executed in a separate thread:

```
context.createProducer().setAsync(new CompletionListener() {

  @Override
  public void onCompletion(Message m) {
    //. . .
  }

  @Override
  public void onException(Message msg, Exception e) {
    //. . .
  }
});
```

For an asynchronous message, part of the work involved in sending the message will be performed in a separate thread, and the specified CompletionListener will be notified when the operation has completed.

When the message has been successfully sent, the JMS provider invokes the callback method onCompletion on the CompletionListener object. If an exception occurs during the attempt to send the message, then the onException callback method is called.

Using the JMS 1.1 classic API, a JMS message can be sent from a stateless session bean:

```
@Resource(mappedName="java:global/jms/myConnection")
ConnectionFactory connectionFactory;

@Resource(mappedName="java:global/jms/myQueue")
Destination inboundQueue;

public void sendMessage(String text) {
  try {
    Connection connection = connectionFactory.createConnection();
    Session session = connection.createSession(false, Session.AUTO_ACKNOWLEDGE);
    MessageProducer messageProducer = session.createProducer(inboundQueue);
    TextMessage textMessage = session.createTextMessage(text);
    messageProducer.send(textMessage);
  } catch (JMSException ex) {
    //. . .
  }
}
```

In this code:

- ConnectionFactory is a JMS-administered object and is used to create a connection with a JMS provider. QueueConnectionFactory or TopicConnectionFactory may be injected instead to perform Queue- or Topic-specific operations, respectively.

  Destination is also an administered object and encapsulates a provider-specific address. A Queue or Topic may be injected here instead. You inject both of these objects by using @Resource and specifying the JNDI name of the resource.

- A Connection represents an active connection to the provider and must be explicitly closed.

- A Session object is created from the Connection that provides a transaction in which the producers and consumers send and receive messages as an atomic unit of work. The first argument to the method indicates whether the session is transacted; the second argument indicates whether the consumer or the client will acknowledge any messages it receives, and is ignored if the session is transacted.

  If the session is transacted, as indicated by a true value in the first parameter, then an explicit call to Session.commit is required in order for the produced messages to be sent and for the consumed messages to be acknowledged. A transaction rollback, initiated by Session.rollback, means that all produced messages are destroyed, and consumed messages are recovered and redelivered unless they have expired.

The second argument indicates the acknowledgment mode of the received message. The permitted values are defined in Table 14-4.

Table 14-4. JMS message acknowledgment mode

Acknowledgment mode	Description
Session.AUTO_ACKNOWLEDGE	Session automatically acknowledges a client's receipt of a message either when the session has successfully returned from a call to receive or when the MessageListener session has called to process the message returns successfully.
Session.CLIENT_ACKNOWLEDGE	Client explicitly calls the Message.acknowledge method to acknowledge all consumed messages for a session.
Session.DUPS_OK_ACKNOWLEDGE	Instructs the session to lazily acknowledge the delivery of messages. This will likely result in the delivery of some duplicate messages (with the JMSRedelivered message header set to true). However, it can reduce the session overhead by minimizing the work the session does to prevent duplicates.

The session must be explicitly closed.

- Use the session and the injected Destination object, inboundQueue in this case, to create a MessageProducer to send messages to the specified destination. A Topic or Queue may be used as the parameter to this method, as both inherit from Destination.

- Use one of the Session.create*XXX*Message methods to create an appropriate message.

- Send the message using messageProducer.send(...).

You can use this code to send messages via both messaging models.

Receiving a Message Synchronously

A JMS message can be received synchronously.

Using the JMS 2 simplified API, you can receive a message:

```
@Inject
private JMSContext context;

@Resource(mappedName="java:global/jms/myQueue")
Destination myQueue;

public void receiveMessage() {
  context.createConsumer(myQueue).receiveBody(String.class, 1000);
  //. . .
}
```

In this code:

- `JMSContext` provides the main entry to the simplified API. It provides a combination of `Connection` and `Session` from the classic API.

- `Destination` is an administered object and encapsulates a provider-specific address. A `Queue` or `Topic` may be injected here instead. You inject both of these objects by using `@Resource` and specifying the JNDI name of the resource.

- When an application needs to receive messages, it uses one of several `createCon sumer` or `createDurableConsumer` methods to create a `JMSConsumer`. A `JMSConsum er` provides methods to receive messages either synchronously or asynchronously.

- The `receiveBody` method is used to receive the next message produced for this `JMSConsumer` within the specified timeout period and returns its body as an object of the specified type. This method does not give access to the message headers or properties (such as the `JMSRedelivered` message header field or the `JMSXDeliver yCount` message property) and should only be used if the application has no need to access them.

  This call blocks until a message arrives, the timeout expires, or this `JMSConsumer` is closed. A timeout of zero never expires, and the call blocks indefinitely.

  If this method is called within a transaction, the JMSConsumer retains the message until the transaction commits.

Using the JMS 1.1 classic API, a JMS message can be received:

```
@Resource(mappedName="java:global/jms/myConnection")
ConnectionFactory connectionFactory;

@Resource(mappedName="java:global/jms/myQueue")
Destination inboundQueue;

public void receiveMessage() {
  try {
    Connection connection = connectionFactory.createConnection();
    Session session = connection.createSession(false, Session.AUTO_ACKNOWLEDGE);
    MessageConsumer consumer = session.createConsumer(inboundQueue);
    connection.start();
    while (true) {
      Message m = consumer.receive();
      // process the message
    }
  } catch (JMSException ex) {
    //. . .
  }
}
```

In this code:

- ConnectionFactory and Destination are administered objects and are injected by the container via the specified JNDI name. This is similar to what was done during the message sending.

- As was the case during message sending, a Connection object and a Session object are created. Instead of MessageProducer, a MessageConsumer is created from session and is used for receiving a message.

- In an infinite loop, consumer.receive waits for a synchronous receipt of the message.

There are multiple publishers and subscribers to a topic. The subscribers receive the message only when they are active. However, a durable subscriber may be created that receives messages published while the subscriber is not active:

```
@Resource(lookup = "myTopicConnection")
TopicConnectionFactory topicConnectionFactory;

@Resource(lookup = "myTopic")
Topic myTopic;

public void receiveMessage() {
  TopicConnection connection = topicConnectionFactory.createTopicConnection();
  TopicSession session = connection
                      .createTopicSession(false, Session.AUTO_ACKNOWLEDGE);
  TopicSubscriber subscriber = session.createDurableSubscriber(myTopic, "myID");
  //. . .
}
```

In this code, TopicConnectionFactory and Topic are injected via @Resource. Topic Connection is created from the factory, which is then used to create TopicSession. TopicSession.createDurableSubscriber creates a durable subscriber. This method takes two arguments: the first is the durable Topic to subscribe to, and the second is the name used to uniquely identify this subscription. A durable subscription can have only one active subscriber at a time. The JMS provider retains all the messages until they are received by the subscriber or expire.

A client may use QueueBrowser to look at messages on a queue without removing them:

```
QueueBrowser browser = session.createBrowser(inboundQueue);
Enumeration messageEnum = browser.getEnumeration();
while (messageEnum.hasMoreElements()) {
  Message message = (Message)messageEnum.nextElement();
  //. . .
}
```

Receiving a Message Asynchronously

You can receive a JMS message asynchronously using a message-driven bean:

```
@MessageDriven(mappedName = "myDestination")
public class MyMessageBean implements MessageListener {

  @Override
  public void onMessage(Message message) {
    try {
      // process the message
    } catch (JMSException ex) {
      //. . .
    }
  }
}
```

In this code:

- @MessageDriven defines the bean to be a message-driven bean.
- The mappedName attribute specifies the JNDI name of the JMS destination from which the bean will consume the message. This is the same destination to which the message was targeted from the producer.
- The bean must implement the MessageListener interface, which provides only one method, onMessage. This method is called by the container whenever a message is received by the message-driven bean and contains the application-specific business logic.

This code shows how a message received by the onMessage method is a text message, and how the message body can be retrieved and displayed:

```
public void onMessage(Message message) {
  try {
    TextMessage tm = (TextMessage)message;
    String message = tm.getText();
  } catch (JMSException ex) {
    //. . .
  }
}
```

Even though a message-driven bean cannot be invoked directly by a session bean, it can still invoke other session beans. A message-driven bean can also send JMS messages.

Quality of Service

By default, a JMS provider ensures that a message is not lost in transit in case of a provider failure. This is called a *durable publisher/producer*. The messages are logged to stable storage for recovery from a provider failure. However, this has performance overheads and requires additional storage for persisting the messages. If a receiver can afford to miss the messages, NON_PERSISTENT delivery mode may be specified. A JMS provider must deliver a NON_PERSISTENT message at most once. This means it may lose the message, but it must not deliver it twice. This does not require the JMS provider to store the message or otherwise guarantee that it is not lost if the provider fails.

Using the JMS 2 simplified API, this delivery mode can be specified:

```
context.createProducer().setDeliveryMode(DeliveryMode.NON_PERSISTENT);
```

All messages sent by `JMSProducer` created here will follow the semantics defined by `NON_PERSISTENT` delivery mode.

Using the JMS 1.1 classic API, you can specify the delivery mode:

```
messageProducer.setDeliveryMode(DeliveryMode.NON_PERSISTENT);
```

Using the JMS 1.1 classic API, you can also specify the delivery mode for each message:

```
messageProducer.send(textMessage, DeliveryMode.NON_PERSISTENT, 6, 5000);
```

In this code, `textMessage` is the message to be sent with the `NON_PERSISTENT` delivery mode. The third argument defines the priority of the message and the last argument defines the expiration time.

JMS defines the priority of a message on a scale of 0 (lowest) to 9 (highest). By default, the priority of a message is 4 (`Message.DEFAULT_PRIORITY`). You can also change message priority by invoking the `Message.setJMSPriority` method.

By default, a message never expires, as defined by `Message.DEFAULT_TIME_TO_LIVE`. You can change this by calling the `Message.setJMSExpiration` method.

Temporary Destinations

Typically, JMS `Destination` objects (i.e., `Queue` and `Topic`) are administered objects and identified by a JNDI name. These objects can also be created dynamically, where their scope is bound to the `JMSContext` or `Connection` from which they are created.

Using the JMS 2 simplified API, you can create a temporary destination object:

```
@Inject
JMSContext context;

TemporaryQueue tempQueue = context.createTemporaryQueue();
TemporaryTopic tempTopic = context.createTemporaryTopic();
```

Using the JMS 1.1 classic API, you can create a temporary topic:

```
TopicConnection connection = topicConnectionFactory.createTopicConnection();
TopicSession session = connection.createTopicSession(false,
                                Session.AUTO_ACKNOWLEDGE);
TemporaryTopic tempTopic = session.createTemporaryTopic();
```

Similarly, you can create a temporary topic:

```
QueueConnection connection = queueConnectionFactory.createQueueConnection();
QueueSession session = connection.createQueueSession(false,
                                Session.AUTO_ACKNOWLEDGE);
TemporaryQueue tempQueue = session.createTemporaryQueue();
```

These temporary destinations are automatically closed and deleted, and their contents are lost when the connection is closed. You can also explicitly delete them by calling the `TemporaryQueue.delete` or `TemporaryTopic.delete` method.

You can use these temporary destinations to simulate a request-reply design pattern by using the `JMSReplyTo` and `JMSCorrelationID` header fields.

CHAPTER 15
Batch Processing

Batch Applications for the Java Platform is defined as JSR 352, and the complete specification can be downloaded (*http://jcp.org/aboutJava/communityprocess/final/jsr352/index.html*).

Batch processing is the execution of a series of *jobs* and is suitable for noninteractive, bulk-oriented, and long-running tasks. Typical examples are end-of-month bank statement generation, end-of-day jobs such as interest calculation, and ETL (extract-transform-load) in a data warehouse. These tasks are typically data or computationally intensive, execute sequentially or in parallel, and may be initiated through various invocation models, including ad hoc, scheduled, and on-demand.

This specification defines a programming model for batch applications and a runtime for scheduling and executing jobs. Key concepts of a batch reference architecture are shown in Figure 15-1 and explained following it.

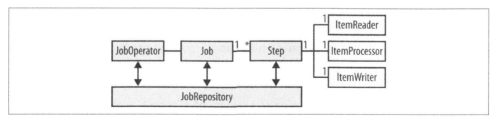

Figure 15-1. Key concepts of a batch reference architecture

- A *job* is an entity that encapsulates an entire batch process. A job is typically put together with a *Job Specification Language* and consists of one or more steps. The Job Specification Language in the Java EE 7 platform is implemented with XML and is referred to as "Job XML".

- A *step* is a domain object that encapsulates an independent, sequential phase of a job. A step contains all of the information necessary to define and control the actual batch processing.

- `JobOperator` provides an interface to manage all aspects of job processing, including operational commands (such as start, restart, and stop) and job repository commands (such as job retrieval and step executions).

- `JobRepository` holds information about jobs currently running and jobs that have run in the past. The `JobOperator` provides access to this repository.

- The `Reader-Processor-Writer` pattern is the primary pattern and uses the *chunk-oriented processing* style, in which `ItemReader` is an abstraction that represents the retrieval of an input for a step, `ItemProcessor` is an abstraction that represents the business processing of an item, and `ItemWriter` is an abstraction that represents the output of a step. `ItemReader` and `ItemProcessor` read and process one item at a time and give it to `ItemWriter` for aggregation. Once the "chunk" number of items is aggregated, they are written out, and the transaction is committed.

  Alternatively, there is a roll-your-own batch pattern, called a *batchlet*. This batch pattern is invoked once, runs to completion, and returns an exit status. This pattern must implement and honor a "cancel" callback to enable operational termination of the batchlet.

Chunk-Oriented Processing

The chunk-oriented processing style is the primary pattern for batch processing in the specification. It is an item-oriented way of processing where multiple items are read and processed to create "chunks" that are then written out, all within a transaction boundary.

The `ItemReader` interface is used to read a stream of items, one item at a time. An `ItemReader` provides an indicator when it has exhausted the items it can supply.

The `ItemProcessor` interface operates on an input item and produces an output item by transforming or applying other business processing. An `ItemProcessor` hands over the processed item to `ItemWriter` for aggregation.

The `ItemWriter` interface is used to write a stream of a "chunk" number of aggregated items. Generally, an item writer has no knowledge of the input it will receive next, only the item that was passed in its current invocation.

The convenience abstract classes `AbstractItemReader` and `AbstractItemWriter` provide implementations of less commonly implemented methods.

Table 15-1 shows the list of interfaces and corresponding abstract classes for different chunk-oriented artifacts.

Table 15-1. Interfaces and classes for chunk-oriented artifacts

Batch artifact	Interface	Abstract class
Reader	ItemReader	AbstractItemReader
Processor	ItemProcessor	None
Writer	ItemWriter	AbstractItemWriter

A simple input record can be defined thusly:

```
public class MyInputRecord {
  private String s;

  public MyInputRecord() { }

  public MyInputRecord(String s) {
    this.s = s;;
  }

  //. . .
}
```

`MyInputRecord` is an item that is read from the input source.

A simple output record can be defined as follows:

```
public class MyOutputRecord {
  private String s;

  public MyOutputRecord() { }

  public MyOutputRecord(String s) {
    this.s = s;
  }

  //. . .
}
```

`MyOutputRecord` is an item that is generated after the item is processed. The `MyInpu` `tRecord` and `MyOutpuRecord` classes look very similar in this case, but they might be very different in the real world. For example, an input record might be reading account information and an output record might be an email statement.

Job XML is used to define the chunk step:

```
<job id="myJob" xmlns="http://xmlns.jcp.org/xml/ns/javaee" version="1.0">
  <step id="myStep">
    <chunk item-count="3">
      <reader ref="myItemReader"/>
      <processor ref="myItemProcessor"/>
      <writer ref="myItemWriter"/>
    </chunk>
```

```
    </step>
  </job>
```

In this code:

- The `job` element identifies a job. It has a logical name `id` and is used for identification purposes.

- A job may contain any number of steps identified by the `step` element. Each step has a logical name `id` and is used for identification purposes.

- The `chunk` element defines a chunk type step. A chunk type step is periodically checkpointed according to a configured checkpoint policy. By default, the checkpoint policy is "item," which means the chunk is checkpointed after a specified number of items are read/processed/written. You can specify a "custom" value using the `checkpoint-policy` attribute, in which case the checkpointing algorithm needs to be specified as well.

  `item-count` specifies the number of items to process per chunk. The default value is 10. This attribute is ignored for the "custom" checkpoint policy.

  This value is used to define the transaction boundary as well.

- `myItemReader` is identified as the reader; its value is the CDI bean name of a class implementing the `ItemReader` interface or extending `AbstractItemReader`.

- `myItemProcessor` is identified as the processor; its value is the CDI bean name of a class implementing the `ItemProcessor` interface.

  This is an optional element. If this item is not specified, then all the elements from the item reader are passed to the item writer for aggregation.

- `myItemWriter` is identified as the writer; its value is the CDI bean name of a class implementing the `ItemWriter` interface or extending the `AbstractItemWriter` class.

The item reader is an implementation of the `ItemReader` interface or extends the `AbstractItemReader` class:

```java
@Named
public class MyItemReader extends AbstractItemReader {

    List<String> list;

    @Override
    public void open(Serializable c) throws Exception {
        list = ...
    }

    @Override
    public MyInputRecord readItem() {
        for (String s : list) {
```

```
        return new MyInputRecord(s);
    }
    return null;
  }
}
```

In this code:

- We mark `MyItemReader` as an item reader by extending the convenient `AbstractI temReader` class.

- The `open` method prepares the reader to read items. `List<String>` is initialized in this method.

  The input parameter `c` represents the last checkpoint for this reader in a given job instance. The checkpoint data is defined by this reader and is provided by the `checkpointInfo` method. The checkpoint data provides the reader whatever information it needs to resume reading items upon restart. A checkpoint value of `null` is passed upon initial start.

- The `readItem` method returns the next item for chunk processing. For all strings read from the `List`, a new `MyInputRecord` instance is created and returned from the `readItem` method. Returning a `null` indicates the end of stream.

- The `@Named` annotation ensures that this bean can be referenced in Job XML.

The item processor is an implementation of the `ItemProcessor` interface:

```
@Named
public class MyItemProcessor implements ItemProcessor {

  @Override
  public MyOutputRecord processItem(Object t) {
    MyOutputRecord o = new MyOutputRecord();
    //. . .
    return o;
  }
}
```

In this code:

- We mark `MyItemProcessor` as an item processor by implementing the `ItemProces sor` interface.

- The `processItem` method is part of a chunk step. This method accepts an input from the item reader and returns an output that gets passed to the output writer for aggregation. In this case, the method receives an item of type `MyInputRecord`, applies the business logic, and returns an output item of type `MyOutputRecord`. The output item is then aggregated and written. In the real world, the business logic of generating an email record from the account will be defined here.

Returning `null` indicates that the item should not continue to be processed. This effectively enables `processItem` to filter out unwanted input items.

- `@Named` ensures that this bean can be referenced in Job XML.

The item writer is an implementation of the `ItemWriter` interface or extends `AbstractItemWriter` class:

```
@Named
public class MyItemWriter extends AbstractItemWriter {

  @Override
  public void writeItems(List list) {
    //. . .
  }
}
```

In this code:

- We mark `MyItemWriter` as an item writer by extending the convenient `AbstractItemWriter` class.
- The `writeItems` method receives the aggregated items and implements the write logic for the item writer. A `List` of `MyOutputRecord` is received in this case.
- `@Named` ensures that this bean can be referenced in Job XML.

If the Job XML is defined in a file named *myJob.xml* and packaged in the *META-INF/batch-jobs* directory in the classpath, then we can start this chunk-oriented job using `JobOperator`:

```
JobOperator jo = BatchRuntime.getJobOperator();
long jid = jo.start("myJob", new Properties());
```

In this code:

- `JobOperator` provides the interface for operating on batch jobs. The `start` method creates a new job instance and starts the first execution of that instance.
- The Job XML describing the job must be available in the *META-INF/batch-jobs* directory for *.jar* files or the *WEB-INF/classes/META-INF/batch-jobs* directory for *.war* files. Job XML files follow a naming convention of *<name>.xml* where *<name>* is the value of the first parameter. The method returns the execution ID for the first instance.

You can restart the job using the `JobOperator.restart` method:

```
Properties props = ...
jo.restart(jid, props);
```

In this code, the execution ID of the job is used to restart a particular job instance. A new set of properties may be specified when the job is restarted.

You can cancel the job using the `JobOperator.abandon` method:

```
jo.abandon(jid);
```

In this code, the execution ID of the job is used to cancel a particular job instance.

You can obtain metadata about the running job:

```
JobExecution je = jo.getJobExecution(jid);
Date createTime = je.getCreateTime();
Date startTime = je.getStartTime();
```

You may specify a different set of properties during multiple executions of the same job. The number of instances of a job with a particular name can be found as follows:

```
int count = jo.getJobInstanceCount("myJob");
```

In this code, the number of `myJob` instances submitted by this application, running or not, are returned.

All job names known to the batch runtime can be obtained like so:

```
Set<String> jobs = jo.getJobNames();
```

This returns the unique set of job names submitted by this application.

Custom Checkpointing

Checkpoints allow a step execution to periodically bookmark its current progress to enable restart from the last point of consistency, following a planned or unplanned interruption. By default, the end of processing for each chunk is a natural point for taking a checkpoint.

You can specify a custom checkpoint policy using the `checkpoint-policy` attribute in Job XML:

```xml
<chunk item-count="3" checkpoint-policy="custom">
  <reader ref="myItemReader"/>
  <processor ref="myItemProcessor"/>
  <writer ref="myItemWriter"/>
  <checkpoint-algorithm ref="myCheckpointAlgorithm"/>
</chunk>
```

In this Job XML fragment:

- The `checkpoint-policy` value is specified to `custom`, indicating that a custom checkpoint algorithm is used.

- `checkpoint-algorithm` is a subelement within the chunk step whose value is a CDI bean name implementing the `CheckpointAlgorithm` interface or extending the `AbstractCheckpointAlgorithm` class.

```java
public class MyCheckpointAlgorithm extends AbstractCheckpointAlgorithm {

    @Override
    public boolean isReadyToCheckpoint() throws Exception {
        if (MyItemReader.COUNT % 5 == 0)
            return true;
        else
            return false;
    }
}
```

In this code, `isReadyToCheckpoint` is invoked by the runtime as each item is read to determine if it is time to checkpoint the current chunk. The method returns `true` if the chunk needs to be checkpointed, and `false` otherwise.

Exception Handling

By default, when any batch artifact that is part of a chunk step throws an exception, the job execution ends with a batch status of `FAILED`. You can override this default behavior for reader, processor, and writer artifacts by configuring exceptions to skip or to retry:

```xml
<chunk item-count="3" skip-limit="3">
  <reader .../>
  <processor .../>
  <writer .../>
  <skippable-exception-classes>
    <include class="java.lang.Exception"/>
    <exclude class="java.io.IOException"/>
  </skippable-exception-classes>
  <retryable-exception-classes>
    <include class="java.lang.Exception"/>
  </retryable-exception-classes>
</chunk>
```

In this code fragment:

- `skip-limit` specifies the number of exceptions this step will skip.

- `skippable-exception-class` specifies a set of exceptions that chunk processing will skip. `retryable-exception-class` specifies a set of exceptions that chunk processing will retry.

- `include` specifies a fully qualified class name of an exception or exception superclass to skip or retry. Multiple `include` elements may be specified.

- `exclude` specifies a fully qualified class name of an exception or exception superclass to not skip or retry. Multiple `exclude` elements may be specified. Classes specified here reduce the number of exceptions eligible to skip or retry as specified by `include`.

- This code fragment will skip all `Exceptions` except `java.io.IOException`.

The `SkipReadListener`, `SkipProcessListener<T>`, and `SkipWriteListener<T>` interfaces can be implemented to receive control when a skippable exception is thrown. The `RetryReadListener`, `RetryProcessListener<T>`, and `RetryWriteListener<T>` interfaces can be implemented to receive control when a retriable exception is thrown.

Batchlet Processing

The batchlet style implements a roll-your-own batch pattern. It is a task-oriented processing style where a task is invoked once, runs to completion, and returns an exit status.

The `Batchlet` interface is used to implement a batch step. The convenience abstract class `AbstractBatchlet` provides implementations of less commonly implemented methods.

Job XML is used to define the batchlet step:

```
<job id="myJob" xmlns="http://xmlns.jcp.org/xml/ns/javaee" version="1.0">
  <step id="myStep" >
    <batchlet ref="myBatchlet"/>
  </step>
</job>
```

In this code:

- The `job` element identifies a job. It has a logical name `id` and is used for identification purposes.

- A job may contain any number of steps identified by the `step` element. It has a logical name `id` and is used for identification purposes.

- The `batchlet` element defines the batchlet type step. It is mutually exclusive with the chunk element. The `ref` attribute is identified as the CDI bean name of a class implementing the `Batchlet` interface or extending `AbstractBatchlet`:

```
@Named
public class MyBatchlet extends AbstractBatchlet {

  @Override
  public String process() {
    //. . .
    return "COMPLETED";
  }
}
```

In this code:

- `MyBatchlet` is the implementation of the batchlet step.

- The `process` method is called to perform the work of the batchlet. Note, in this case, an explicit status of `COMPLETE` is returned as the job status. If this method throws an exception, the batchlet step ends with a status of `FAILED`.

- `@Named` ensures that this bean can be referenced in Job XML.

Listeners

Listeners can be used to intercept batch execution. Listeners can be specified on job, step, chunk, reader/writer/processor for a chunk, skipping, and retrying exceptions. Table 15-2 lists the interfaces and abstract classes that can be implemented to intercept batch execution.

Table 15-2. Batch listeners

Interface	Abstract class	Receive control
`JobListener`	`AbstractJobListener`	Before and after a job execution runs, and also if an exception is thrown during job processing
`StepListener`	`AbstractStepListener`	Before and after a step runs, and also if an exception is thrown during step processing
`ChunkListener`	`AbstractChunkListener`	At the beginning and end of chunk processing and before and after a chunk checkpoint is taken
`ItemReadListener`	`AbstractItemReadListener`	Before and after an item is read by an item reader, and also if the reader throws an exception
`ItemProcessListener`	`AbstractItemProcessListener`	Before and after an item is processed by an item processor, and also if the processor throws an exception
`ItemWriteListener`	`AbstractItemWriteListener`	Before and after an item is written by an item writer, and also if the writer throws an exception
`SkipReadListener, SkipProcessListener, SkipWriteListener`	None	When a skippable exception is thrown from an item reader, processor, or writer
`RetryReadListener, RetryProcessListener, RetryWriteListener`	None	When a retriable exception is thrown from an item reader, processor, or writer

The listeners can be specified in Job XML:

```
<job id="myJob" xmlns="http://xmlns.jcp.org/xml/ns/javaee" version="1.0">
  <listeners>
    <listener ref="myJobListener"/>
  </listeners>
  <step id="myStep" >
    <listeners>
      <listener ref="myStepListener"/>
      <listener ref="myChunkListener"/>
      <listener ref="myItemReadListener"/>
      <listener ref="myItemProcessorListener"/>
      <listener ref="myItemWriteListener"/>
    </listeners>
    <chunk>
    . . .
    </chunk>
  </step>
</job>
```

The listeners for the job are specified as a child of `<job>`. All other listeners are specified as a child of `<step>`. The value of the `ref` attribute is the CDI bean name of a class implementing the corresponding listener.

Job Sequence

A step is a basic execution element that encapsulates an independent, sequential phase of a job.

A job may contain any number of steps. Each step may be either a chunk type step or batchlet type step. By default, each step is the last step in the job. The next step in the job execution sequence needs to be explicitly specified via the `next` attribute:

```
<job id="myJob" xmlns="http://xmlns.jcp.org/xml/ns/javaee" version="1.0">
  <step id="step1" next="step2">
    <chunk item-count="3">
      <reader ref="myItemReader"></reader>
      <processor ref="myItemProcessor"></processor>
      <writer ref="myItemWriter"></writer>
    </chunk>
  </step>
  <step id="step2" >
    <batchlet ref="myBatchlet"/>
  </step>
</job>
```

In this Job XML:

- We define a job using two steps with the logical names `step1` and `step2`.

- `step1` is defined as a chunk type step and `step2` is defined as a batchlet type step.

- step1 is executed first and then followed by step2. The order of steps is identified by the next attribute on step1. step2 is the last step in the job; this is the default.

Other than the step, the specification outlines other execution elements that define the sequence of a job:

Flow

Defines a sequence of execution elements that execute together as a unit.

Split

Defines a set of flows that execute concurrently.

Decision

Provides a customized way of determining sequencing among steps, flows, and splits.

The first step, flow, or split defines the first step (flow or split) to execute for a given Job XML.

Flow

A flow execution element defines a sequence of execution elements that execute together as a unit. When the flow is finished, it is the entire flow that transitions to the next execution element:

```
<job id="myJob" xmlns="http://xmlns.jcp.org/xml/ns/javaee" version="1.0">
  <flow id="flow1" next="step3">
    <step id="step1" next="step2">
      . . .
    </step>
    <step id="step2" >
      . . .
    </step>
  </flow>
  <step id="step3" >
    . . .
  </step>
</job>
```

In this Job XML:

- We define a job using a flow with the logical name flow1 and a step with the logical name step3.

- We define flow1 using two steps: step1 and step2. Within the flow, step1 is followed by step2.

  A flow may contain any of the execution elements. The execution elements within a flow may only transition among themselves; they may not transition to elements outside of the flow.

- By default, flow is the last execution element in the job. We can specify the next execution element using the `next` attribute. `step3` is executed after all steps in `flow1` are finished. The value of the `next` attribute can be a logical name of a step, flow, split, or decision.

Split

A split execution element defines a set of flows that execute concurrently:

```
<job id="myJob" xmlns="http://xmlns.jcp.org/xml/ns/javaee" version="1.0">
  <split id="split1" next="step3">
    <flow id="flow1">
      <step id="step1">
        . . .
      </step>
    </flow>
    <flow id="flow2">
      <step id="step2">
        . . .
      </step>
    </flow>
  </split>
  <step id="step3">
    . . .
  </step>
</job>
```

In this Job XML:

- We define a job using a `split` with the logical name `split1` and a step with the logical name `step3`.

- A split can only contain `flow` elements. This split contains two `flow` elements with the logical names `flow1` and `flow2`. `flow1` has a step, `step1`, and `flow2` has a step, `step2`.

  Each flow runs on a separate thread.

- By default, split is the last execution element in the job. You can specify the next execution element using the `next` attribute. The split is finished after all flows complete. When the split is finished, the entire split transitions to the next execution element. `step3` is executed after all steps in the `split1` are finished.

  The value of the `next` attribute can be a logical name of a step, flow, split, or decision.

Decision

A decision execution element provides a customized way of determining sequencing among steps, flows, and splits.

Four transition elements are defined to direct job execution sequence or to terminate job execution:

next
> Directs execution flow to the next execution element.

fail
> Causes a job to end with a FAILED batch status.

end
> Causes a job to end with a COMPLETED batch status.

stop
> Causes a job to end with a STOPPED batch status.

The decision uses any of the transition elements to select the next transition:

```
<job id="myJob" xmlns="http://xmlns.jcp.org/xml/ns/javaee" version="1.0">
  <step id="step1" next="decider1">
    . . .
  </step>
  <decision id="decider1" ref="myDecider">
    <next on="DATA_LOADED" to="step2"/>
    <end on="NOT_LOADED"/>
  </decision>
  <step id="step2">
    . . .
  </step>
</job>
```

In this Job XML:

- We define a job using a step with the logical name step1, a decision execution element with the logical name decider1, and another step with the logical name step2.

- A decision element is the target of the next attribute from a job-level step, flow, split, or another decision. In this case, decider1 is specified as the value of the next attribute of step1.

- The decision element follows a step, flow, or split execution element.

  This element has a reference to the Decider batch artifact. A decider receives control as part of a decision element in a job and decides the next transition. The decide method receives an array of StepExecution objects as input. These objects represent the execution element that transitions to this decider. The decider method returns an exit status that updates the current job execution's exit status. This exit status value also directs the execution transition using transition elements configured on the same decision element as the decider:

  ```
  public class MyDecider implements Decider {
  ```

```
      @Override
      public String decide(StepExecution[] ses) throws Exception {
        //. . .
        if (...)
          return "NOT_LOADED";
        if (...)
          return "DATA_LOADED";
      }
    }
```

This method returns NOT_LOADED and DATA_LOADED exit status.

• The decision execution element uses the next transition element to transfer the control to step2 if the exit status is DATA_LOADED. The job is terminated via the end transition element if the exit status is NOT_LOADED.

Fail, end, and stop are *terminating elements*, because they cause a job execution to terminate.

Partitioning the Job

A batch step can run as a partitioned step. A partitioned step runs as multiple instances of the same step definition across multiple threads, one partition per thread. Each partition can have unique parameters that specify on which data it should operate. This allows a step to be partitioned and run across multiple threads, without any change in the existing Java code.

The number of partitions and the number of threads is controlled through a static specification in the Job XML:

```
<step id="myStep" >
  <chunk item-count="3">
    <reader ref="myItemReader">
      <properties>
        <property name="start" value="#{partitionPlan['start']}"  />
        <property name="end" value="#{partitionPlan['end']}"  />
      </properties>
    </reader>
    <processor ref="myItemProcessor"></processor>
    <writer ref="myItemWriter"></writer>
  </chunk>
  <partition>
    <plan partitions="4" threads="2">
      <properties partition="0">
        <property name="start" value="1"/>
        <property name="end" value="10"/>
      </properties>
      <properties partition="1">
        <property name="start" value="11"/>
        <property name="end" value="20"/>
```

```
          </properties>
        </plan>
      </partition>
    </step>
```

In this code:

- `<partition>`, an optional element, is used to specify that a `<step>` is a partitioned step. The partition plan is specified for a chunk step but can be specified for a batchlet step as well.

- Each `<partition>` has a plan that specifies the number of partitions via the `partitions` attribute, the number of partitions to execute concurrently via the `threads` attribute, and the properties for each partition via the `<properties>` element. The partition to which the properties belong is specified via the `partition` attribute.

  By default, the number of `threads` is equal to the number of `partitions`.

- Unique property values are passed to each partition via the `property` element. If these properties need to be accessed in the item reader, then they are specified with `#{partitionPlan['<PROPERTY-NAME>']}` where PROPERTY-NAME is the name of the property. Each partition specifies two properties, `start` and `end`, which are then made available to the item reader as `#{partitionPlan['start']}` and `#{partitionPlan['end']}`.

  These properties are then accessible in the item reader as:

  ```
  @Inject
  @BatchProperty(name = "start")
  private String startProp;

  @Inject
  @BatchProperty(name = "end")
  private String endProp;
  ```

  These properties are then available in the open method of the item reader.

Each thread runs a separate copy of the step: chunking and checkpointing occur independently on each thread for chunk type steps.

The number of partitions and the number of threads can also be specified through a batch artifact called a *partition mapper*:

```
<partition>
  <mapper ref="myMapper"/>
</partition>
```

In this code:

- The `<mapper>` element provides a programmatic means for calculating the number of partitions and threads for a partitioned step. The `ref` attribute refers to the CDI bean name of a class implementing `PartitionMapper` interface.

The <mapper> element and the <plan> element are mutually exclusive.

You can define the mapper batch artifact by implementing the PartitionMapper interface:

```
public class MyMapper implements PartitionMapper {

  @Override
  public PartitionPlan mapPartitions() throws Exception {
    return new PartitionPlanImpl() {

      @Override
      public int getPartitions() {
        return 2;
      }

      @Override
      public int getThreads() {
        return 2;
      }

      @Override
      public Properties[] getPartitionProperties() {
        Properties[] props = new Properties[getPartitions()];

        for (int i=0; i<getPartitions(); i++) {
          props[i] = new Properties();
          props[i].setProperty("start", String.valueOf(i*10+1));
          props[i].setProperty("end", String.valueOf((i+1)*10));
        }
        return props;
      }
    };
  }
}
```

In this code:

- The mapPartitions method returns an implementation of the PartitionPlan interface. This code returns PartitionPlanImpl, a convenient basic implementation of the PartitionPlan interface.

- The getPartitions method returns the number of partitions.

- The getThreads method returns the number of threads used to concurrently execute the partitions. By default, the number of threads is equal to the number of partitions.

- The getPartitionProperties method returns an array of Properties for each partition.

The partitions of a partitioned step may need to share results with a control point to decide the overall outcome of the step. The `PartitionCollector` and `PartitionAnalyzer` batch artifact pair provide for this need.

CHAPTER 16

Build an End-to-End Application

Introduction

This chapter provides self-paced instructions for building a typical three-tier end-to-end application using the following Java EE 7 technologies:

- Java Persistence API 2.1
- Java API for RESTful Web Services 2.0
- Java Message Service 2.0
- JavaServer Faces 2.2
- Contexts and Dependency Injection 1.1
- Bean Validation 1.1
- Batch Applications for the Java Platform 1.0
- Java API for JSON Processing 1.0
- Java API for WebSocket 1.0
- Java Transaction API 1.2

Software Requirements

You need to download and install the following software:

1. JDK 7 (*http://www.oracle.com/technetwork/java/javase/downloads/index.html*)
2. NetBeans 7.4 or higher (All or Java EE version) (*http://netbeans.org/downloads/*)

   Figure 16-1 shows a preview of the downloads page and highlights the exact Download button to click.

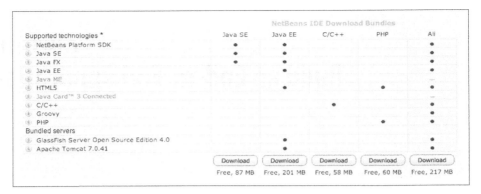

Figure 16-1. NetBeans download bundles

NetBeans comes prebundled with GlassFish 4, which provides a complete deployment and runtime environment for Java EE 7 applications.

Problem Statement

This hands-on lab builds a typical three-tier Java EE 7 web application that allows customers to view the show times for a movie in a seven-theater cineplex and make reservations. Users can add new movies and delete existing movies. Customers can discuss the movie in a chat room. Total sales from each showing are calculated at the end of the day. Customers also accrue points for watching movies.

Figure 16-2 shows the key components of the application. The User Interface initiates all the flows in the application. Show Booking, Add/Delete Movie, and Ticket Sales interact with the database; Movie Points may interact with the database (but this is out of scope for this application); and Chat Room does not interact with the database.

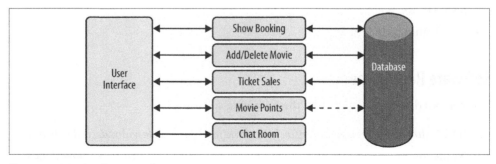

Figure 16-2. Application flow

The different functions of the application, as previously detailed, utilize various Java technologies and web standards in their implementation. Figure 16-3 shows how different Java EE technologies are used in different flows.

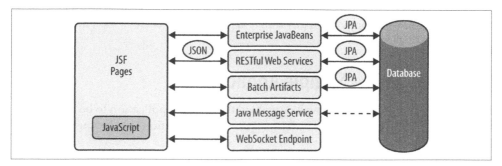

Figure 16-3. Technologies used in the application

Table 16-1 details the components and the selected technology used in its implementation.

Table 16-1. Technologies used in the application

Flow	Description
User Interface	Written entirely in JavaServer Faces (JSF).
Show Booking	Uses lightweight Enterprise JavaBeans to communicate with the database using the Java Persistence API.
Add/Delete Movie	Implemented using RESTful Web Services. JSON is used as on-the-wire data format.
Ticket Sales	Uses Batch Applications for the Java Platform to calculate the total sales and persist to the database.
Movie Points	Uses Java Message Service (JMS) to update and obtain loyalty reward points; an optional implementation using database technology may be performed.
Chat Room	Uses client-side JavaScript and JSON to communicate with a WebSocket endpoint.

Lab Flow

The attendees will start with an existing maven application, and by following the instructions and guidance provided by this lab, they will:

- Read existing source code to gain an understanding of the structure of the application and use of the selected platform technologies.
- Add new and update existing code with provided fragments in order to demonstrate usage of different technology stacks in the Java EE 7 platform.

This lab is not a comprehensive tutorial of Java EE. You can learn Java EE concepts by reading through the previous chapters of this book. The Java EE 7 Tutorial (*http://docs.oracle.com/javaee/7/tutorial/doc/*) is also a good place to learn the concepts.

This is a sample application and the code may not follow the best practices to prevent SQL injection, cross-side scripting attacks, escaping parameters, and other similar features expected of a robust enterprise application. This is intentional so as to stay focused on explaining the technology. It is highly recommended that you make sure that the code copied from this sample application is updated to meet those requirements.

Walkthrough of a Sample Application

PURPOSE: In this section, you will download the sample application to be used in this hands-on lab. Then I'll give you a walkthrough of the application to help you understand the application architecture.

1. Download the sample application (*http://glassfish.org/hol/movieplex7-starting-template.zip*) and unzip it. This will create a *movieplex7* directory and unzip all the content there.

2. In the NetBeans IDE, select File and then Open Project, select the unzipped directory, and click Open Project. The project structure is shown in Figure 16-4.

3. Maven coordinates: expand Project Files and double-click *pom.xml*. In the *pom.xml* file, the Java EE 7 API is specified as a <dependency>:

```
<dependencies>
  <dependency>
    <groupId>javax</groupId>
    <artifactId>javaee-api</artifactId>
    <version>7.0</version>
    <scope>provided</scope>
  </dependency>
</dependencies>
```

This will ensure that Java EE 7 APIs are retrieved from Maven. Note that the APIs are specified in the "provided" scope and thus are not bundled with the application and instead provided by the container.

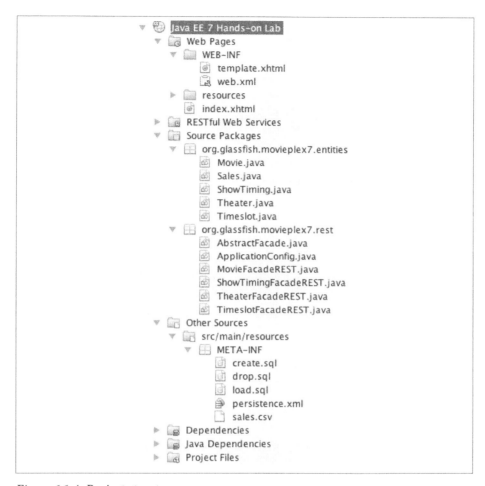

Figure 16-4. Project structure

4. Default `DataSource`: expand Other Sources, *src/main/resources*, *META-INF*, and double-click *persistence.xml*. By default, NetBeans opens the file in Design view. Click the Source tab to view the XML source.

It looks like Figure 16-5.

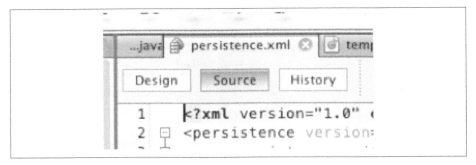

Figure 16-5. persistence.xml source tab

```xml
<?xml version="1.0" encoding="UTF-8"?>
<persistence version="2.1"
  xmlns="http://xmlns.jcp.org/xml/ns/persistence"
  xmlns:xsi="http://www.w3.org/2001/XMLSchema-instance"
  xsi:schemaLocation="http://xmlns.jcp.org/xml/ns/persistence
          http://xmlns.jcp.org/xml/ns/persistence/persistence_2_1.xsd">
  <persistence-unit name="movieplex7PU" transaction-type="JTA">
    <!--
    <jta-data-source>java:comp/DefaultDataSource</jta-data-source>
    -->
    <properties>
      <property
        name="javax.persistence.schema-generation.database.action"
        value="drop-and-create"/>
      <property
        name="javax.persistence.schema-generation.create-source"
        value="script"/>
      <property
        name="javax.persistence.schema-generation.create-script-source"
        value="META-INF/create.sql"/>
      <property
        name="javax.persistence.sql-load-script-source"
        value="META-INF/load.sql"/>
      <property
        name="eclipselink.logging.exceptions"
        value="false"/>
    </properties>
  </persistence-unit>
</persistence>
```

In this code:

a. The default `DataSource` is used, as `<jta-data-source>` is commented out. For GlassFish 4, the default `DataSource` is bound to the JDBC resource `jdbc/__de fault`.

b. The database schema will be dropped and generated by way of scripts. The create script is in *META-INF/create.sql* and the data load script is in *META-INF/load.sql*.

Feel free to open and read through the SQL scripts. The database schema is shown in Figure 16-6.

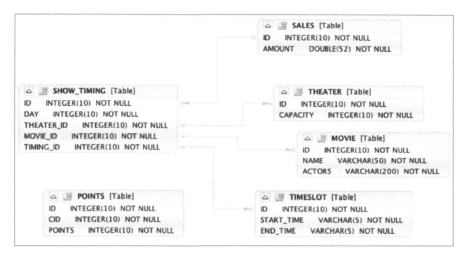

Figure 16-6. Database schema

This folder also contains *sales.csv*, which carries some comma-separated data used later in the application.

c. A persistence-provider-specific property is mentioned to suppress exception logging.

Clicking back and forth between the Design and Source views may prompt the error shown in Figure 16-7.

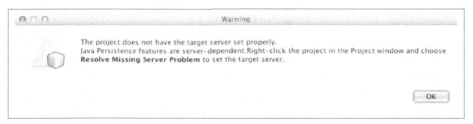

Figure 16-7. Missing server error message

This will get resolved when we run the application. Click OK to dismiss the dialog.

5. JPA entities, stateless EJBs, and REST endpoints: expand Source Packages. The package `org.glassfish.movieplex7.entities` contains the JPA entities corresponding to the database table definitions. Each JPA entity has several convenient `@NamedQuery` annotations defined and uses Bean Validation constraints to enforce validation.

The package `org.glassfish.movieplex7.rest` contains stateless EJBs corresponding to different JPA entities.

Each EJB has methods to perform CRUD operations on the JPA entity and convenience query methods. Each EJB is also EL-injectable (`@Named`) and published as a REST endpoint (`@Path`). The `ApplicationConfig` class defines the base path of the REST endpoint. The path for the REST endpoint is the same as the JPA entity class name.

The mapping between JPA entity classes, EJB classes, and the URI of the corresponding REST endpoint is shown in Table 16-2.

Table 16-2. JPA entity and EJB class mapping with RESTful path

JPA entity class	EJB class	RESTful path
Movie	MovieFacadeREST	/webresources/movie
Sales	SalesFacadeREST	/webresources/sales
ShowTiming	ShowTimingFacadeREST	/webresources/showtiming
Theater	TheaterFacadeREST	/webresources/theater
Timeslot	TimeslotFacadeREST	/webresources/timeslot

Feel free to browse through the code.

6. JSF pages: *WEB-INF/template.xhtml* defines the template of the web page and has a header, left navigation bar, and a main content section. *index.xhtml* uses this template and the EJBs to display the number of movies and theaters.

By default, Java EE 7 enables CDI discovery of beans. There is no need to bundle *beans.xml*, and you'll notice none exists in the *WEB-INF* folder.

Note, *template.xhtml* is in the *WEB-INF* folder, as it allows the template to be accessible from the pages bundled with the application only. If it were bundled with the rest of the pages, it would be accessible outside the application and thus would allow other external pages to use it as well.

7. Run the sample: right-click the project and select Run. This will download all the Maven dependencies on your machine, build a WAR file, deploy on GlassFish 4, and show the URL *localhost:8080/movieplex7* in the browser.

During the first run, the IDE will ask you to select a deployment server. Choose the configured GlassFish server and click OK.

The output looks like Figure 16-8.

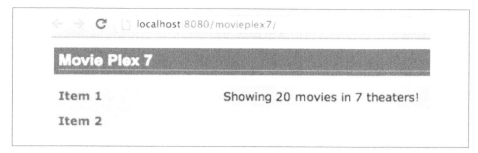

Figure 16-8. Output from the packaged application

Show Booking (JavaServer Faces)

PURPOSE: Build pages that allow a user to book a particular movie in a theater. A new feature of JavaServer Faces 2.2 will be introduced and demonstrated in this application.

This application will build a Faces Flow that allows the user to make a movie reservation. Starting from the home page, the flow will contain four pages, shown in Figure 16-9.

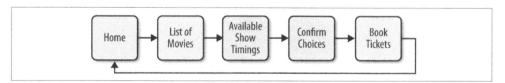

Figure 16-9. Show booking flow

1. Items in a flow are logically related to each other, so they must be kept together in a directory (Figure 16-10).

   In the NetBeans IDE, right-click the Web Pages, select New and then Folder, specify the folder name *booking*, and click Finish.

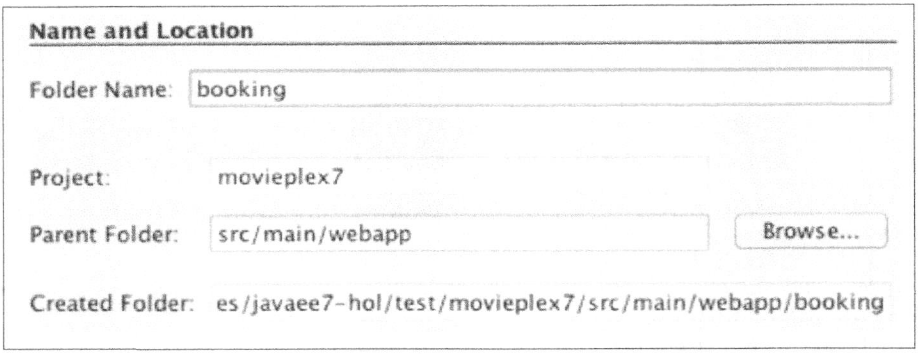

Name and Location	
Folder Name:	booking
Project:	movieplex7
Parent Folder:	src/main/webapp
Created Folder:	es/javaee7-hol/test/movieplex7/src/main/webapp/booking

Figure 16-10. Create a new folder

2. Right-click the newly created folder; select New and then Facelets Template Client; and click Next >.

    Specify the filename as *booking*. Click Browse next to Template:, expand Web Pages and then WEB-INF, select *template.xhtml*, and click Select File such that it looks like Figure 16-11. Click Finish.

    In this file, remove the `<ui:define>` sections with "top" and "left" names, as these are inherited from the template.

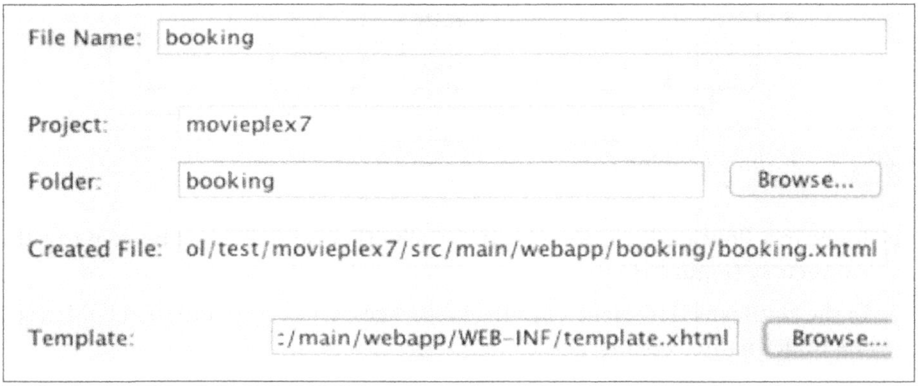

File Name:	booking	
Project:	movieplex7	
Folder:	booking	Browse...
Created File:	ol/test/movieplex7/src/main/webapp/booking/booking.xhtml	
Template:	:/main/webapp/WEB-INF/template.xhtml	Browse...

Figure 16-11. Facelets template client filename

3. *booking.xhtml* is the entry point to the flow (more on this later). Replace the "content" `<ui:define>` section such that it looks like the following code fragment:

```
<ui:define name="content">
  <h2>Pick a movie</h2>
  <h:form prependId="false">

    <h:selectOneRadio value="#{booking.movieId}"
```

```
                    layout="pageDirection"
                    required="true">
        <f:selectItems value="#{movieFacadeREST.all}"
                    var="m"
                    itemValue="#{m.id}"
                    itemLabel="#{m.name}"/>
    </h:selectOneRadio>

    <h:commandButton id="shows" value="Pick a time" action="showtimes" />
    </h:form>
</ui:define>
```

The code builds an HTML form that displays the list of movies as radio button choices. The chosen movie is bound to `#{booking.movieId}`, which will be defined as a flow-scoped bean. The value of the `action` attribute on `commandButton` refers to the next view in the flow—*showtimes.xhtml* in the same directory, in our case.

Click the hint (shown as a yellow lightbulb) and click the suggestion to add the namespace prefix. Do the same for the `f:` prefix, as shown in Figure 16-12.

Figure 16-12. Resolve namespace prefix/URI mapping for h: and f:

4. Right-click Source Packages and select New and then Java Class. Specify the class name as `Booking` and the package name as `org.glassfish.movieplex7.booking`.

Add the `@Named` class-level annotation to make the class EL-injectable. Add `@Flow Scoped("booking")` to define the scope of the bean as the flow. The bean is automatically activated and passivated as the flow is entered or exited.

Add the following field:

```
int movieId;
```

and generate getters/setters by going to Source and then Insert Code, selecting Getter and Setter, and then selecting the field.

Add the following convenience method:

```
public String getMovieName() {
    try {
        return em.createNamedQuery("Movie.findById", Movie.class)
                .setParameter("id", movieId)
```

```
                    .getSingleResult()
                    .getName();
        } catch (NoResultException e) {
            return "";
        }
    }
```

This method will return the movie name based upon the selected movie. Inject `EntityManager` in this class by adding the following code:

```
@PersistenceContext
EntityManager em;
```

Alternatively, the movie ID and name may be passed from the selected radio button and parsed in the backing bean. This will save an extra trip to the database.

5. Create *showtimes.xhtml* in the *booking* folder following the directions in step 2 on page 284. Replace the "content" `<ui:define>` section such that it looks like:

```
<ui:define name="content">
  <h2>Show Timings for <font color="red">#{booking.movieName}</font></h2>
  <h:form>
    <h:selectOneRadio value="#{booking.startTime}"
                      layout="pageDirection"
                      required="true">
      <c:forEach items="#{timeslotFacadeREST.all}" var="s">
        <f:selectItem itemValue="#{s.id},#{s.startTime}"
                      itemLabel="#{s.startTime}"/>
      </c:forEach>
    </h:selectOneRadio>
    <h:commandButton value="Confirm" action="confirm" />
    <h:commandButton id="back" value="Back" action="booking" />
  </h:form>
</ui:define>
```

This code builds an HTML form that displays the chosen movie name and all the showtimes. `#{timeslotFacadeREST.all}` returns the list of all the movies and iterates over them via a `c:forEach` loop. The ID and start time of the selected show are bound to `#{booking.startTime}`. One command button (`value="Back"`) allows the user to go back to the previous page, and the other command button (`value="Confirm"`) takes the user to the next view in the flow—*confirm.xhtml*, in our case.

Typically a user will expect the showtimes only for the selected movie, but all the showtimes are shown here. This allows us to demonstrate going back and forth within a flow if an incorrect showtime for a movie is chosen. You could write a different query that displays only the shows available for the chosen movie; however, this is not part of the application.

6. Add the following fields to the `Booking` class:

```
String startTime;
int startTimeId;
```

And the following methods:

```
public String getStartTime() {
    return startTime;
}

public void setStartTime(String startTime) {
    StringTokenizer tokens = new StringTokenizer(startTime, ",");
    startTimeId = Integer.parseInt(tokens.nextToken());
    this.startTime = tokens.nextToken();
}

public int getStartTimeId() {
    return startTimeId;
}
```

These methods will parse the values received from the form. Also add the following method:

```
public String getTheater() {
  // for a movie and show
  try {
    // Always return the first theater
    List<ShowTiming> list =
        em.createNamedQuery("ShowTiming.findByMovieAndTimingId",
                            ShowTiming.class)
        .setParameter("movieId", movieId)
        .setParameter("timingId", startTimeId)
        .getResultList();
    if (list.isEmpty())
      return "none";

    return list
      .get(0)
      .getTheaterId()
      .getId().toString();
  } catch (NoResultException e) {
    return "none";
  }
}
```

This method will find the first theater available for the chosen movie and show timing.

Additionally, a list of theaters offering that movie may be shown in a separate page.

7. Create a *confirm.xhtml* page in the *booking* folder by following the directions defined in step 2 on page 284. Replace the "content" <ui:define> section:

```
<ui:define name="content">
  <c:choose>
    <c:when test="#{booking.theater == 'none'}">
      <h2>No theater found, choose a different time</h2>
      <h:form>
```

```
        Movie name: #{booking.movieName}<p/>
        Starts at: #{booking.startTime}<p/>
        <h:commandButton id="back" value="Back" action="showtimes"/>
      </h:form>
    </c:when>
    <c:otherwise>
      <h2>Confirm ?</h2>
      <h:form>
        Movie name: #{booking.movieName}<p/>
        Starts at: #{booking.startTime}<p/>
        Theater: #{booking.theater}<p/>
        <p/><h:commandButton id="next" value="Book" action="print"/>
        <h:commandButton id="back" value="Back" action="showtimes"/>
      </h:form>
    </c:otherwise>
  </c:choose>
</ui:define>
```

The code displays the selected movie, showtime, and theater if available. The reservation can proceed if all three are available. *print.xhtml*, identified by the `action` of `commandButton` with `Book` value, is the last page that shows the confirmed reservation.

You can add `actionListener` to `commandButton` to invoke the business logic for making the reservation. Additional pages may be added to take the credit card details and email address.

8. Create the *print.xhtml* page in the *booking* folder by following the directions defined in step 2 on page 284 and replace the "content" `<ui:define>` section such that it looks like:

```
<ui:define name="content">
  <h2>Reservation Confirmed</h2>
  <h:form>
    Movie name: #{booking.movieName}<p/>
    Starts at: #{booking.startTime}<p/>
    Theater: #{booking.theater}<p/>
    <p/><h:commandButton id="home" value="home" action="goHome" /></p>
  </h:form>
</ui:define>
```

This code displays the movie name, showtimes, and the selected theater.

The `commandButton` initiates exit from the flow. The `action` attribute defines a navigation rule that will be defined in the next step.

9. *booking.xhtml*, *showtimes.xhtml*, *confirm.xhtml*, and *print.xhtml* are all in the same directory. Now we need to inform the runtime that the views in this directory are to be treated as view nodes in a flow. We can do this by adding *booking/booking-flow.xml* or by having a class that has a method with `@Produces @FlowDefinition`.

Right-click the *Web Pages/booking* folder; select New, Other, XML, and then XML Document; specify the name as *booking-flow*; click Next >; leave the default of Well-Formed Document; and click Finish. Edit the file such that it looks like:

```
<faces-config version="2.2" xmlns="http://xmlns.jcp.org/xml/ns/javaee"
    xmlns:xsi="http://www.w3.org/2001/XMLSchema-instance"
    xsi:schemaLocation="
        http://xmlns.jcp.org/xml/ns/javaee
        http://xmlns.jcp.org/xml/ns/javaee/web-facesconfig_2_2.xsd">

    <flow-definition id="booking">
      <flow-return id="goHome">
        <from-outcome>/index</from-outcome>
      </flow-return>
    </flow-definition>

</faces-config>
```

This defines the flow graph. It uses the standard parent element used in any *faces-config.xml* file but defines a `<flow-definition>`.

`<flow-return>` defines a return node in a flow graph. `<from-outcome>` contains the node value, or an EL expression that defines the node, to return to. In this case, the navigation returns to the home page.

10. Finally, invoke the flow by editing *WEB-INF/template.xhtml* and changing:

```
<h:commandLink action="item1">Item 1</h:commandLink>
```

to:

```
<h:commandLink action="booking">Book a movie</h:commandLink>
```

commandLink renders an HTML anchor tag that behaves like a form submit button. The action attribute points to the directory where all views for the flow are stored. This directory already contains *booking-flow.xml*, which defines the flow of the pages.

11. Run the project by right-clicking the project and selecting Run. The browser shows the updated output (Figure 16-13).

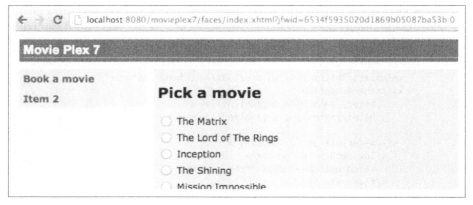

Figure 16-13. "Pick a movie" page output

Click "Book a movie" to see the page shown in Figure 16-14.

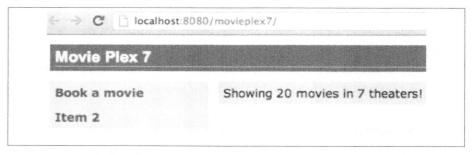

Figure 16-14. The "Book a movie" link

Select a movie, say *The Shining*, and click "Pick a time" to see the page output shown in Figure 16-15.

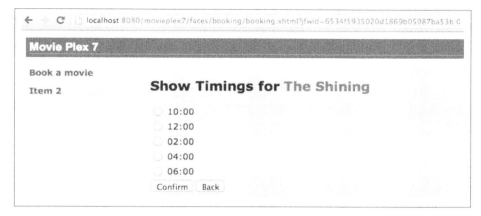

Figure 16-15. Showtimes page output

Pick a time slot, say "04:00," to see the output shown in Figure 16-16.

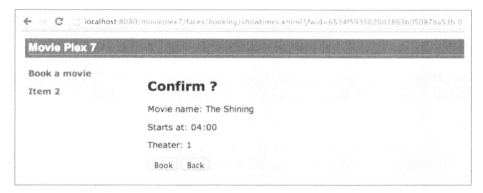

Figure 16-16. "Confirm booking" page output

Click Book to confirm and see the output in Figure 16-17.

Figure 16-17. "Reservation confirmed" page output

Feel free to enter other combinations, go back and forth in the flow, and notice how the values in the bean are preserved.

Clicking Home takes the user to the main application page as shown in Figure 16-13.

Chat Room (Java API for WebSocket)

PURPOSE: Build a chat room for viewers. Several new features of the Java API for WebSocket 1.0 will be introduced and demonstrated in this application.

This section will build a chat room for movie viewers.

1. Right-click Source Packages; select New and then Java Class. Specify the class name as ChatServer and the package as `org.glassfish.movieplex7.chat`, and click Finish.

2. Change the class such that it looks like:

```
@ServerEndpoint("/websocket")
public class ChatServer {

    private static final Set<Session> peers =
            Collections.synchronizedSet(new HashSet<Session>());

    @OnOpen
    public void onOpen(Session peer) {
      peers.add(peer);
    }

    @OnClose
    public void onClose(Session peer) {
      peers.remove(peer);
    }
```

```
@OnMessage
public void message(String message, Session client)
        throws IOException, EncodeException {
    for (Session peer : peers) {
        peer.getBasicRemote().sendObject(message);
    }
}
}
```

In this code:

- @ServerEndpoint decorates the class to be a WebSocket endpoint. The value defines the URI where this endpoint is published.

- @OnOpen and @OnClose decorate the methods that must be called when the Web-Socket session is opened or closed. The peer parameter defines the client requesting connection initiation and termination.

- @OnMessage decorates the message that receives the incoming WebSocket message. The first parameter, message, is the payload of the message. The second parameter, client, defines the other end of the WebSocket connection. The method implementation transmits the received message to all clients connected to this endpoint.

Resolve the imports. Make sure to pick the java.websocket.Session instead of the default.

3. In Web Pages, select New and then Folder, specify the folder name as *chat*, and click Finish.

4. Create *chatroom.xhtml* in the *chat* folder following the directions outlined in step 2 on page 284. Replace the "content" <ui:define> section such that it looks like:

```
<ui:define name="content">
  <form action="">
    <table>
      <tr>
        <td>
          Chat Log<br/>
          <textarea readonly="true" rows="6" cols="50" id="chatlog">
          </textarea>
        </td>
        <td>
          Users<br/>
          <textarea readonly="true" rows="6" cols="20" id="users">
          </textarea>
        </td>
      </tr>
      <tr>
        <td colspan="2">
          <input id="textField" name="name" value="Duke" type="text"/>
          <input onclick="join();" value="Join" type="button"/>
```

```
                    <input onclick="send_message();" value="Send" type="button"/><p/>
                    <input onclick="disconnect();" value="Disconnect" type="button"/>
                </td>
            </tr>
        </table>
    </form>
    <div id="output"></div>
    <script language="javascript"
            type="text/javascript"
            src="${facesContext.externalContext.requestContextPath}
                /chat/websocket.js">
    </script>
</ui:define>
```

The code builds an HTML form that has two textareas—one to display the chat log and the other to display the list of users currently logged in. A single text box is used for the username or the chat message. Clicking the Join button takes the username as the value, while clicking Send takes the chat message as the value. JavaScript methods, which will be explained in the next section, are invoked when these buttons are clicked. The chat messages are sent and received as WebSocket payloads. There is an explicit button to disconnect the WebSocket connection. The output div is the placeholder for status messages. The WebSocket initialization occurs in the *websocket.js* file included at the bottom of the fragment. See Figure 16-18.

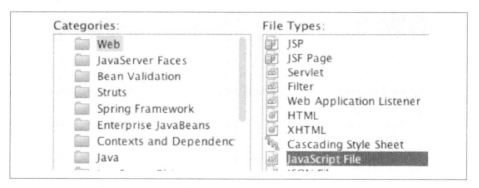

Figure 16-18. Select JavaScript file type

5. Right-click "chat" in Web Pages and then select New, Web, and JavaScript File. Specify the name as "websocket" and click Finish.

6. Edit the contents of *websocket.js* such that it looks like:

```
var wsUri = 'ws://' + document.location.host
                + document.location.pathname.substr(0,
                    document.location.pathname.indexOf("/faces"))
                + '/websocket';
console.log(wsUri);
```

```
var websocket = new WebSocket(wsUri);

var textField = document.getElementById("textField");
var users = document.getElementById("users");
var chatlog = document.getElementById("chatlog");

var username;
websocket.onopen = function(evt) { onOpen(evt); };
websocket.onmessage = function(evt) { onMessage(evt); };
websocket.onerror = function(evt) { onError(evt); };
websocket.onclose = function(evt) { onClose(evt); };
var output = document.getElementById("output");

function join() {
    username = textField.value;
    websocket.send(username + " joined");
}

function send_message() {
    websocket.send(username + ": " + textField.value);
}

function onOpen() {
    writeToScreen("CONNECTED");
}

function onClose() {
    writeToScreen("DISCONNECTED");
}

function onMessage(evt) {
  writeToScreen("RECEIVED: " + evt.data);
  if (evt.data.indexOf("joined") !== -1) {
    users.innerHTML +=
      evt.data.substring(0, evt.data.indexOf(" joined")) + "\n";
  } else {
    chatlog.innerHTML += evt.data + "\n";
  }
}

function onError(evt) {
  writeToScreen('<span style="color: red;">ERROR:</span> ' + evt.data);
}

function disconnect() {
    websocket.close();
}

function writeToScreen(message) {
    var pre = document.createElement("p");
    pre.style.wordWrap = "break-word";
    pre.innerHTML = message;
```

```
        output.appendChild(pre);
    }
```

You calculate the WebSocket endpoint URI by using standard JavaScript variables and appending the URI specified in the ChatServer class. You initialize the Web-Socket by calling new WebSocket(...). Event handlers are registered for life-cycle events via onXXX messages. The listeners registered in this script are explained in Table 16-3.

Table 16-3. WebSocket event listeners

Listeners	Called when
onOpen(evt)	WebSocket connection is initiated
onMessage(evt)	WebSocket message is received
onError(evt)	Error occurs during the communication
onClose(evt)	WebSocket connection is terminated

Any relevant data is passed along as a parameter to the function. Each method prints the status on the browser using the writeToScreen utility method. The join method sends a message to the endpoint indicating that a particular user has joined. The endpoint then broadcasts the message to all the listening clients. The send_mes sage method appends the logged-in username and the value of the text field and broadcasts to all the clients similarly. The onMessage method updates the list of logged-in users as well.

7. Edit *WEB-INF/template.xhtml* and change:

```
<h:outputLink value="item2.xhtml">Item 2</h:outputLink>
```

to:

```
<h:outputLink
   value="${facesContext.externalContext.requestContextPath}/faces
         /chat/chatroom.xhtml">
   Chat Room</h:outputLink>
```

The outputLink tag renders an HTML anchor tag with an href attribute. ${face sContext.externalContext.requestContextPath} provides the request URI that identifies the web application context for this request. This allows the links in the left navigation bar to be fully qualified URLs.

8. Run the project by right-clicking the project and selecting Run. The browser shows *localhost:8080/movieplex7*, as shown in Figure 16-19.

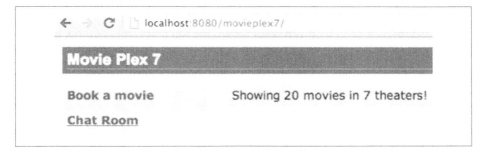

Figure 16-19. Chat room link

Click Chat Room to see the output shown in Figure 16-20.

The "CONNECTED" status message is shown and indicates that a WebSocket connection with the endpoint has been established.

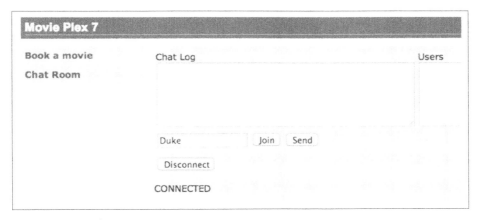

Figure 16-20. Chat room page output

Please make sure your browser supports WebSocket in order for this page to show up successfully. Chrome 14.0+, Firefox 11.0+, Safari 6.0+, and IE 10.0+ are the browsers that support WebSocket. A complete list of supported browsers is available at *caniuse.com/websockets*.

Open the URI *localhost:8080/movieplex7* in another browser window. Enter **Duke** in the text box in the first browser and click Join. Notice that the user list and the status message in both the browsers gets updated. Enter **Duke2** in the text box of the second browser and click Join. Once again, the user list and the status message in both the browsers is updated. Now you can type any message in either browser and click Send to send the message.

The output from two different browsers after the initial greeting looks like Figure 16-21. Chrome output is shown on the top and Firefox on the bottom.

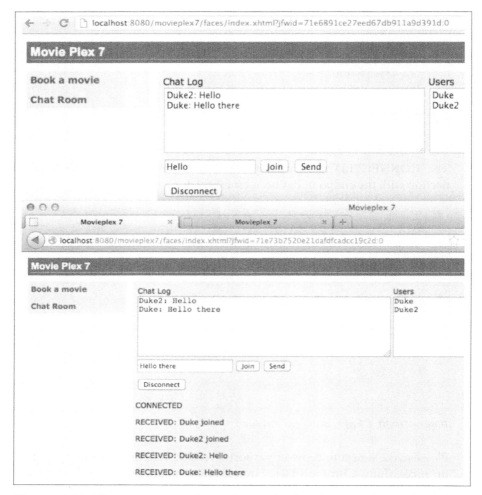

Figure 16-21. Chat room output from Chrome (top) and Firefox (bottom)

Chrome Developer Tools can be used to monitor WebSocket traffic.

View and Delete Movies (Java API for RESTful Web Services)

PURPOSE: View and delete a movie. Several new features of JAX-RS 2 will be introduced and demonstrated in this application.

This section will enable us to view all the movies, view details of a selected movie, and delete an existing movie using the JAX-RS Client API.

1. Right-click Source Packages and then select New and Java Class. Specify the class name as `MovieClientBean` and the package as `org.glassfish.movieplex7.client`, and click Finish.

   This bean will be used to invoke the REST endpoint.

2. Add the `@Named` and `@RequestScoped` class-level annotations. This allows the class to be injected in an EL expression and also defines the bean to be automatically activated and passivated with the request.

   Make sure to resolve the imports by clicking the yellow lightbulb or right-clicking the editor pane and selecting Fix Imports (use the Command + Shift + I shortcut on Mac).

3. Add the following code to the class:

```java
Client client;
WebTarget target;

@PostConstruct
public void init() {
    client = ClientBuilder.newClient();
    target = client
        .target("http://localhost:8080/movieplex7/webresources/movie/");
}

@PreDestroy
public void destroy() {
    client.close();
}
```

   In this code:

   - `ClientBuilder` is used to create an instance of `Client`.
   - The `Client` instance is created and destroyed in the life-cycle callback methods. We set the endpoint URI on this instance by calling the `target` method.
   - We set the URI of the endpoint on the `Client` instance using the `target` method.

4. Add the following code to the class:

```
public Movie[] getMovies() {
    return target
            .request()
            .get(Movie[].class);
}
```

Prepare a request by calling the `request` method. Invoke the HTTP `GET` method by calling the `get` method. The response type is specified in the last method call, so the return value is of the type `Movie[]`.

5. In NetBeans IDE, right-click Web Pages, select New and then Folder, specify the folder name *client*, and click Finish.

   In this folder, create *movies.xhtml* following the directions outlined in step 2 on page 284.

6. Replace the content within `<ui:define>` with the following code fragment:

```
<h:form prependId="false">
  <h:selectOneRadio
    value="#{movieBackingBean.movieId}"
    layout="pageDirection">
    <c:forEach items="#{movieClientBean.movies}" var="m">
      <f:selectItem itemValue="#{m.id}" itemLabel="#{m.name}"/>
    </c:forEach>
  </h:selectOneRadio>

  <h:commandButton value="Details" action="movie" />
</h:form>
```

This code fragment invokes the `getMovies` method from `MovieClientBean`, iterates over the response in a `for` loop, and displays the name of each movie with a radio button. The selected radio button value is bound to the EL expression #{movie BackingBean.movieId}.

The code also has a button with the label Details and looks for *movie.xhtml* in the same directory. We will create this file later.

Click the yellow lightbulb in the left bar to resolve the namespace prefix-to-URI resolution. This needs to be repeated three times—for the `h:`, `c:`, and `f:` prefixes (see Figure 16-22).

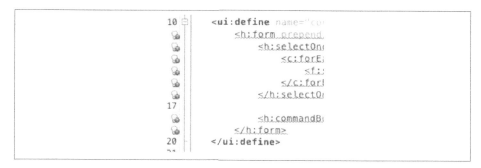

Figure 16-22. Resolve namespace prefix/URI mapping for h:, c:, f:

7. Right-click the `org.glassfish.movieplex7.client` package, select New and then Java Class, specify the value as `MovieBackingBean`, and click Finish.

   Add the following field:

   ```
   int movieId;
   ```

   Add getters/setters by right-clicking on the editor pane and selecting Insert Code (use the Control + I shortcut on Mac). Select the field and click Generate.

   Add the `@Named` and `@RequestScoped` class-level annotations.

   Resolve the imports. Make sure to import `javax.enterprise.context.RequestScoped`.

8. In *template.xhtml*, add the following code in `<ui:insert>` with `name="left"`:

   ```
   <p/>
   <h:outputLink
       value="${facesContext.externalContext.requestContextPath}/faces
               /client/movies.xhtml">
       Movies</h:outputLink>
   ```

Running the project (Fn + F6 on Mac) and clicking Movies in the left navigation bar shows the output in Figure 16-23. All movies are displayed in a list with a radio button next to them. This output uses a REST endpoint for querying instead of a traditional EJB/JPA-backed endpoint.

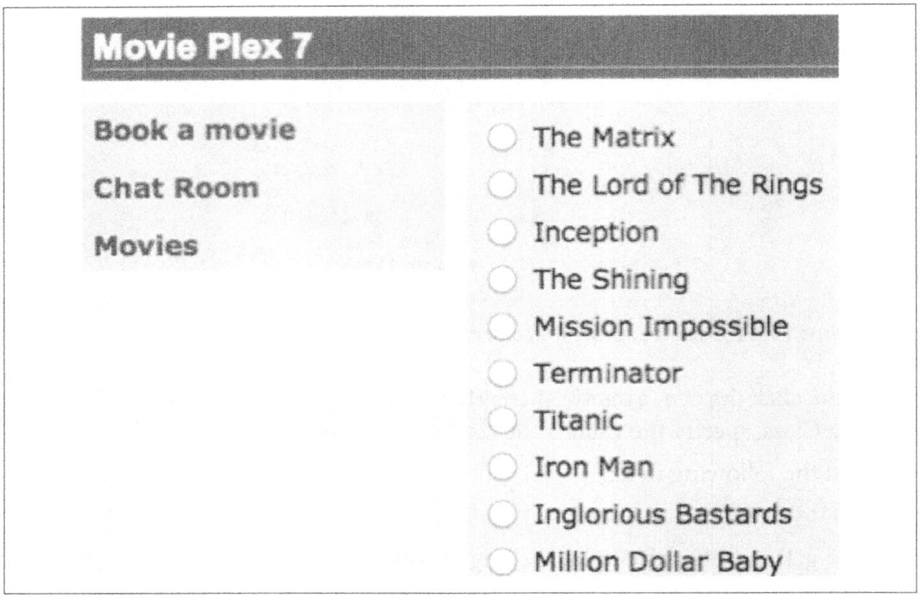

Figure 16-23. Movies page output

9. In `MovieClientBean`, inject `MovieBackingBean` to read the value of the selected movie from the page. Add the following code:

```
@Inject
MovieBackingBean bean;
```

10. In `MovieClientBean`, add the following method:

```
public Movie getMovie() {
    Movie m = target
                .path("{movie}")
                .resolveTemplate("movie", bean.getMovieId())
                .request()
                .get(Movie.class);
    return m;
}
```

This code reuses the `Client` and `WebTarget` instances created in `@PostConstruct`. It also adds a variable part to the URI of the REST endpoint, defined via `{movie}`, and binds it to a concrete value via the `resolveTemplate` method. The return type is specified as a parameter to the `get` method.

11. Create *movie.xhtml* following the directions in step 2 on page 284. Change the `<ui:define>` element such that its content looks like:

```
<h1>Movie Details</h1>
<h:form>
    <table cellpadding="5" cellspacing="5">
```

```
        <tr>
            <th align="left">Movie Id:</th>
            <td>#{movieClientBean.movie.id}</td>
        </tr>
        <tr>
            <th align="left">Movie Name:</th>
            <td>#{movieClientBean.movie.name}</td>
        </tr>
        <tr>
            <th align="left">Movie Actors:</th>
            <td>#{movieClientBean.movie.actors}</td>
         </tr>

    </table>
    <h:commandButton value="Back" action="movies" />
</h:form>
```

Click the yellow lightbulb to resolve the namespace prefix-URI mapping for h:.
Display the output values by calling the getMovie method and using the id, name,
and actors property values.

12. Run the project, select Movies in the left navigation bar, select a radio button next
    to any movie, and click on details to see the output shown in Figure 16-24.

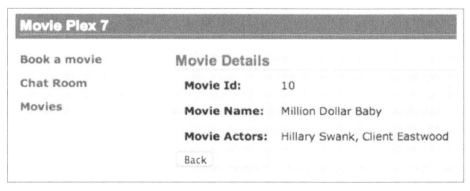

Figure 16-24. "Movie details" page output

Click the Back button to select another movie.

13. Add the ability to delete a movie. In *movies.xhtml*, add the following code with the
    other commandButton:

```
<h:commandButton
    value="Delete"
    action="movies"
    actionListener="#{movieClientBean.deleteMovie()}"/>
```

This button displays a Delete label, invokes the method deleteMovie from Movie
ClientBean, and then renders *movie.xhtml*.

14. Add the following code to `MovieClientBean`:

```
public void deleteMovie() {
    target
        .path("{movieId}")
        .resolveTemplate("movieId", bean.getMovieId())
        .request()
        .delete();
}
```

This code again reuses the `Client` and `WebTarget` instances created in `@PostCon` `struct`. It also adds a variable part to the URI of the REST endpoint, defined via `{movieId}`, and binds it to a concrete value via the `resolveTemplate` method. The URI of the resource to be deleted is prepared and the `delete` method is called to delete the resource.

Make sure to resolve the imports.

Running the project yields the output shown in Figure 16-25.

Figure 16-25. Delete button

Select a movie and click the Delete button. This deletes the movie from the database and refreshes the page.

Add Movie (Java API for JSON Processing)

PURPOSE: Add a new movie. Several new features of the Java API for JSON Processing 1.0 will be introduced and demonstrated in this application.

This section will define JAX-RS entity providers that will allow reading and writing JSON for a `Movie` POJO. The JAX-RS Client API will request this JSON representation.

This section will enable us to add a new movie to the application. Typically, this functionality will be available after proper authentication and authorization.

1. Right-click Source Packages, select New and then Java Package, specify the value as `org.glassfish.movieplex7.json`, and click Finish.

2. Right-click the newly created package, select New and then Java Class, specify the name as `MovieReader`, and click Finish. Add the following class-level annotations:

```
@Provider
@Consumes(MediaType.APPLICATION_JSON)
```

`@Provider` allows this implementation to be discovered by the JAX-RS runtime during the provider scanning phase. `@Consumes` indicates that this implementation will consume a JSON representation of the resource.

3. Make the class `implements MessageBodyReader<Movie>`. See Figure 16-26.

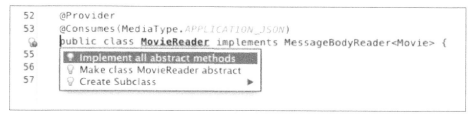

Figure 16-26. Implement abstract methods for MessageBodyReader

Click on the hint (shown as a yellow lightbulb) on the class definition and select "Implement all abstract methods."

4. Add an implementation of the `isReadable` method as:

```
@Override
public boolean isReadable(Class<?> type,
                          Type type1,
                          Annotation[] antns,
                          MediaType mt) {
    return Movie.class.isAssignableFrom(type);
}
```

This method ascertains if the `MessageBodyReader` can produce an instance of a particular type.

5. Add an implementation of the `readFrom` method as:

```
@Override
public Movie readFrom(Class<Movie> type,
                      Type type1,
                      Annotation[] antns,
                      MediaType mt,
                      MultivaluedMap<String, String> mm,
                      InputStream in)
              throws IOException, WebApplicationException {
    Movie movie = new Movie();
    JsonParser parser = Json.createParser(in);
    while (parser.hasNext()) {
      switch (parser.next()) {
```

```
        case KEY_NAME:
          String key = parser.getString();
          parser.next();
          switch (key) {
            case "id":
                movie.setId(parser.getInt());
                break;
            case "name":
                movie.setName(parser.getString());
                break;
            case "actors":
                movie.setActors(parser.getString());
                break;
            default:
                break;
          }
          break;
        default:
          break;
      }
    }
    return movie;
}
```

This code reads a type from the input stream in. JsonParser, a streaming parser, is created from the input stream. Key values are read from the parser and a Movie instance is populated and returned.

Resolve the imports.

6. Right-click the newly created package, select New and then Java Class, specify the name as MovieWriter, and click Finish. Add the following class-level annotations:

```
@Provider
@Produces(MediaType.APPLICATION_JSON)
```

@Provider allows this implementation to be discovered by the JAX-RS runtime during the provider-scanning phase. @Produces indicates that this implementation will produce a JSON representation of the resource.

7. Make the class implements MessageBodyWriter<Movie>. See Figure 16-27.

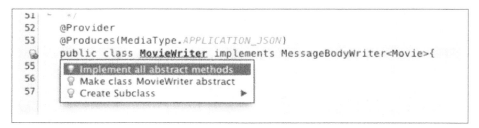

Figure 16-27. Implement abstract methods for MessageBodyWriter

Click the hint (shown as a yellow lightbulb) on the class definition and select "Implement all abstract methods."

8. Add an implementation of the isWritable method as:

```
public boolean isWriteable(Class<?> type,
                           Type type1,
                           Annotation[] antns,
                           MediaType mt) {
    return Movie.class.isAssignableFrom(type);
}
```

This method ascertains if the MessageBodyWriter supports a particular type.

9. Add an implementation of the getSize method as:

```
public long getSize(Movie t,
                    Class<?> type,
                    Type type1,
                    Annotation[] antns,
                    MediaType mt) {
    return -1;
}
```

Originally, this method was called to ascertain the length in bytes of the serialized form of t. In JAX-RS 2.0, this method is deprecated, and the value returned by the method is ignored by a JAX-RS runtime. All MessageBodyWriter implementations are advised to return −1.

10. Add an implementation of the writeTo method as:

```
public void writeTo(Movie t,
                    Class<?> type,
                    Type type1,
                    Annotation[] antns,
                    MediaType mt,
                    MultivaluedMap<String, Object> mm,
                    OutputStream out)
        throws IOException, WebApplicationException {
    JsonGenerator gen = Json.createGenerator(out);
    gen.writeStartObject()
            .write("id", t.getId())
            .write("name", t.getName())
            .write("actors", t.getActors())
            .writeEnd();
    gen.flush();
}
```

This method writes a type to an HTTP message. JsonGenerator writes JSON data to an output stream in a streaming way. Overloaded write methods are used to write different data types to the stream.

Resolve the imports.

11. In Web Pages, in the *client* folder, create *addmovie.xhtml* following the directions in step 2 on page 284. Change the `<ui:define>` element (the "top" and "left" elements need to be removed) such that its content looks like:

```
<h1>Add a New Movie</h1>
<h:form>
    <table cellpadding="5" cellspacing="5">
        <tr>
            <th align="left">Movie Id:</th>
            <td><h:inputText value="#{movieBackingBean.movieId}"/></td>
        </tr>
        <tr>
            <th align="left">Movie Name:</th>
            <td><h:inputText value="#{movieBackingBean.movieName}"/> </td>
        </tr>
        <tr>
            <th align="left">Movie Actors:</th>
            <td><h:inputText value="#{movieBackingBean.actors}"/></td>
        </tr>

    </table>
    <h:commandButton
        value="Add"
        action="movies"
        actionListener="#{movieClientBean.addMovie()}"/>
</h:form>
```

This code creates a form to accept as input the movie's `id`, `name`, and `actors`. These values are bound to fields in `MovieBackingBean`. The click of the command button invokes the `addMovie` method from `MovieClientBean` and then renders *movies.xhtml*.

Click the hint (shown as a yellow lightbulb) to resolve the namespace prefix/URI mapping.

12. Add `movieName` and `actors` fields to `MovieBackingBean` as:

```
String movieName;
String actors;
```

Generate getters and setters.

13. Add the following code to *movies.xhtml*:

```
<h:commandButton value="New Movie" action="addmovie" />
```

along with rest of the `<commandButton>`s.

14. Add the following method in `MovieClientBean`:

```
public void addMovie() {
    Movie m = new Movie();
    m.setId(bean.getMovieId());
    m.setName(bean.getMovieName());
    m.setActors(bean.getActors());
```

```
target
    .register(MovieWriter.class)
    .request()
    .post(Entity.entity(m, MediaType.APPLICATION_JSON));
}
```

This method creates a new Movie instance, populates it with the values from the backing bean, and POSTs the bean to the REST endpoint. The register method registers a MovieWriter that enables conversion from the POJO to JSON. We specify a media type of application/json using MediaType.APPLICATION_JSON.

Resolve the imports.

15. Run the project to see the updated main page as shown in Figure 16-28.

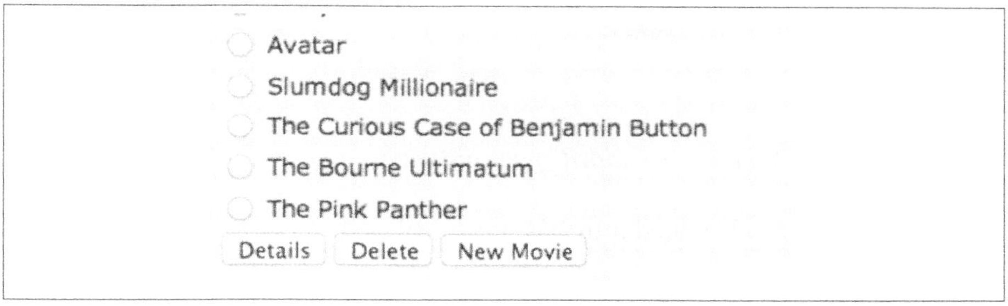

Figure 16-28. "New movie button" page output

You can add a new movie by clicking the New Movie button.

16. Enter the details as shown in Figure 16-29.

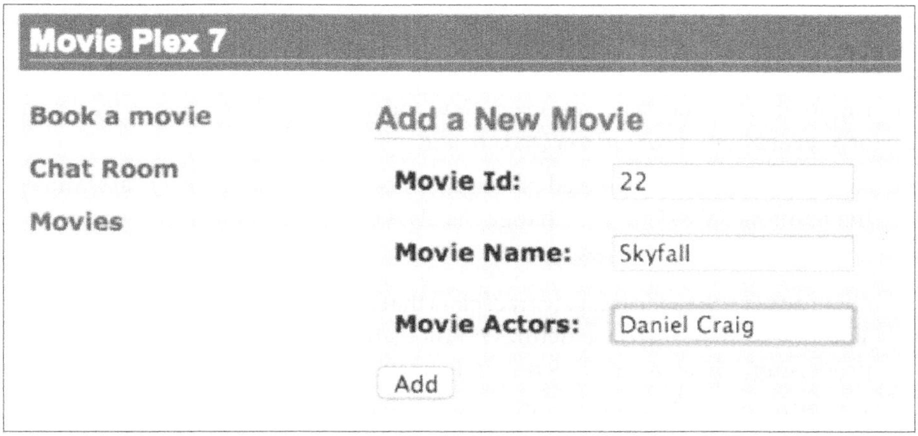

Figure 16-29. "Add a new movie" page output

Click the Add button. The Movie Id value has to be greater than 20; otherwise, the primary key constraint will be violated. The table definition may be updated to generate the primary key based upon a sequence; however, this is not done in the application.

The updated page looks like Figure 16-30.

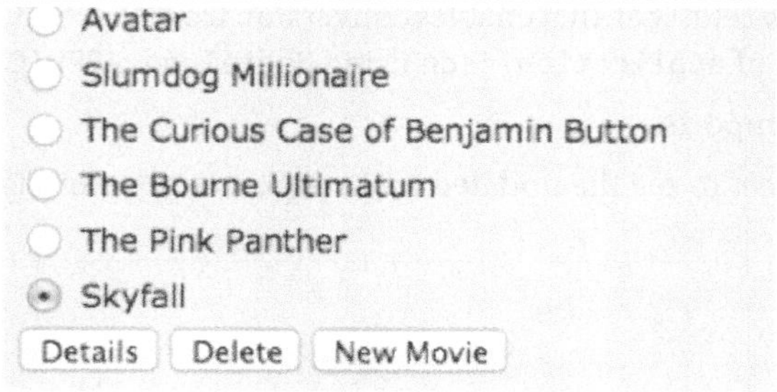

Figure 16-30. "New movie added" page output

Note that the newly added movie is now displayed.

Ticket Sales (Batch Applications for the Java Platform)

PURPOSE: Read the total sales for each show and populate the database. Several new features of the Java API for Batch Processing 1.0 will be introduced and demonstrated in this application.

This section will read the cumulative sales for each show from a CSV file and populate them in a database.

1. Right-click Source Packages, select New and then Java Package, specify the value as `org.glassfish.movieplex7.batch`, and click Finish.

2. Right-click the newly created package, select New and then Java Class, and specify the name as `SalesReader`. Change the class definition and add:

   ```
   extends AbstractItemReader
   ```

   `AbstractItemReader` is an abstract class that implements the `ItemReader` interface. The `ItemReader` interface defines methods that read a stream of items for chunk processing. This reader implementation returns a `String` item type.

   Add `@Named` as a class-level annotation; it allows the bean to be injected in Job XML. Add `@Dependent` as another class-level annotation to mark this bean as a bean-defining annotation so that this bean is available for injection.

   Resolve the imports.

3. Add the following field:

```
private BufferedReader reader;
```

Override the open method to initialize the reader:

```
public void open(Serializable checkpoint) throws Exception {
  reader = new BufferedReader(
              new InputStreamReader(
                Thread.currentThread()
                  .getContextClassLoader()
                  .getResourceAsStream("META-INF/sales.csv")));
}
```

This method initializes a BufferedReader from *META-INF/sales.csv* that is bundled with the application and is shown in Figure 16-31.

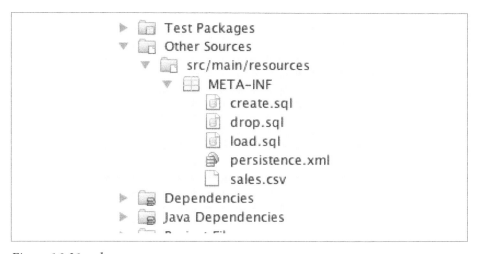

Figure 16-31. sales.csv

The following is a sampling of the first few lines from *sales.csv*:

```
1,500.00
2,660.00
3,80.00
4,470.00
5,1100.x0
```

Each line has a show identifier comma-separated by the total sales for that show. Note that the last line (5th record in the sample) has an intentional typo. In addition, the 17th record has a typo. The lab will use these lines to demonstrate how to handle parsing errors.

4. Override the following method from the abstract class:

```
@Override
public String readItem() {
    String string = null;
    try {
        string = reader.readLine();
    } catch (IOException ex) {
        ex.printStackTrace();
    }
    return string;
}
```

The `readItem` method returns the next item from the stream. It returns `null` to indicate end of stream. Note that the end of the stream indicates the end of the chunk, so the current chunk will be committed and the step will end.

Resolve the imports.

5. Right-click the `org.glassfish.movieplex7.batch` package, select New and then Java Class, and specify the name as `SalesProcessor`. Change the class definition and add:

```
implements ItemProcessor
```

`ItemProcessor` is an interface that defines a method that is used to operate on an input item and produce an output item. This processor accepts a `String` input item from the reader, `SalesReader` in our case, and returns a `Sales` instance to the writer (coming shortly). `Sales` is the prepackaged JPA entity with the application starter source code.

Add `@Named` and `@Dependent` as class-level annotations to allow the bean to be injected in Job XML.

Resolve the imports.

6. Add an implementation of the abstract method from the interface as:

```
@Override
public Sales processItem(Object s) {
    Sales sales = new Sales();

    StringTokenizer tokens = new StringTokenizer((String)s, ",");
    sales.setId(Integer.parseInt(tokens.nextToken()));
    sales.setAmount(Float.parseFloat(tokens.nextToken()));

    return sales;
}
```

This method takes a `String` parameter coming from the `SalesReader`, parses the value, populates it in the `Sales` instance, and returns it. This is then aggregated with the writer.

The method can return `null`, indicating that the item should not be aggregated. For example, the parsing errors can be handled within the method and return `null` if the values are not correct. However, this method is implemented where any parsing errors are thrown as exceptions. Job XML can be instructed to skip these exceptions, and thus that particular record is skipped from aggregation as well (shown later).

Resolve the imports.

7. Right-click the `org.glassfish.movieplex7.batch` package, select New and then Java Class, and specify the name as `SalesWriter`. Change the class definition and add:

```
extends AbstractItemWriter
```

`AbstractItemWriter` is an abstract class that implements the `ItemWriter` interface. The `ItemWriter` interface defines methods that write to a stream of items for chunk processing. This writer writes a list of `Sales` items.

Add `@Named` and `@Dependent` as class-level annotations to allow the bean to be injected in Job XML.

Resolve the imports.

8. Inject `EntityManager` as:

```
@PersistenceContext EntityManager em;
```

Override the following method from the abstract class:

```
@Override
@Transactional
public void writeItems(List list) {
    for (Sales s : (List<Sales>)list) {
      em.persist(s);
    }
}
```

The batch runtime aggregates the list of `Sales` instances returned from the `Sales Processor` and makes it available as a `List` in this method. This method iterates over the list and persists each item in the database.

The method also has a `@Transactional` annotation that provides transactional semantics to this method.

Resolve the imports.

9. Create a Job XML that defines the job, step, and chunk.

In the Files tab, expand the project → *src* → *main* → *resources*; right-click *resources* and then *META-INF*; select New and then Folder; specify the name as `batch-jobs`; and click Finish.

Right-click the newly created folder, select New and then Other, select XML and then XML Document, click Next >, specify the name as `eod-sales`, click Next, leave the default, and click Finish.

Replace the contents of the file with the following:

```
<job>
  id="endOfDaySales"
  xmlns="http://xmlns.jcp.org/xml/ns/javaee"
  version="1.0">
    <step id="populateSales" >
        <chunk item-count="3" skip-limit="5">
            <reader ref="salesReader"/>
            <processor ref="salesProcessor"/>
            <writer ref="salesWriter"/>
            <skippable-exception-classes>
                <include class="java.lang.NumberFormatException"/>
            </skippable-exception-classes>
        </chunk>
    </step>
</job>
```

In this code:

- job has one step of chunk type.

- The <reader>, <processor>, and <writer> elements define the CDI bean name
  of the implementations of the ItemReader, ItemProcessor, and ItemWriter
  interfaces.

- The item-count attribute indicates that three items are read/processed/aggre-
  gated and then given to the writer. The entire reader/processor/writer cycle is
  executed within a transaction.

- The <skippable-exception-classes> element specifies a set of exceptions to
  be skipped by chunk processing.

The CSV file used for this lab has intentionally introduced a couple of typos that
would generate a NumberFormatException. Specifying this element allows the application to skip the exception, ignore that particular element, and continue processing. If this element is not specified, then the batch processing will halt. The
skip-limit attribute specifies the number of exceptions a step will skip.

10. Invoke the batch job.

    Right-click the org.glassfish.movieplex7.batch package, and select New and
    then Session Bean. Enter the name as **SalesBean** and click Finish.

    Add the following code to the bean:

```
public void runJob() {
    try {
        JobOperator jo = BatchRuntime.getJobOperator();
        long jobId = jo.start("eod-sales", new Properties());
        System.out.println("Started job: with id: " + jobId);
    } catch (JobStartException ex) {
        ex.printStackTrace();
    }
}
```

This method uses `BatchRuntime` to get an instance of `JobOperator`, which is then used to start the job. `JobOperator` is the interface for operating on batch jobs. It can be used to start, stop, and restart jobs. It can additionally inspect job history, to discover what jobs are currently running and what jobs have previously run.

Add `@Named` and `@RequestScoped` as a class-level annotation; it allows the bean to be injectable in an EL expression and automatically activated and passivated with the request.

Resolve the imports.

11. Inject `EntityManager` in the class as:

```
@PersistenceContext EntityManager em;
```

and add the following method:

```
public List<Sales> getSalesData() {
    return em.createNamedQuery("Sales.findAll", Sales.class)
            .getResultList();
}
```

This method uses a predefined `@NamedQuery` to query the database and return all rows from the table.

Resolve the imports.

12. Add the following code in *template.xhtml* along with other `<outputLink>`s:

```
<p/>
<h:outputLink
    value="${facesContext.externalContext.requestContextPath}
            /faces/batch/sales.xhtml">
    Sales</h:outputLink>
```

13. Right-click Web Pages, select New and then Folder, specify the name as `batch`, and click Finish. Create *sales.xhtml* in that folder following the directions explained in step 2 on page 284.

Copy the following code inside `<ui:define>` with `name="content"`:

```
<h1>Movie Sales</h1>
<h:form>
    <h:dataTable value="#{salesBean.salesData}" var="s" border="1">
        <h:column>
            <f:facet name="header">
                <h:outputText value="Show ID" />
            </f:facet>
            #{s.id}
        </h:column>
        <h:column>
            <f:facet name="header">
                <h:outputText value="Sales" />
            </f:facet>
            #{s.amount}
```

```
            </h:column>
        </h:dataTable>

        <h:commandButton
            value="Run Job"
            action="sales"
            actionListener="#{salesBean.runJob()}"/>
        <h:commandButton
            value="Refresh"
            action="sales" />
    </h:form>
```

This code displays the show identifier and sales from that show in a table by invoking `SalesBean.getSalesData()`. The first command button invokes the job that processes the CSV file and populates the database. The second command button refreshes the page.

Right-click the yellow lightbulb to fix the namespace prefix/URI mapping. Repeat this process for the `h:` and `f:` prefixes.

14. Run the project to see the output shown in Figure 16-32.

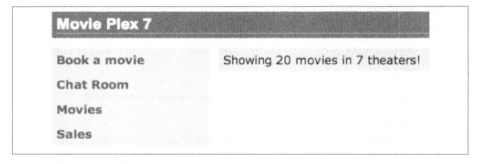

Figure 16-32. Sales link

Notice that a new Sales entry is displayed in the left navigation bar.

15. Click Sales to see the output shown in Figure 16-33.

The empty table indicates that there is no sales data in the database.

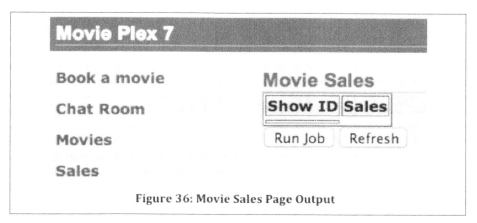

Figure 36: Movie Sales Page Output

Figure 16-33. "Movie sales" page output

16. Click the Run Job button to initiate data processing of the CSV file. Wait a couple of seconds for the processing to finish and then click the Refresh button to see the updated output, as shown in Figure 16-34.

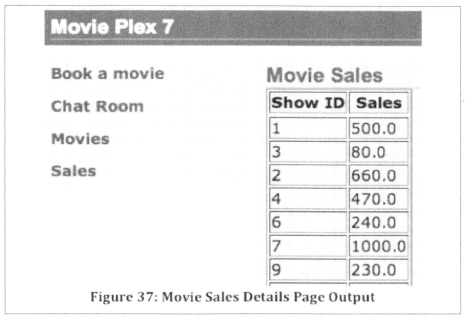

Show ID	Sales
1	500.0
3	80.0
2	660.0
4	470.0
6	240.0
7	1000.0
9	230.0

Figure 37: Movie Sales Details Page Output

Figure 16-34. "Movie sales details" page output

Now the table is populated with the sales data.

Note that record 5 is missing from the table, as this record did not have the correct numeric entries for the sales total. The Job XML for the application explicitly states to skip such errors.

Movie Points (Java Message Service 2)

PURPOSE: Customers accrue points for watching a movie.

This section will provide a page to simulate submission of movie points accrued by a customer. These points are submitted to a JMS queue that is then read synchronously by another bean. The JMS queue can continue further processing, possibly storing messages in the database using JPA.

1. Right-click Source Packages, select New and then Java Package, specify the value as `org.glassfish.movieplex7.points`, and click Finish.

2. Right-click the newly created package, select New and then Java Class, and specify the name as `SendPointsBean`.

   Add the following class-level annotations:

   ```
   @Named
   @RequestScoped
   ```

   This marks the bean to be EL-injectable and automatically activated and passivated with the request.

3. Typically, a message to a JMS queue is sent after the customer has bought the tickets. Another bean will then retrieve this message and update the points for that customer. This allows the two systems, one generating the data about tickets purchased and the other about crediting the account with the points, to be completely decoupled.

   This lab will mimic the sending and consuming of a message via an explicit call to the bean from a JSF page.

   Add the following field to the class:

   ```
   @NotNull
   @Pattern(regexp = "^\\d{2},\\d{2}",
    message = "Message format must be 2 digits, comma, 2 digits, e.g. 12,12")
   private String message;
   ```

This field contains the message sent to the queue. This field's value is bound to an inputText in a JSF page (created later). It also has a Bean Validation constraint that enables validation of data on form submit. It requires the data to consist of two digits, followed by a comma, and then two more digits. If the message does not meet the validation criteria, then the error message to be displayed is specified via a message attribute.

You could think of this as conveying the customer identifier and the points accrued by that customer.

Generate getter/setters for this field. Right-click in the editor pane, select Insert Code (use the Control + I shortcut on Mac), select "Getter and Setter," select the field, and click Generate.

4. Add the following code to the class:

```
@Inject
JMSContext context;

@Resource(lookup = "java:global/jms/pointsQueue")
Queue pointsQueue;

public void sendMessage() {
    System.out.println("Sending message: " + message);

    context.createProducer().send(pointsQueue, message);
}
```

This code uses the default factory to inject an instance of container-managed JMSContext.

All messages are then sent to a Queue instance (created later) identified by the java:global/jms/pointsQueue JNDI name. The actual message is obtained from the value entered in the JSF page and bound to the message field.

Resolve the imports.

Make sure the Queue class is imported from javax.jms.Queue instead of the default java.util.Queue, as shown in Figure 16-35.

Select the fully qualified name to use in the import statement.

Import Statements:

Resource	⬚ javax.annotation.Resource
ConnectionFactory	⊶ javax.jms.ConnectionFactory
Queue	⊶ javax.jms.Queue
Serializable	⊶ java.io.Serializable
JMSContext	⊶ javax.jms.JMSContext
Named	⬚ javax.inject.Named
SessionScoped	⬚ javax.enterprise.context.SessionScoped

☑ Remove unused imports

Figure 16-35. Resolve imports for Queue

Click OK.

5. Right-click the `org.glassfish.movieplex7.points` package, select New and then Java Class, and specify the name as `ReceivePointsBean`.

   Add the following class-level annotations:

```
@JMSDestinationDefinition(name = "java:global/jms/pointsQueue",
        interfaceName = "javax.jms.Queue")
@Named
@RequestScoped
```

   This marks the bean to be referenced from an EL expression. It also activates and passivates the bean with the session.

   `JMSDestinationDefinition` will create `Queue` with the JNDI name `java:global/jms/pointsQueue`.

6. Add the following code to the class:

```
@Inject
JMSContext context;

@Resource(lookup ="java:global/jms/pointsQueue")
Queue pointsQueue;

public String receiveMessage() {
  String message = context
                    .createConsumer(pointsQueue)
                    .receiveBody(String.class);
  System.out.println("Received message: " + message);
```

```
      return message;
  }
```

This code is very similar to `SendPointsBean`. The `createConsumer` method creates `JMSConsumer`, which is then used to synchronously receive a message.

7. Add the following method to the class:

```
public int getQueueSize() {
  int count = 0;
  try {
    QueueBrowser browser = context.createBrowser(pointsQueue);
    Enumeration elems = browser.getEnumeration();
    while (elems.hasMoreElements()) {
      elems.nextElement();
      count++;
    }
  } catch (JMSException ex) {
    ex.printStackTrace();
  }
  return count;
}
```

This code creates a `QueueBrowser` to look at the messages on a queue without removing them. It calculates and returns the total number of messages in the queue.

Resolve the imports.

8. Right-click Web Pages, select New and then Folder, specify the name as `points`, and click Finish. Create *points.xhtml* in that folder following the directions explained in step 2 on page 284.

Copy the following code inside `<ui:define>` with `name="content"`:

```
<h1>Points</h1>
<h:form>
    Queue size:
    <h:outputText value="#{receivePointsBean.queueSize}"/><p/>
    <h:inputText value="#{sendPointsBean.message}"/>

    <h:commandButton
        value="Send Message"
        action="points"
        actionListener="#{sendPointsBean.sendMessage()}"/>
</h:form>
<h:form>
    <h:commandButton
        value="Receive Message"
        action="points"
        actionListener="#{receivePointsBean.receiveMessage()}"/>
</h:form>
```

Click the yellow lightbulb to resolve namespace prefix/URI mapping for the `h:` prefix.

This page displays the number of messages in the current queue. It provides a text box for entering the message that can be sent to the queue. The first command button invokes the sendMessage method from SendPointsBean and refreshes the page. An updated queue count, incremented by 1 in this case, is displayed. The second command button invokes the receiveMessage method from Receive PointsBean and refreshes the page. The queue count is updated again, decremented by 1 in this case.

If the message does not meet the validation criteria, then the error message is displayed on the screen.

9. Add the following code in *template.xhtml* along with other <outputLink>s:

```
<p/>
<h:outputLink
    value="${facesContext.externalContext.requestContextPath}
            /faces/points/points.xhtml">
    Points</h:outputLink>
```

10. Run the project. The update page looks like Figure 16-36.

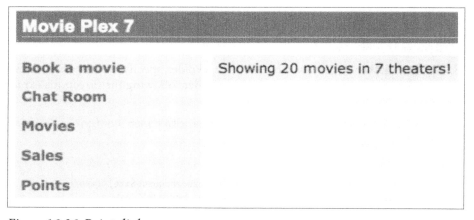

Figure 16-36. Points link

Click Points to see the output in Figure 16-37.

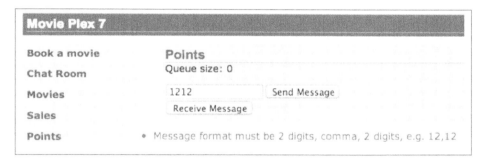

Figure 16-37. Points page default output

The output shows that the queue has 0 messages. Enter the message **1212** in the text box and click Send Message to see the output shown in Figure 16-38.

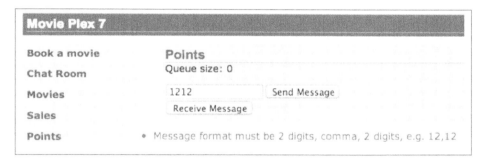

Figure 16-38. Bean Validation error message

This message does not meet the validation criteria, so the error message is displayed.

Enter the message **12,12** in the text box and click the Send Message button to see the output in Figure 16-39.

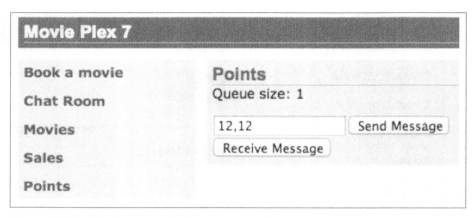

Figure 16-39. Points page output: one message in queue

The updated count now shows that there is one message in the queue.

Click the Receive Message button to see the output in Figure 16-40.

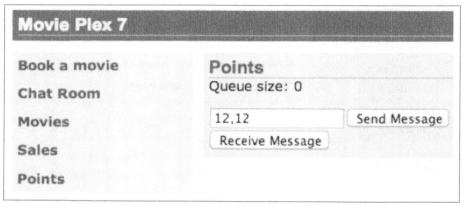

Figure 16-40. Points page output: zero messages in queue

The updated count now shows that the message has been consumed and the queue has zero messages.

Click Send Message four times to see the output in Figure 16-41.

Figure 16-41. Points page output: four messages in queue

The updated count now shows that the queue has four messages.

Click Receive Message twice to see the output in Figure 16-42.

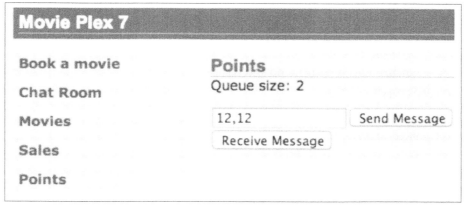

Figure 16-42. Points page output: two messages in queue

The count is once again updated to reflect the two consumed and two remaining messages in the queue.

Conclusion

This hands-on lab built a trivial three-tier web application using Java EE 7 and demonstrated the following features of the platform:

- Java EE 7 Platform
  - Maven coordinates
  - Default `DataSource`
  - Default `JMSConnectionFactory`
- Java Persistence API 2.1
  - Schema generation properties
- Java API for RESTful Web Services 2.0
  - Client API
  - Custom entity providers
- Java Message Service 2.0
  - Default JMS `ConnectionFactory`
  - Injecting `JMSContext`
  - Synchronous message send and receive
- JavaServer Faces 2.2
  - Faces Flow
- Contexts and Dependency Injection 1.1
  - Automatic discovery of beans
  - Injection of beans
- Bean Validation 1.1
  - Integration with JavaServer Faces
- Batch Applications for the Java Platform 1.0
  - Chunk-style processing
  - Exception handling
- Java API for JSON Processing 1.0
  - Streaming API for generating JSON
  - Streaming API for consuming JSON
- Java API for WebSocket 1.0
  - Annotated server endpoint

— JavaScript client

- Java Transaction API 1.2

  — @Transactional

Hopefully, this has piqued your interest in trying out Java EE 7 applications using GlassFish 4.

Send us feedback at *users@glassfish.java.net*.

Troubleshooting

1. How can I start/stop/restart GlassFish from within the IDE?

   In the Services tab, right-click GlassFish Server 4. All the commands to start, stop, and restart are available from the pop-up menu. View the server log by clicking View Server Log, and view the web-based administration console by clicking View Admin Console.

2. I accidentally closed the GlassFish output log window. How do I bring it back?

   In the Services tab of NetBeans, expand Servers, choose the GlassFish node, and select View Domain Server Log.

Completed Solution

The completed solution can be downloaded as a zip (*http://glassfish.org/hol/movieplex7-solution.zip*).

Further Reading

This appendix provides a reference to the specifications for different technologies included in the Java EE 7 platform.

Web Technology Specifications

- JSR 45: Debugging Support for Other Languages 1.0 (*http://bit.ly/1e6mrrq*)
- JSR 52: Standard Tag Library for JavaServer Pages (JSTL)1.2 (*http://bit.ly/11qaUk4*)
- JSR 245: JavaServer Pages (JSP) 2.3 (*http://bit.ly/15396AI*)
- JSR 340: Java Servlet 3.1 (*http://bit.ly/11qaWsk*)
- JSR 341: Expression Language 3.1 (*http://bit.ly/14dZKTB*)
- JSR 344: JavaServer Faces (JSF) 2.2 (*http://bit.ly/11qaYjY*)
- JSR 353: Java API for JSON Processing (JSON-P) 1.0 (*http://bit.ly/15rok02*)
- JSR 356: Java API for WebSocket 1.0 (*http://bit.ly/1aT42yz*)

Enterprise Technology Specifications

- JSR 236: Concurrency Utilities for Java EE 1.0 (*http://bit.ly/15ZXWcJ*)
- JSR 250: Common Annotations for the Java Platform 1.2 (*http://bit.ly/12yzxOk*)
- JSR 318: Interceptors 1.2 (*http://bit.ly/15ZY107*)
- JSR 322: Java EE Connector Architecture 1.7 (*http://bit.ly/15roqVy*)
- JSR 330: Dependency Injection for Java 1.0 (*http://bit.ly/17Pc8GN*)
- JSR 338: Java Persistence API (JPA) 2.1 (*http://bit.ly/17bCbpg*)
- JSR 343: Java Message Service (JMS) 2.0 (*http://bit.ly/1ch5TPl*)

- JSR 345: Enterprise JavaBeans (EJB) 3.2 (*http://bit.ly/16fbtix*)
- JSR 346: Contexts and Dependency Injection (CDI) for the Java EE Platform 1.1 (*http://bit.ly/13hceqI*)
- JSR 349: Bean Validation 1.1 (*http://bit.ly/13hcgyR*)
- JSR 352: Batch Applications for Java Platform 1.0 (*http://bit.ly/12Y8o29*)
- JSR 907: Java Transaction API (JTA) 1.2 (*http://bit.ly/1ch6sZz*)
- JSR 919: JavaMail 1.5 (*http://bit.ly/14e0mIU*)

Web Service Technologies

- JSR 93: Java API for XML Registries (JAXR) 1.0 (*http://bit.ly/1bCdevg*)
- JSR 101: Java API for XML-based RPC (JAX-RPC) 1.1 (*http://bit.ly/1aT4Nrs*)
- JSR 109: Implementing Enterprise Web Services 1.4 (*http://bit.ly/13U6xyL*)
- JSR 181: Web Services Metadata for the Java Platform 2.1 (*http://bit.ly/18J7YkO*)
- JSR 222: Java Architecture for XML Binding (JAXB) 2.2 (*http://bit.ly/11qbE8X*)
- JSR 224: Java API for XML Web Services (JAX-WS) 2.2 (*http://bit.ly/13U6EdQ*)
- JSR 339: Java API for RESTful Web Services (JAX-RS) 2.0 (*http://bit.ly/15ZZ7J8*)

Management and Security Technologies

- JSR 77: J2EE Management API 1.1 (*http://bit.ly/18NcQsE*)
- JSR 88: Java Platform EE Application Deployment API 1.2 (*http://bit.ly/17PcOMl*)
- JSR 115: Java Authorization Contract and Containers (JACC) 1.5 (*http://bit.ly/19t3oKd*)
- JSR 196: Java Authentication Service Provider Interface for Containers (JASPIC) 1.0 (*http://bit.ly/11qbK0k*)

Index

A

absolute-ordering element, 24
AbstractBatchlet class, 265
AbstractCheckpointAlgorithm class, 264
AbstractChunkListener class, 266
AbstractItemProcessListener class, 266
AbstractItemReader class, 258, 260, 261
AbstractItemReadListener class, 266
AbstractItemWriter class, 258, 260, 262
AbstractJobListener class, 266
AbstractStepListener class, 266
AbstractWriteListener class, 266
ActionEvent class, 45
@AdministeredObjectDefinition annotation, 10
AfterBeanDiscovery event, 184
AfterDeploymentValidation event, 184
Ajax, JSF support for, 43–46, 72
@Alternative annotation, 172–173, 182
alternative beans, CDI, 172–173, 182
annotated client endpoints, WebSocket, 132–135
annotated server endpoints, WebSocket, 122–127
annotations, 5
  (see also specific annotations)
@Any annotation, 172
Application class, 74, 82
application-managed entity manager, 222
@ApplicationPath annotation, 74

@ApplicationScoped annotation, 180
apply request values phase, JSF, 42
@AroundConstruct annotation, 9, 151
@AroundInvoke annotation, 175
@AssertFalse annotation, 204
@AssertTrue annotation, 204
async-supported element, 21
AsyncContext class, 21
asynchronous processing
  client invocations with JAX-RS, 86, 87
  dispatch-based dynamic client, 106
  JMS messages, 249, 253–254
  message-driven beans, 154
  programmatic client endpoints, 135
  programmatic server endpoints, 129
  server requests with Ajax, 43
  server responses with JAX-RS, 76
  servlets, 20–22
  session bean methods, 159–160
  tasks, 189–194
AsyncListener interface, 20, 22
attached objects, server-side, 47–49
@AttributeOverrides annotation, 220
auth-constraint element, 26
authentication, WebSocket endpoints, 142–143

B

Batch Applications, 3, 7, 257–258
  batchlets, 258, 265–266

We'd like to hear your suggestions for improving our indexes. Send email to index@oreilly.com.

View and Delete Movies component, 299–304

exception handling
    chunk-oriented batch processing, 264
    mapping exceptions, 29, 87–88
exception-type element, 30
exclude element, 168, 264
explicit bean archive, 168
Expression Language (see EL)
extended persistence context, 225
extension points, client-side, 47–49

F

f: prefix, 34
f:ajax element, 43–46, 49, 72
f:convertDateTime element, 47
f:converter element, 46
f:convertNumber element, 47
f:event element, 46
f:passThroughAttribute element, 60
f:passThroughAttributes element, 60
f:validateBean element, 49, 211
f:validateDoubleRange element, 48
f:validateLength element, 48
f:validator element, 46, 49
f:valueChangeListener element, 49
f:view element, 58
facelets, 34–37
    tag libraries for, 34
    template client pages for, 36–37
    templates for, 35–37, 57
Faces Flow, 51–57
    defining flows, 53
    nodes in, 52
    packaging flows, 53–57
    scope of beans in a flow, 53
faces-config.xml file, 51
@FacesBehavior annotation, 49
@FacesConverter annotation, 48
FacesMessage class, 49
@FacesValidator annotation, 49
fail element, 270
FetchType enumeration, 221
filter chains, JAX-RS, 92
filter element, 16
filter-mapping element, 16
filters
    JAX-RS, 88–92
    servlet, 16–17

flow element, 268
flow-call element, 56
flow-definition element, 53, 56
flow-return element, 56
FlowBuilder class, 53
flows, JSF (see Faces Flow)
@FlowScoped annotation, 53
fn: prefix, 34
@ForeignKey annotation, 228
@FormParam annotation, 77, 81
@Future annotation, 206

G

@GET annotation, 74, 77
GlassFish server, 6, 327
@GroupSequence annotation, 211

H

h: prefix, 34, 40
h:body element, 64
h:button element, 47, 63
h:commandButton element, 41, 44, 61, 72
h:commandLink element, 61
h:dataTable element, 61
h:form element, 62, 71
h:graphicImage element, 62
h:inputFile element, 71
h:inputHidden element, 62
h:inputSecret element, 63
h:inputText element, 40, 44, 63
h:inputTextArea element, 63
h:link element, 47, 64
h:outputFormat element, 64
h:outputLabel element, 64
h:outputLink element, 65
h:outputScript element, 43, 65
h:outputStylesheet element, 66
h:outputText element, 65
h:panelGrid element, 66
h:selectBooleanCheckbox element, 67
h:selectManyCheckbox element, 69
h:selectManyListbox element, 70
h:selectManyMenu element, 71
h:selectOneListbox element, 68
h:selectOneMenu element, 68
h:selectOneRadio element, 67
handlers, JAX-WS, 107–109
@HEAD annotation, 77, 78

@HeaderParam annotation, 7, 81
HTML5, 2
HTTP cookies, sending and receiving, 12, 14
HTTP headers, filters for, 88
HTTP messages, entity interceptors for, 88
HTTP methods, binding with JAX-RS, 77–79
HTTP requests
    binding resources to, 81–82
    JAX-RS client API handling, 84–87
    JSF support for, 46–47
    servlets handling, 12–13
HTTP upgrade processing, 31–32
http-method-omission element, 27
@HttpConstraint annotation, 25
HttpHeaders interface, 82
HttpMethod class, 79
@HttpMethodConstraint annotation, 25
HttpServlet class, 11
    (see also servlets)
HttpServletRequest bean type, 186
HttpServletRequest class, 12
    authenticate method, 28
    getPart method, 30
    getParts method, 30
    getRequestDispatcher method, 15
    login method, 28
    logout method, 28
    upgrade method, 31
HttpServletResponse class, 12
HttpServletResponse.sendRedirect method, 15
HttpSession bean type, 186
HttpSession interface, 14
HttpSessionActivationListener interface, 18
HttpSessionAttributeListener interface, 19
HttpSessionBindingListener interface, 19
HttpSessionListener interface, 18
HttpUpgradeHandler interface, 31

I

I/O, nonblocking, 22–23
@Id annotation, 220, 228
IETF RFC 6455 Protocol, 121
if element, 51
implicit bean archive, 168
inbound-parameter element, 56
include element, 264
@Index annotation, 228
@Inheritance annotation, 221
inheritance from superclasses, 221

@Inject annotation, 170–171, 248
injection points, 35, 170–171
input element, 59
@Interceptor annotation, 175
interceptor chains, JAX-RS, 93
@InterceptorBinding annotation, 175
interceptors, 5, 9, 174–178
interceptors element, 177
InvocationCallback interface, 86
invoke application phase, JSF, 42
ItemProcessListener interface, 266
ItemProcessor interface, 258, 261
ItemReader interface, 258, 260
ItemReadListener interface, 266
ItemWriteListener interface, 266
ItemWriter interface, 258, 260

J

Java API for XML Binding (see JAXB)
Java API for XML Web Services (see JAX-WS)
Java Community Process (see JCP)
Java EE 6 Pocket Guide (O'Reilly), xiii
Java EE 7, 1–3
    architecture, 5–6
    component specifications, 3–5
    deliverables, 3
    new features, 6
    specifications, list of, 329–330
    tutorial for, 277
Java EE Connector Architecture (see JCA)
Java Message Service (see JMS)
Java Persistence API (see JPA)
Java Persistence Query Language (see JPQL)
Java Specification Request (see JSR)
Java Transaction API (see JTA)
JavaMail, 10
JavaScript Object Notation (see JSON)
JavaServer Faces (see JSF)
javax.ejb package, 164
javax.faces library, 43
javax.persistence.criteria package, 229
javax.persistence.metamodel package, 229
JAX-RS (Java API for RESTful Web Services), 7,
    73
    Bean Validation with, 94–96
    binding HTTP methods, 77–79
    client API, 84–87
    entity interceptors, 88, 92–94
    entity providers, 82–84, 86

taskDone method, 193
taskStarting method, 193
taskSubmitted method, 193
ManagedThreadFactor interface, 197–198
Management and Security Technologies, 4
@ManyToMany annotation, 221
@ManyToOne annotation, 221, 228
@MapKey annotation, 222
@MapKeyClass annotation, 222
@MapKeyColumn annotation, 222
MapMessage type, 247
@MappedSuperclass annotation, 221
mapper element, 272
@MatrixParam annotation, 81
@Max annotation, 204
MDB (message-driven beans), 154–156, 253
message payload (see entity providers)
message-driven beans (see MDB)
message-oriented middleware (see MOM)
Message.setJMSExpiration method, 255
MessageBodyReader interface, 80, 83
MessageBodyWriter interface, 80, 83
MessageConsumer interface, 253
@MessageDriven annotation, 154, 254
MessageDrivenContext class, 156
MessageHandler class, 128, 135
MessageListener interface, 155
MessageListener.onMessage method, 254
MessageProducer interface, 251, 253
messages, JMS (see JMS: messages)
metadata-complete element, 14, 25
methods, constraints for, 212–214
@Min annotation, 204
Model-View-Controller (see MVC)
MOM (message-oriented middleware), 245
movie application example (see example movie application)
@MultipartConfig annotation, 30
MVC (Model-View-Controller), 33

N

@NameBinding annotation, 91
@Named annotation, 35, 172, 261
@NamedQueries annotation, 230
@NamedQuery annotation, 230, 231, 241
@NamedStoredProcedureQuery annotation, 235–236
namespaces
    for composite components, 39

for facelets tag libraries, 34
navigation rules, JSF, 51
navigation-rule element, 51
NetBeans, 275
@New annotation, 172
next element, 270
nonblocking I/O, 22–23
@NotNull annotation, 204, 207, 237
@Null annotation, 204

O

Object Model API, JSON Processing, 116–119
ObjectMessage type, 247
observer beans, 182
@OnClose annotation, 126, 132
@OnError annotation, 126, 132
@OneToMany annotation, 221
@OneToOne annotation, 221
@Oneway annotation, 100
@OnMessage annotation, 123, 133
@OnOpen annotation, 126, 132
optimistic concurrency control, 240
@OPTIONS annotation, 77, 79
Oracle GlassFish Server, 6
ordering element, 24
orm.xml file, 234

P

Part.getSubmittedFileName method, 31
partial page rendering, 43
partial view processing, 43
partition element, 272
PartitionMapper interface, 273
@Past annotation, 205
@Path annotation, 73, 74
@PathParam annotation, 74, 124
@Pattern annotation, 206, 207
payload (see entity providers)
PbC (Programming by Contract), 212
@PermitAll annotation, 27
@PerPersist annotation, 232
persistence, 9 (see JPA)
persistence context, 222–226
persistence element, 224
persistence unit, 222–226
persistence-unit element, 224
persistence-unit-metadata element, 234
persistence.xml file, 223, 226, 238, 241

SOAPHandler interface, 108
specifications, 3–5, 329–330
    (see also component specifications; JSR)
SPI (Service Provider Interface), 183–185
split element, 269
SQL queries, 229–232
@SQLResultSetMapping annotation, 229
@Startup annotation, 150
@Stateful annotation, 146
stateful session beans, 145–148
@Stateless annotation, 35, 148
stateless session beans, 35, 148–150
step element, 259, 265, 267
StepListener interface, 266
@Stereotype annotation, 181
stereotypes, CDI, 181–182
stop element, 270
stored procedures, 235–236
streaming API, JSON Processing, 112–115
StreamMessage type, 247
superclasses, entities inheriting from, 221
synchronous communication, JMS messages,
    251–253

T

tag libraries, for facelets, 34
@Target annotation, 175, 207
tasks
    CDI beans as, 191
    scheduling, 194–197
    submitting asynchronously, 189–194
TCK (Technology Compliance Kit), 3, 6
template client pages, for facelets, 36–37
templates, for facelets, 35–37, 57
templating system, 34
@Temporal annotation, 221
TemporaryQueue.delete method, 256
TemporaryTopic.delete method, 256
TextMessage type, 247
threads, managed (see managed threads)
@Timeout annotation, 162
Timer Service, EJB, 160–164
TimerService class, 161
Topic interface, 251, 253
TopicConnection interface, 253
TopicConnectionFactory interface, 250, 253
topics, JMS, 246
TopicSession.createDurableSubscriber method,
    253

@Transactional annotation, 2, 10, 177, 216–218
transactional observers, 183
@Transactional.TxType annotation, 217
@TransactionAttribute annotation, 158
@TransactionManagement annotation, 157
TransactionManager.getStatus method, 218
transactions, 10
    for asynchronous tasks, 192
    committing, 250
    container-managed, 157–159, 216–218
    bean-managed, 157–159
    entity, 239–241
    rolling back, 250
    user-managed, 215–216
@TransactionScoped annotation, 10, 218
@TransportProtected annotation, 27
type attribute, input element, 59

U

ui: prefix, 34
ui:component element, 36
ui:composition element, 36
ui:define element, 36, 37
ui:fragment element, 36
ui:include element, 36
ui:insert element, 36, 57
UIComponent class, 60
update model values phase, JSF, 42
UriInfo interface, 82
user-data-constraint element, 26
user-managed transactions, 215–216
User.nameUpdated method, 49
UserTransaction bean type, 185
UserTransaction interface, 157, 192, 215–216
UserTransaction.getStatus method, 218
using page, 38

V

@Valid annotation, 96, 209, 237
@ValidateExecutable annotation, 213
validation (see Bean Validation; constraints; val-
    idators, JSF)
Validator.validate method, 239
ValidatorException class, 49
validators, JSF, 48
ValueChangeListener interface, 49
@Version annotation, 240
@Vetoed annotation, 9, 169

About the Author

Arun Gupta is a Java Evangelist working at Oracle. As a founding member of the Java EE team, he works to create and foster the community around Java EE, GlassFish, and WebLogic. He led a cross-functional team to drive the global launch of the Java EE 7 platform through strategy, planning, and execution of content, marketing campaigns, and programs. He is extremely passionate about developers and loves to engage with partners, customers, Java user groups, Java champions, and others around the world to spread the goodness of Java. Arun has extensive speaking experience in more than 30 countries on myriad topics. An author, a prolific blogger at *blogs.oracle.com/arungupta*, an avid runner, and a globe trotter, Arun is easily accessible at @arungupta.

Colophon

The animals on the cover of *Java EE 7 Essentials* are Asiatic glassfish (members of the family *Ambassidae*). Found only in the waters of Asia and Oceania, the fish in this family are divided into eight genera that include around 40 species. In addition to the Asiatic glassfish, the family also includes the Striped Glass Catfish, the Borneo Glass Catfish, the Duskyfin glassfish, and the Three-Striped African Glass Catfish. Most members of this family are quite small, but the larger species can grow to a maximum of 10 inches.

The most popular member of *Ambassidae* among aquarium hobbyists is the Indian glassfish, due to its distinctive transparent body. In many species of glassfish, the internal organs and skeleton are visible through the skin. Unfortunately, this remarkable trait has led to the practice of injecting dye directly into fish to produce neon stripes or spots. This process is incredibly harmful to the fish, and most die during the procedure. Any that live are sold as "painted" or "disco" fish, but they are very susceptible to infection and disease and usually die within weeks or months. In 1997, the UK publication *Practical Fishkeeping* started a largely successful campaign to stop merchants from stocking fish that have been dyed. While the movement was able to halt the sale of these fish in almost half the stores in the UK, the problem still persists in global markets.

Despite a reputation of being difficult to keep, glassfish actually make excellent aquarium additions if given the right environment. Their natural habitats range from fresh to salt water depending on the species, but most prefer standing freshwater as opposed to brackish salt water. It is better to keep a school instead of an individual or a pair, as a group of these fish will act much more energetically and boldly than would one or two alone.

The cover image is from a loose plate, origin unknown. The cover font is Adobe ITC Garamond. The text font is Adobe Minion Pro; the heading font is Adobe Myriad Condensed; and the code font is Dalton Maag's Ubuntu Mono.

Get even more for your money.

Join the O'Reilly Community, and register the O'Reilly books you own. It's free, and you'll get:

- $4.99 ebook upgrade offer
- 40% upgrade offer on O'Reilly print books
- Membership discounts on books and events
- Free lifetime updates to ebooks and videos
- Multiple ebook formats, DRM FREE
- Participation in the O'Reilly community
- Newsletters
- Account management
- 100% Satisfaction Guarantee

Signing up is easy:

1. **Go to: oreilly.com/go/register**
2. **Create an O'Reilly login.**
3. **Provide your address.**
4. **Register your books.**

Note: English-language books only

To order books online:
oreilly.com/store

For questions about products or an order:
orders@oreilly.com

To sign up to get topic-specific email announcements and/or news about upcoming books, conferences, special offers, and new technologies:
elists@oreilly.com

For technical questions about book content:
booktech@oreilly.com

To submit new book proposals to our editors:
proposals@oreilly.com

O'Reilly books are available in multiple DRM-free ebook formats. For more information:
oreilly.com/ebooks

O'REILLY®

Lightning Source UK Ltd.
Milton Keynes UK
UKOW06f1102240913

217747UK00007B/11/P